African Development in a
Comparative Perspective

Published for and on behalf
of the United Nations

UNCTAD
Geneva

James Currey
Oxford

Africa World Press
Trenton NJ

Published for and behalf
of the United Nations

UNCTAD
United Nations Conference on Trade and Development
Palais des Nations CH-1211 Geneva 10

James Currey
www.jamescurrey.com
is an imprint of Boydell & Brewer Ltd
PO Box 9. Woodbridge, Suffolk IP12 3DF, UK
and of Boydell & Brewer Inc.
668 Mt Hope Avenue, Rochester, NY 14620, USA
www.boydellandbrewer.com

Africa World Press
P.O. Box 1892 Trenton NJ 08607

© United Nations 1998 and 1999

A catalogue record is available from the British Library
ISBN 978-0-85255-165-3 (James Currey)

A catalog record for this book is available from the Library of Congress

United Nations Sales No. GV.E.99.0.21
ISBN 978-92-1-101004-6 (United Nations)

Contents

Chapter I

GROWTH AND DEVELOPMENT IN AFRICA: TRENDS AND PROSPECTS

Chapter II

THE ROLE, STRUCTURE AND PERFORMANCE OF AGRICULTURE

List of text tables

List of charts and boxes

PREFACE

After 15 years of almost continuous economic decline, Africa began a recovery in the mid-1990s. In 1995, for the first time in many years, the region as a whole experienced an increase in per capita income, a performance that was repeated in 1996 and again in 1997. Some analysts concluded that a turning-point had been reached in African development and that structural adjustment programmes were finally working. However, even during this upturn, only a handful of countries were able to reach or surpass the 6 per cent growth target for Africa set by the United Nations. Moreover, the effects of the financial crisis which began in East Asia in 1997, have demonstrated the fragility of recovery.

Because of their relatively marginal position in global financial integration, most African countries, with the notable exception of South Africa, have been spared the large swings in market sentiment associated with international financial flows. However, their economies have been adversely affected by falling commodity prices for key Africa exports, slower growth in world trade, and a loss of competitiveness to Asian countries following the latter's currency devaluations. With civil strife flaring up and also drawing in a number of countries, output growth in 1998 barely kept pace with population growth and real per capita incomes actually declined again throughout much of sub-Saharan Africa.

In order to make a dent in widespread poverty, domestic policymakers and the international community must engineer an economic take-off in which growth rates of 6 per cent per annum are sustained. There should be no illusions about the difficulties of meeting this challenge. Nor should faith be placed in quick fixes or outside panaceas. However, there are important lessons that can be drawn from other developing countries which have emerged from economic and social instability and stagnation into periods of fast and sustainable growth.

Africa can regain the development momentum which underpinned the social and economic gains of many countries in the decade following their independence. But this requires a comprehensive reassessment of current approaches and a bold vision for the future.

Since the early 1980s many governments have pursued reforms under structural adjustment programmes that place emphasis on macroeconomic stability, a reduced role for the State, greater reliance on market forces and a rapid opening up to international competition as the key to unlocking growth potential. Greater macroeconomic stability and removal of large price distortions in key areas have no doubt made an important contribution to economic recovery in some countries. However, despite many years of policy reform, barely any country in the region has successfully completed its adjustment programme with a return to sustained growth. Indeed, the path from adjustment to improved performance is, at best, a rough one and, at worst, a disappointing dead-end. Of the 15 countries identified as "core adjusters" by the World Bank as recently as 1993, only three are now classified by IMF as "strong performers". Mainstream assessments of Africa's growth prospects have almost invariably proved over-optimistic largely because they have been based on an act of faith in growth-enhancing market forces, rather than on a careful examination of constraints and opportunities.

Such assessments, as well as the policy advice proffered, have not always taken proper account of the external constraints. Indeed, declining export prices and a sharp deterioration in external financial conditions in the early 1980s brought the already shaky foundations of many African economies to a state of near collapse. These losses were not offset by rises in official development assistance (ODA) or official lending; less than 15 per cent of the trade loss was compensated by ODA. Predictably, the resulting adjustment took the form of severe import compression and a sharp decline in investment; the share of investment in GDP, which had averaged over 25 per cent in the 1970s, had fallen to 16 per cent by the early 1990s. The region was caught in a vicious circle: the existing economic structure was unable to generate the growth in export earnings needed to maintain imports and investment, which in turn impeded structural change and economic growth.

The recovery of the mid-1990s was greatly helped by improved external conditions. The 25 per cent rise in non-oil commodity prices from 1993 to 1996 accounts for much of the increase in export earnings. However, these gains proved transitory as commodity prices turned down, markedly in 1998. The medium-term outlook is not promising. Moreover, the downward trend in real ODA that emerged at the beginning of the decade continues unabated.

The international community should not, and need not, adopt a passive stance on African economic development. Indeed, on one key issue, that of debt, it can make a demonstrable commitment to the new generation of African policymakers.

There is now ample evidence that Africa's external debt burden is having a severe adverse impact on investment and renewed growth. Not only does it impede public investment in physical and human infrastructure, but also it deters private investment, including foreign investment. As a proportion of exports and GDP the external debt of Africa is the highest of any developing region. Most of it is public and owed to official creditors, and a good deal is simply unpayable. The extent of the debt overhang is indicated by accumulated arrears which, by 1996, had reached over $64 billion, amounting to more than a quarter of the total debt. Of even more concern is that two thirds of the increase in debt since 1988 has been due to arrears.

The launching of the Heavily Indebted Poor Countries Debt Initiative (HIPC Initiative) has allowed a more comprehensive, coordinated and equitable approach to be taken. However, it needs significant revision if it is to help decisively in establishing the conditions for sustained growth; the basic concerns relate to eligibility for, and the adequacy of, debt reduction as well as to the speed at which relief should be granted. A comprehensive assessment of the sustainability of African debt is now needed; it should be carried out by an independent body that would not be unduly influenced by the interest of creditors. Such a body could be composed of eminent persons experienced in questions of finance and development who could be appointed by mutual agreement between creditors and debtors, with a commitment by creditors to implement fully and swiftly any recommendations that may be made. Such a course of action would be in complete harmony with the recognized principles of debt workouts.

Raising net resource transfers through debt relief will not succeed, however, unless it is accompanied by appropriate domestic policies to overcome low productivity and heavy dependence on a small number of primary commodities. Expanding investment in both primary and secondary industries and in both the public and the private sector is a vital prerequisite for, if not a guarantee of, rapid structural change and productivity growth. Whilst there is a growing consensus on this point, the analysis in this book suggests that the current approach to structural adjustment is unlikely to achieve such an outcome.

The most disturbing feature of policy reforms in SSA is their failure so far to bring about an investment recovery; the average ratio of investment to GDP during 1995-1997 was 17 per cent, only slightly above that of the early 1990s and well below that of other developing regions. Public investment has borne the brunt of the adjustment impact, but private investment has not, as conventional wisdom might suggest, stepped into the breach. Indeed, as a share of GDP, it is lower than in the 1970s.

One important reason for poor economic performance is slippage in programme implementation. Another is the failure to address the debt problem and to provide adequate external financing in designing the programmes. More importantly, while there is consensus that structural constraints and institutional weaknesses prevent an effective functioning of markets and impede a positive response to private incentives, these obstacles are often neglected. Thus, policies are promoted to get prices "right" when some of the more important agents and institutions of a modern market economy are underdeveloped or totally absent. Again, there is no proper sequencing of liberalization of product and factor markets with prior institutional reforms needed for its success. The outcome has been sadly predictable: greater instability in key prices and failure to generate appropriate incentives. Even when incentives are generated, structural constraints and institutional weaknesses prevent their resulting in a vigorous supply response:

- Weak supply response to liberalization of agricultural markets largely reflects inadequate assessment of the factors constraining production. Evidence strongly suggests that the assumptions about the taxation of agricultural producers through pricing policies which underline these reforms are not entirely valid. While for some products African farmers have been heavily taxed compared with more successful exporters in other regions, that has not been so for all products or all countries;

- Agricultural liberalization has not been associated with a strengthening of price incentives. The domestic terms of trade have generally turned against farmers more in those countries which have sought to link domestic prices to world prices. The shift from public to private marketing agents has not increased the proportion of export prices passed on to producers, mainly because of imperfect and underdeveloped markets;

- Dismantling of marketing boards has tended to enlarge the institutional hiatus, as private institutions are generally unable to take up many of the functions previously rendered by marketing boards;

- Financial liberalization has often been undertaken without first ensuring the conditions for its success, including a high degree of price stability and fiscal discipline, sound financial institutions and corporate finance, depth in financial markets, and effective prudential regulation. Consequently, it has lead to high and unstable interest rates, widespread insolvencies, a rapid accumulation of public domestic debt and fiscal instability;

- While there was certainly a need to move towards more realistic and flexible exchange rates, the pendulum has swung too far. Leaving exchange rates to markets has resulted in highly unstable rates as markets proved to be very thin. Instability has further been exacerbated by arrangements that have resulted in *de facto* liberalization of the capital account;

- Trade policy reforms have largely been driven by theoretical notions of neutral incentives, to be attained through low and uniform tariffs, rather than by pragmatism. Nor have tariff reforms always been supplemented by adequate arrangements to support exports and investment. As a result, while exports and investment are sometimes too heavily taxed, imports of luxury goods occasionally receive favourable treatment. Numerous exemptions from duties, large-scale smuggling, and tariff reductions create serious difficulties for domestic firms with the potential to form the basis of a more export-oriented industrial base.

A rethinking of policies is now needed that recognizes and addresses directly the structural constraints and institutional hiatus that pervade the African economies. It should draw on successful development experiences in Africa and elsewhere, and focus on capital accumulation and nurturing and building the institutions needed for an efficient market economy.

Policy intervention should also be based on the recognition by governments that in market-based systems capital accumulation is closely linked to the consolidation of property rights and the emergence of a strong and dynamic indigenous entrepreneurial class willing to commit its resources to investment. Fears associated with the emergence of such a class as a rival economic power to ruling elites need to be overcome if market-based development is to succeed.

There is no universal recipe, but some general principles can be laid down that are appropriate to Africa, in the light of its market imperfections and volatile economic environment:

- As elsewhere, private investment requires complementary public investment in physical and human infrastructure. Undercapitalization, including inadequate public investment, is the principal obstacle to sustained agricultural development in Africa. Neglect of agriculture in public spending is a more serious source of urban bias than pricing policies. At less than 5 per cent of GDP the current level of public investment is barely sufficient to meet the development challenge;

- The poor past performance of many marketing boards and *caisses de stabilisation* does not imply that their original rationale is no longer valid. Some of the needs which they were established to satisfy can now be met by the private sector, but government action remains indispensable in several areas of commodity trade such as financing, risk management, market promotion, and the provision of infrastructure and services unlikely to be forthcoming from other sources. Thus there is a strong case for institutional pluralism in which reformed and depoliticized marketing boards and *caisses* are part of a landscape that also includes private organizations, parastatals and co-operatives;

- A more pragmatic approach would be to reconsider the case for financial restraint linked to administered interest rates and institutions that would mobilize domestic savings, direct credits toward investment and meet the diverse needs of small- and medium-sized enterprises in the primary and secondary sectors;

- In a continent seeking export-led growth, the exchange rate is too important a variable to leave to shallow and volatile markets and the vagaries of capital flows. Its management requires, *inter alia*, certain kinds of regulations and controls. Opening up the capital account is not likely to bring back flight capital, which on some estimates accounts for 70 per cent of non-land private wealth in SSA. Much of the flight capital appears to have originated from the illicit diversion of public funds rather than to have been constituted by business incomes seeking economic stability or high yields abroad. A change in the banking regulations of those developed countries where these funds are hidden could produce effective results in this respect;

- The marginalization of SSA in world trade is a reflection of its inability to expand productive capacity, rather than a consequence of its resistance to openness. A gradual approach to trade liberalization is desirable in view of the existing weaknesses in supply capabilities. A trade regime that provides exporters with easy access to inputs at world prices, facilitates investment and discourages luxury consumption should also be built on a differentiated approach, supplemented by arrangements such as duty drawbacks and export retention schemes. The case for infant industry protection and industrial policies to promote learning and develop skills in domestic firms is no less relevant today in SSA than it has been for all successful late developers in this century. While WTO Agreements have reduced the scope for some policy options, selective strategies can still be applied, and exemptions provided under the agreements cover most countries in Africa. However, any such support must be time-bound and closely tied to performance criteria.

The experience of countries which have successfully launched a sustained process of economic growth based on a dynamic investment-export nexus built around primary activities gives ground for optimism that a similar process can be initiated in SSA. For most countries in the region the opportunities are ample, and their exploitation should be the initial focus of policy. As the successful experiences of resource-rich countries in Latin America and East Asia have shown, policy requirements at such early stages of export promotion and accumulation are less demanding and can yield rapid results. Those countries have indeed succeeded in initiating strong and sustained export and output growth following many years of instability and economic stagnation, and they did not always start from more favourable conditions than those now prevailing in Africa.

After a decade or more of reform in SSA premised on the assumption that government failures are far worse than market failures, the need to ensure complementarity between States and markets is now increasingly recognized. However, acknowledging market imperfections should not give way to a false ideology of state infallibility. Reforms are desperately needed if the African State is once again to assume its developmental role. This is a daunting task, and any comprehensive agenda of institutional reform can only emerge at the country level, where ownership of reforms can be ensured and the chances of success thereby increased. In general, governments need to diffuse a sense of national purpose. More specifically, there is an urgent need for a more efficient, dedicated and better remunerated civil service. At the same time, it is necessary to build greater trust and partnership between the state and private actors.

Political instability on account of social, especially ethnic, fragmentation is not an intrinsically African problem. While Africa is highly diversified in terms of social and ethnic minorities, there is less discrimination than in most other regions. But efforts since independence to build multi-ethnic political coalitions have entailed heavy economic costs. The experience of some South-East Asian countries illustrates that it is possible to achieve social and political harmony while nevertheless accelerating growth.

African countries should strengthen their regional economic ties, as they have already begun to do with their political ties. Special attention should be paid to a division of labour whereby trade and investment flows link countries at different levels of development. Intra-regional trade has been growing in SSA but is still very small. However, even marginal increases in such trade can help develop export capacities, which in turn can generate regional growth dynamics by easing balance-of-payments constraints and providing learning effects which will eventually make African exporters competitive globally.

Rubens Ricupero
Secretary-General of UNCTAD

Acknowledgements

This book is based on the *Trade and Development Report 1998, Part Two*. It was prepared by a team led by Yilmaz Akyüz and comprising Alberto Gabriele, Charles Gore, Shigesha C. Kasahara, Detlef Kotte, Richard Kozul-Wright, Jörg Mayer and Anthony Woodfield. Research assistance was provided by Serra Ayral and Erna Borneck.

The book draws on background studies prepared by Korkut Boratav, L. Amedee Darga, Martin Fransman, Alberto Gabriele, Massoud Karshenas, Friedrich von Kirchbach, Jörg Mayer, Thandika Mkandawire, Lynn Mytelka, Machiko Nissanke, Hendrik Roelofsen, Charles Soludo, Taffere Tesfachew, Samuel Wangwe, Adrian Wood and Marc Wuyts. These studies were prepared within the framework of a research project funded by the Japan Trust Fund for International Cooperation for Development. The project was directed by Yilmaz Akyüz and managed by Shigesha C. Kasahara, and the research was coordinated by Charles Gore.

Research issues were originally identified in discussions with government representatives and academics at a workshop held in Harare (Zimbabwe) in January 1997, and preliminary findings were discussed at a workshop in Mauritius in December 1997. These meetings provided the background for a conference held in Mauritius on 24-25 September 1998, on "African Development in a Comparative Perspective", attended by policy-makers from 34 African countries, and organized in collaboration with the Trade Division of the Ministry of Foreign Affairs of Mauritius and the Ministry of Foreign Affairs of Japan.

Kamran Kousari, UNCTAD Coordinator for Africa, was closely involved in all aspects of the project. Sidney Fairmont and Graham Grayston edited the final text, and Petra Hoffmann was responsible for desk-top publishing. General secretarial support was provided by Vivianne Njume-Ebong, Heather Wicks, and Nicole Winch.

The financial assistance of the Government of Japan (projects RAF/96/A40 and RAF/97/A28) is gratefully acknowledged. Thanks are also due to the Government of Zimbabwe for their logistical support for the first workshop, and the Government of Mauritius for their logistical and financial support for the second workshop and the international conference.

Explanatory notes

Classification by country or commodity group

The classification of countries in this book generally follows that of the UNCTAD *Handbook of International Trade and Development Statistics 1995.*[1] Unless otherwise stated, the classification by commodity group used also generally follows that employed in the same publication.

The term "country" refers, as appropriate, also to territories or areas. The designations employed and the presentation of the material in this publication do not imply the expression of any opinion whatsoever on the part of the Secretariat of the United Nations concerning the legal status of any country, territory, city or area, or of its authorities, or concerning the delimitation of its frontiers or boundaries.

The term "North Africa" denotes Algeria, Egypt, Libyan Arab Jamahiriya, Morocco and Tunisia. The term "sub-Saharan Africa" (and the abbreviation "SSA") refers to the rest of Africa, other than South Africa, unless otherwise specified.

References to "Latin America" in the text or tables include the Caribbean countries unless otherwise indicated.

Other notes

References in the text to *TDR* are to the *Trade and Development Report* (of a particular year). For example, *TDR 1997* refers to *Trade and Development Report, 1997* (United Nations publication, Sales No. E.97.II.D.8).

The term "dollar" ($) refers to United States dollars, unless otherwise stated.

The term "billion" signifies 1,000 million.

The term "tons" refers to metric tons.

Annual rates of growth and change refer to compound rates.

Exports are valued f.o.b. and imports c.i.f., unless otherwise specified.

Use of a hyphen (-) between dates representing years, e.g. 1988-1990, signifies the full period involved, including the initial and final years.

An oblique stroke (/) between two years, e.g. 1990/91, signifies a fiscal or crop year.

Two dots (..) indicate that the data are not available, or are not separately reported.

A dash (-) or a zero (0) indicates that the amount is nil or negligible.

A dot (.) indicates that the item is not applicable.

A plus sign (+) before a figure indicates an increase; a minus sign (-) before a figure indicates a decrease.

Details and percentages do not necessarily add to totals because of rounding.

---

[1]   United Nations publication, Sales No.E/F.97.II.D.7.

Abbreviations

ACP	African, Caribbean and Pacific (group of States)
CEPR	Centre for Economic Policy Research (London)
CFA	Communauté financière africaine (franc zone)
c.i.f.	cost, insurance and freight
ECA	Economic Commission for Africa
ECLAC	Economic Commission for Latin America and the Caribbean
ESAF	Enhanced Structural Adjustment Facility (of IMF)
EU	European Union
FAO	Food and Agriculture Organization of the United Nations
FDI	foreign direct investment
f.o.b.	free on board
GDP	gross domestic product
GNP	gross national product
HIPCs	heavily indebted poor countries
IFAD	International Fund for Agricultural Development
IFI	international financial institution
IMF	International Monetary Fund
ISI	import-substitution industrialization
LDC	least developed country
MBs	marketing boards
MVA	manufacturing value added
NBER	National Bureau of Economic Research (United States)
NIEs	newly industrializing economies
NPC	nominal protection coefficient
NTMs	non-tariff measures
ODA	official development assistance
OECD	Organisation for Economic Cooperation and Development
PORIM	Palm Oil Research Institute of Malaysia
R&D	research and development
SACU	South African Customs Union
SADC	Southern African Development Community
SAF	Structural Adjustment Facility
SAP	Structural Adjustment Programme
SDR	special drawing right
SITC	Standard International Trade Classification
SSA	sub-Saharan Africa
TNCs	transnational corporations
TRIMs	trade-related investment measures
TRIPs	trade-related intellectual property rights
UNCTAD	United Nations Conference on Trade and Development
UNDP	United Nations Development Programme
UNIDO	United Nations Industrial Development Organization
UNU	United Nations University
VAT	value-added tax
WIDER	World Institute for Development Economics Research
WTO	World Trade Organization

Introduction

After about a decade of relatively satisfactory growth, economic performance worsened in most countries in sub-Saharan Africa (SSA) in the second half of the 1970s; with few exceptions, the region as a whole experienced thereafter two decades of almost continuous economic decline. Since the early 1980s, many countries have adopted economic policy reforms under structural adjustment programmes sponsored by the Bretton Woods institutions. Emphasis has been placed on a reduced role for the State, greater reliance on market forces and a rapid opening up to international competition as the keys to unlocking Africa's growth potential. However, despite many years of policy reform, hardly any country in the region has successfully completed its adjustment programme with a return to sustained growth.

The recovery that began in 1994, with per capita income rising by about 1 per cent per annum in the subsequent three years, has given grounds for renewed optimism. Indeed, policy efforts may have been able to arrest Africa's long-standing economic decline, and the medium-term prospects may not be as bleak as the performance over the past two decades. However, during the past three years, only a few countries have been able to sustain growth rates reaching or surpassing the 6 per cent target set by the United Nations New Agenda for the Development of Africa in the 1990s. Moreover, the recovery is not underpinned by a strong investment performance. Rather, it reflects a greater utilization of existing capacity and owes much to what appears to be a temporary upswing in commodity prices. Even if the growth reached during the three years ending in 1996 could be sustained in the next decade, that would not reverse the marginalization of the region or have much of an effect on widespread poverty, and would constitute little more than the recovery of ground lost during the past 20 years.

A bold vision is now needed for African economic development, involving a comprehensive reassessment of international and domestic policy approaches in order to translate the current recovery into stronger and sustained growth. This book makes an initial attempt in that direction.

At the international level, the book emphasizes a rapid removal of the debt overhang as the single most important step that should be taken. While representing an important departure in terms of its coverage, the HIPC Initiative needs significant revision if it is to help decisively in establishing the conditions for rapid and sustained growth.

However, increasing net resource transfers through debt relief will not succeed unless it is accompanied by appropriate domestic policies designed to break out of the vicious circle of low productivity and heavy dependence on a small number of primary commodities prevailing in a large majority of African economies. Such a structural change calls for a considerably higher rate of investment than has so far been achieved, in both primary and secondary industries and by both the public and the private sector. Although there is a growing consensus on this point, the book suggests that the current approach to structural adjustment is unlikely to achieve such an outcome.

While it is recognized that structural constraints and institutional weaknesses prevent an efficient functioning of markets, in practice these obstacles are often neglected, and policies are designed to get the prices "right" in economies characterized by the total absence of markets or their imperfection. Furthermore, there is also often no proper sequencing of liberalization of product and factor markets with the institutional reforms needed for its success. Consequently, liberalization often leads to greater instability and fails to generate appropriate incentives, while structural constraints and institutional weaknesses prevent incentives from being translated into a vigorous supply response through new investment for the expansion and rationalization of productive capacity.

A new policy orientation is now needed that recognizes and addresses directly the structural constraints and institutional hiatus in the African economies. In identifying these impediments and the policies needed to overcome them, the book places the African experience in a comparative perspective and draws on successful development experiences elsewhere. It focuses on capital accumulation and on nurturing and building the institutions needed for an efficient market economy, including a dynamic indigenous entrepreneurial class.

It is argued that to achieve the required structural change accumulation needs to be linked to trade so as to enhance productive capacity, efficiency and competitiveness. In this respect, the existence of ample unexploited opportunities in primary sectors gives reasonable grounds for optimism. Realizing this potential will provide the focus for initial policy efforts in many countries, since increasing productivity and output in the primary sector is essential for generating investable resources needed for structural change. The successful experiences of resource-rich countries show that policy requirements at early stages of export promotion are relatively less demanding and can yield rapid results. A number of such countries in East Asia and Latin America have managed to initiate strong and sustained export and economic growth based on primary sectors, after many years of stagnation and instability, and not always starting from better initial conditions than those currently prevailing in Africa.

Chapter I briefly reviews the African growth experience during the past three decades and examines prospects over the medium term. While recognizing the importance of domestic policies, the chapter stresses the role of the external environment in shaping the economic performance. It is argued that the mainstream assessment of prospects for Africa is based on faith in growth-enhancing market forces, rather than on a careful examination of constraints and opportunities. Also, such an assessment serves to underestimate the importance of removing the debt overhang in initiating a self-sustaining process of growth.

Chapter II discusses the structure and performance of African agriculture. While there has been some improvement in agricultural performance over the past decade, undercapitalization, including inadequate public investment, remains the principal obstacle to sustained agricultural development. Chapter III examines agricultural policy reforms and supply behaviour. The evidence presented strongly suggests that the assumptions about the taxation of agricultural producers through pricing policies in the 1970s, which underlie the subsequent reforms are not entirely valid. Rather than generating the desired incentives, the recent emphasis on liberalization and dismantling of marketing boards has tended to exacerbate the institutional hiatus, since private institutions are generally unable to take up many of the functions previously performed by marketing boards.

Chapter IV deals with trade, accumulation and industry. It argues that the marginalization of SSA in world trade is a reflection of its failure to expand its productive capacity, rather than a consequence of its resistance to openness. The conventional emphasis on trade, as opposed to investment and accumulation, is thus misplaced. The chapter goes on to examine the composition of African trade, in terms of the relative importance of primary products and manufactures. Although some countries appear to be underperforming in exports of manufactures compared to their capacity, for most countries in the region the challenge is to increase total exports while diversifying their composition in favour of more dynamic and high-value-added products. Intraregional trade offers important opportunities in this respect.

Chapter V considers the domestic policy options open to governments and the institutional reforms that need to be pursued to create a pro-investment climate and reinvigorate growth. It attempts to identify the principal weaknesses of financial, trade and agricultural policies and their effects on stability, private incentives and public investment, and discusses alternative policy options. The purpose is not to offer a recipe that works under all circumstances, but to highlight the kind of approach that could be adopted when some of the more important agents and institutions of a modern market economy are underdeveloped or missing. The chapter ends with a discussion of policy challenges to be met in filling the institutional hiatus in Africa.

Chapter I

GROWTH AND DEVELOPMENT IN AFRICA: TRENDS AND PROSPECTS

A. Post-independence take-off

It has become increasingly common to describe Africa as a continent of missed growth opportunities, subjected to heavy-handed state interventions and misguided, inward-looking development strategies from which it is only now escaping. The historical record is not so simple. The conventional account downplays the challenges that faced many African countries at independence and overlooks the respectable, and for some countries spectacular, growth rates achieved immediately after independence. Nor is it always appreciated that Africa's integration into the world economy has been long and close, albeit shaped in large part by colonial ties and legacies.

Although there were considerable differences in initial conditions and income levels in African countries at independence, in almost all cases little had been done to create the necessary conditions for national economic development, including in particular physical infrastructure and sufficient educational opportunities. The main positive colonial legacy was the development of primary export sectors which appeared to offer strong growth potential.

Set against the very high expectations of the newly independent African States, the practical difficulties of building vibrant national economies and the problems posed by demographic transition, Africa's growth performance was quite strong from the mid-1960s until the first oil shock.[1] Although GDP growth in sub-Saharan Africa was faster than in the 1950s under colonial rule, aver-

aging an annual rate of 4.5 per cent or more than 1 per cent per capita, it was lower than in other developing regions, with the exception of South Asia, during the same period.

There were, however, considerable differences in growth among SSA countries, with average rates ranging from 0.5 per cent per annum (in Chad) to 14.7 per cent per annum (in Botswana). Many of the countries that performed least well after independence were ones that suffered years of civil turmoil. Others experiencing stagnation included those lacking natural resources in demand in the developed countries, and countries that were landlocked and did not have adequate transport links and port arrangements with neighbouring countries. On the other hand, a group of star performers emerged during this period with growth rates comparable to those of the best-performing economies elsewhere in the developing world. In this group of eight countries six achieved growth in excess of 8 per cent per annum (Botswana, Burundi, Côte d'Ivoire, Kenya, Nigeria and Zimbabwe) and two had growth rates of more than 6 per cent (Congo and Gabon).

This post-colonial growth was driven by a strong investment performance. On average, investment in SSA grew in volume by 6.4 per cent annually during 1965-1973 (chart 1). Investment shares were rising steadily everywhere, from less than 14 per cent of GDP in 1965 to over 18 per cent in 1973 for the region as a whole, and exceeding 20 per cent in many countries as protectionist

Chart 1

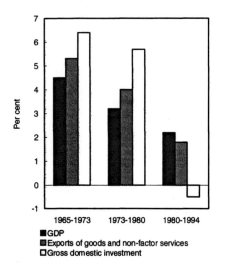

AVERAGE REAL GROWTH RATES OF GDP, EXPORTS, AND INVESTMENT IN SUB-SAHARAN AFRICA, 1965-1994

(Per cent per annum)

- ■GDP
- ▨Exports of goods and non-factor services
- ☐Gross domestic investment

Source: UNCTAD secretariat calculations, based on World Bank, *Trends in Developing Economies 1990* (Washington, D.C., 1990); and World Bank, *World Development Report 1996* (Washington, D.C., 1996).

Note: The figures underlying the chart are unweighted averages.

barriers increased average returns on investment. In agriculture, investment in the cultivation of new land helped to increase output. In most cases, public sector investment played a leading role in the accumulation process, made possible both by development aid and by a growing revenue base.

Before independence, foreign direct investment (FDI) had been limited mainly to minerals and oil extraction, and in some cases to the production of wage goods such as beverages and textiles. This pattern continued after independence, albeit with a growing enthusiasm to attract FDI into infant industries by using various incentives, including import protection. The stock of FDI doubled between 1960 and 1970, and as a percentage of GDP was in fact twice the amount directed to East and South-East Asia at the time.[2]

It has become fashionable to dismiss Africa's post-independence performance on the grounds that it was accompanied by only weak integration into the world economy. This is a partial assessment. The colonial experience had led policymakers in Africa, as elsewhere, to adopt a cautious approach to integration into the world economy. Nevertheless, most post-colonial economic strategies accepted that Africa's growth prospects lay in exploiting its comparative advantage in natural resources, on which basis it could begin to industrialize and diversify its exports. Moreover, and contrary to accounts that assume a radical policy shift in the early years of independence, this starting point coincided in many cases with the establishment of institutions and structures towards the end of the colonial era, such as export marketing boards, multi-purpose state development corporations and import-substitution measures.[3]

Between 1965 and 1973 export revenues in SSA grew very strongly, averaging over 15 per cent per annum. Export volumes rose with rapid growth in key commodities such as tea, coffee and cocoa, and were helped by preferential treatment of exports by the former colonial powers. Moreover, the earlier trend of falling terms of trade came to a halt in 1965 and the share of exports in GDP grew steadily for most countries after independence. Increasing export revenues eased the foreign-exchange constraint in the non-CFA countries, and whilst import volumes grew more slowly than exports in this period, the share of imports in GNP remained high.

Faced with small domestic markets and restrictive colonial trading legacies, some African countries sought to create new regional trade arrangements or to strengthen existing ones. However, different initial conditions among members often led to tensions (as in East Africa), and more generally such arrangements were constrained by the export composition of most African economies, and by infrastructural weaknesses. Consequently, the share of regional trade in total external trade stagnated at around 5 per cent, and more than half of SSA's external trade continued to be conducted with Europe.[4]

The rhetoric of the post-independence economic strategy emphasized structural change away from dependence on primary sector employment and traditional exports. However, even as growth accelerated, the pace and pattern of structural change in many African economies lagged behind.

Box 1

NURTURING INDIGENOUS CAPITALISM IN SUB-SAHARAN AFRICA

Compared with other developing regions, indigenous capitalism developed late in SSA.[1] During the colonial period, little industrial investment took place that could have been a threat to foreign enterprises. Most manufacturing was in small-scale, light-industry consumer goods such as soap, beverages, textiles, footwear and furniture. Apart from isolated cases such as that of Kano in northern Nigeria, Africans owned very few of even these small enterprises. Indigenous entrepreneurs were largely relegated to artisanship and commercial activities in the informal sector. In the years leading up to independence, colonial businessmen in many cases sought to avoid expropriation by entering into partnership arrangements with African entrepreneurs.

As for the rural areas, the best land had been alienated to colonial settlers. Indigenous rural capitalism was discouraged by the colonial authorities, which preferred cooperating (through marketing boards) with small African cocoa and coffee producers with limited bargaining power. Other factors that conspired to discourage large-farm capitalism were the region's abundant land, which limited the number of landless labourers available to work for wages on large farms, and property systems that were based on traditional rather than freehold forms of tenure. Only starting in the 1950s did the colonial countries encourage the emergence of African agricultural capitalism as part of their effort to secure national successors for continuing production and export of those primary commodities that the metropolitan countries needed. Agricultural capitalism took root in those pre-independence years among, for example, the Bugandan producers of coffee in Uganda, the Yoruba cocoa farmers of Nigeria and the Kikuyu cash-crop growers of Kenya.

After independence, African farmers continued the process of accumulation in the countryside, but part of the rural surplus was channelled into urban property, and much of it was taxed to help finance government investments. In some cases, as in Côte d'Ivoire, the new land-based capitalists included many Africans holding high political and administrative positions after independence.

As for town-based investments, African civil servants were sometimes able to obtain loans to invest in urban businesses, but such credits were generally more easily available for investment in land and property, which, given the region's rapid urbanization, provided attractive and reasonably secure returns. Most private urban businesses and industries, therefore, were launched by African small-scale entrepreneurs with initial capital from private savings or relatives, and further capital for expansion coming mainly from reinvested profits. Many of these enterprises, however, found it difficult to compete with local subsidiaries of TNCs with superior access to imported technology. Also, indigenous capitalists were sometimes discriminated against by their governments, as when special privileges such as tax exemptions were conferred on foreign interests, or when large public enterprises were established with the aim of rapidly increasing the pace of industrialization and growth. Indeed, upon independence only a few countries, such as Kenya and Nigeria, nurtured indigenous capitalists as a primary vehicle for capital accumulation, modernization and economic growth. However, even under the best conditions it proved difficult for them to make the leap from micro- and small-scale to medium- and large-scale entrepreneurship in manufacturing. The principal constraints were high costs due to unreliable supplies, inadequate infrastructure and deficient human resources, as well as limited demand due to small market sizes.

[1] For a more detailed account of the history of capitalist development in sub-Saharan Africa, see J. Iliffe, *The Emergence of African Capitalism* (Minneapolis: University of Minnesota Press, 1983).

Industry was the fastest-growing sector, thanks in large part to mining and transportation. Manufacturing activity grew by a robust 7.3 per cent per annum during 1965-1973, but in most cases from a very low starting point. By 1973, in only one country (Zimbabwe) was more than 20 per cent of output generated by manufacturing; in the large majority of countries the proportion was less than 10 per cent. However, in some countries, including Côte d'Ivoire, Kenya and Nigeria, robust infant industries emerged during this period. In some instances, private entrepreneurs were prominent in this early industrialization drive, but in most cases the State took the lead (see box 1).

Chart 2

GROWTH IN INDUSTRY AND AGRICULTURE IN SUB-SAHARAN AFRICA, 1965-1994

(Per cent per annum)

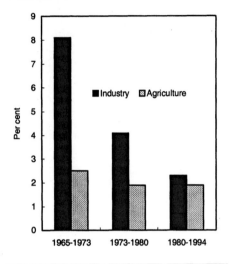

Source: See chart 1.
Note: See chart 1.

Despite these desirable structural shifts, a process of "positive" de-agrarianization did not begin in most African economies during this period. Growth of agricultural value-added in SSA was generally very weak, averaging only 2.5 per cent per annum (chart 2). This rate was much lower than in other developing regions, and in many countries agricultural growth did not keep up with population increases. While there was an expansion in the cultivated land area during this period, private and public investment was not forthcoming on a scale needed to transform the technological profile of agricultural production and to enhance productivity growth. Consequently, export expansion was in most cases based on very traditional commodities with little diversification, either vertically towards processed commodities and manufactures, or horizontally within the primary sector.[5]

In the light of these broad developments it is interesting to consider trends during this period in the group of star performers mentioned above. Investment took the lead in most cases, often linked to strong export performance. Even when export growth was relatively slow, as in Kenya, the countries concerned were often starting from a high level. In all these countries, an emerging investment-export nexus was linked both to a shift towards industrial activity, with an average rise in output of 11 per cent per annum compared with 7 per cent for SSA as a whole, and to strong agricultural growth, averaging close to 7 per cent per annum compared with only 2.5 per cent for the SSA average. Nevertheless, even for these star performers export diversification was quite limited.

B. Faltering growth in the 1970s

The 1973 oil price increase and the subsequent slowdown of growth in the developed world had a particularly adverse impact on Africa, except for a few oil exporters, since exposure and vulnerability to external influences were greater than in other developing regions. Indeed, countries registering a break in growth performance between 1973 and 1980 were far more numerous than in other developing regions, where the break came primarily in the early 1980s.[6] With population growth still accelerating, this meant a fairly significant drop in average per capita growth rates in Africa, from 1.2 per cent per annum in the previous period to 0.7 per cent per annum. Moreover, almost half the countries in Africa actually experienced negative per capita growth rates in this period.

Two persistent features characterized African growth performance in the 1970s: increased diversity among economies and lack of continuity in growth. Variations among countries' growth rates increased significantly compared with the previous period, with declines in output reaching as much as 7 per cent per annum in some countries while other countries were growing at 10 per cent per annum. The lack of continuity resulted from the weakening performance of earlier star performers. Significantly slower growth occurred in all these economies, but the weakening of growth in some of the larger countries, which had grown strongly in the earlier period, was of particular importance. On the other hand, many smaller African countries witnessed a dramatic revival of growth.

The slowdown reflected a continued deterioration in agriculture, where the average growth rate for SSA as a whole fell from 2.5 per cent in the previous period to below 2 per cent during 1973-1980, failing to keep pace with population growth (chart 2). More significantly, industrial growth was halved compared with 1965-1973, and there was a sharp deceleration in manufacturing growth, which fell to 3 per cent per annum for the region as a whole. While a number of countries achieved high rates of growth in manufacturing during this period many countries, including Zimbabwe (which had been among the star performers in the previous period), experienced negative manufacturing growth, whereas in no country had manufacturing output declined in the earlier period.

There was a significant volatility of growth rates from year to year that tended to coincide with fluctuations in countries' external terms of trade (chart 3). These fluctuations reflected not only the negative effects on most SSA countries of the 1973 oil price shock and the recession that followed in the developed countries, but also the short-lived boom that resulted from the rebound in world prices for a number of non-oil primary exports in 1976. While a large majority of SSA countries were hurt by the 1973 oil shock, oil-exporting countries such as Gabon and Nigeria benefited substantially from the 1973 windfall, although their growth subsequently contracted when oil prices declined during 1977-1979. For the non-oil-exporting countries in the region, export volumes, which had been increasing almost constantly for two decades, peaked in 1973 and showed a slight downward trend during the rest of the 1970s. Despite rising nominal prices of a number of non-oil commodities, export earnings

Chart 3

TERMS OF TRADE OF SUB-SAHARAN AFRICA, 1954-1996

(Index numbers, 1954-1956 = 100)

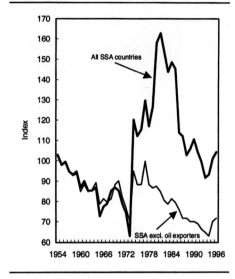

Source: UNCTAD, *Handbook of International Trade and Development Statistics*, various issues.

slowed down, growing at an average rate of 4 per cent per annum during 1973-1980. However, as import prices rose dramatically because of oil and accelerating inflation in the industrialized countries, the purchasing power of the non-oil countries' exports stagnated in the mid-1970s, whereas that of the oil exporters increased sharply.

In the 1970s many SSA countries benefited from the expansion of international bank lending to developing countries. Initially, this expansion improved the access to international finance for a number of countries, and some countries, notably the oil exporters, used such lending to finance additional import growth. From 1976 onwards, however, bank lending was increasingly used to compensate export shortfalls due to terms-of-trade losses and declines in the purchasing power of exports in non-oil countries. Net new long-term borrowing by SSA from all sources rose from $3 billion in 1976 to $11.5 billion in 1980. The share of long-term commercial bank lending in total disbursements increased rapidly, accounting for more

Chart 4

DISBURSEMENTS ON LONG-TERM DEBT TO SUB-SAHARAN AFRICA, 1970-1996, BY SOURCE OF LENDING

(Billions of dollars)

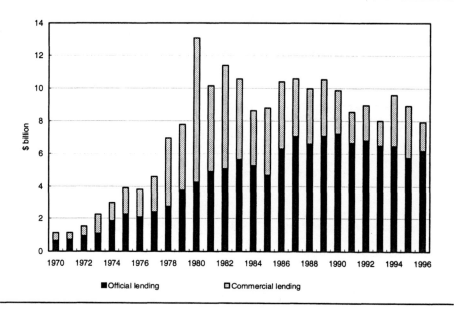

■ Official lending   ▨ Commercial lending

Source: World Bank, *Global Development Finance 1997* (Washington, D.C., 1997).
Note: Figures are for public and publicly guaranteed debt.

than two-thirds of the total borrowing at the end of the decade (chart 4). The major borrowers from this source were Cameroon, Côte d'Ivoire, the Democratic Republic of the Congo, Gabon, Kenya and Nigeria. Short-term lending to SSA also rose dramatically, from $2.5 billion in 1976 to $22.6 billion in 1980.

This increase in international private lending to SSA coincided with sharp declines in the return on investment. Such declines were not generally experienced elsewhere in the developing world; indeed, figures for South Asia show that returns there increased slightly. Although investment decelerated during this period, it rose as a share of GDP, averaging over 20 per cent, compared with 15 per cent in 1961-1973. In a small number of countries, investment accelerated in response to favourable price shifts in traditional

exports and export diversification linked to the exploitation of previously untapped oil and mineral reserves. By contrast, other countries experienced a sharp slowdown in investment growth and in some cases absolute declines.

Only government expenditure maintained its strong growth and consequently accounted for a rising share of GDP, with government consumption equivalent to 4 per cent more of GDP in 1980 than in 1973. However, declining revenues led to growing fiscal deficits and inflationary pressures. Because many SSA countries had pegged the value of their currencies to major convertible currencies, exchange rates appreciated significantly in real terms; according to some estimates, they appreciated on average by some 40 per cent between 1973 and 1980. The current account deficit (before official transfers) for SSA as a whole in this period more than doubled compared with the earlier period, averaging 15 per cent of the regional GDP. This situation was also reflected in a rapid rise in total SSA long-term external public and private debt, from 18 per cent of GDP in 1970 to 40 per cent in 1980. The growing fiscal and current account imbalances and rising debt and inflation levels of the 1970s were exceptional by the standards of the post-independence period.

Thus, many countries in SSA ended the decade with increased external indebtedness, greater macroeconomic imbalances and instability, a lagging agricultural sector, and a weak and uncompetitive industrial base. Coming on top of such structural weaknesses, the external shocks of the 1980s drove a large majority of the countries into a deep crisis that wiped out the earlier gains in living standards.

C. The crisis of the 1980s and thereafter

The period between 1980 and 1994 witnessed a noticeable deterioration in the performance of most SSA countries. Population grew faster than output, with per capita incomes falling, on average, by 0.6 per cent per annum. The dispersion of growth rates among countries, which had increased during the 1970s, was greatly reduced and there was a downward convergence of growth rates during these years of crisis. For every country which experienced positive per capita output growth during 1980-1994, two had negative per capita rates of growth. There were in fact only nine countries that had positive per capita growth and of these only in Botswana and Mauritius (both already middle-income countries in 1980) was growth sufficient to tackle the challenges of economic development and poverty alleviation. The fact that the star performers of the previous period also registered negative growth rates further underscores the damaging lack of continuity in Africa's growth performance.

The performance of agriculture did not deteriorate drastically in the 1980s compared with the previous decade: for SSA as a whole agricultural growth was maintained, on average, at about 2 per cent per annum between 1980 and 1994, mostly on account of a turnaround after the mid-1980s (see chapter II). In many countries, growth was faster in agriculture than in industry, where it dropped to around 2 per cent per annum – a dramatic decline from the 8 per cent attained in the initial post-independence period.

The factors underlying the poor economic performance in Africa are well known and were discussed in some detail in previous *TDRs*. Africa, like many other parts of the developing world, failed to adjust to a more hostile external environment characterized by terms-of-trade deterioration, sharp increases in international interest rates, and stagnation and declines in net transfer of external resources, resulting from a turnaround in the policy stance in the major industrial countries. However, Africa fell further behind than other developing regions, in large part because its structural weaknesses were deeper and its room for manoeuvre was narrower.

After peaking in 1977, the terms of trade of non-oil SSA countries declined almost every year until 1994 (chart 3). For North Africa and the SSA oil exporters the downward trend started after 1981; it was steeper but did not last as long. Unlike previous episodes, when the terms of trade declined in the context of rising prices of both primary commodities and manufactures, the declines in the 1980s were associated with rising prices of manufactures and falling prices of commodities. Deflationary policies in the major industrial countries took much longer to have a tangible impact on prices of manufactures than on commodity prices, which tend to be much more sensitive to market pressures.[7]

World prices for most commodities exported by SSA were at historically low levels in the late 1980s and early 1990s. In real terms, prices for coffee and cocoa – two of SSA's main non-oil commodity exports – were down from their levels in the 1950s by around 40 per cent. In 1992, coffee prices were at a 17-year low. Real prices of other

Chart 5

COMPOSITION OF NET RESOURCE FLOWS TO SUB-SAHARAN AFRICA, 1970-1996

(Billions of dollars)

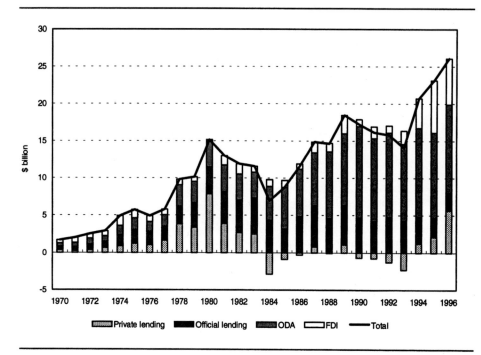

Private lending   Official lending   ODA   FDI   Total

Source: As for chart 4.

Note: FDI includes portfolio investment; ODA corresponds to the item "grants" as defined by the World Bank in *Global Development Finance* and excludes funds allocated through technical cooperation.

major export items were also well below the level of the 1950s – by over 50 per cent for tea and cotton, one third for copper and sugar, and a quarter for tobacco.

The terms of trade of the SSA non-oil countries fell by more than one third between 1977 and 1993, compared with a decline of about 20 per cent for other non-oil developing countries. Thus, in 1993, the SSA countries would have needed to increase the volume of their exports by more than 50 per cent above their 1977 level in order to be able to import the same volume of goods as in that year. In the event, export volumes did rise, but not enough to compensate for this decline in the terms of trade. In some cases (e.g. cocoa) success in increasing export volumes proved self-defeating by depressing prices further.[8]

Of the 29 non-oil countries in the region for which data are available, there are only two (Mauritius and Zimbabwe) that did not suffer terms-of-trade losses between 1977 and 1993, while in 16 countries of the other 27 such losses exceeded 30 per cent. The countries relying heavily on exports of tropical beverages (Cameroon, Ethiopia, Ghana, Kenya, Rwanda, Uganda and the United Republic of Tanzania) were hit the hardest, with terms-of-trade losses of between 50 and 77 per cent. Among the 27 countries, only six (Benin, Cameroon, Côte d'Ivoire, Mauritania, Niger and Rwanda) were able to offset the fall in export prices by expanding export volumes.

The decline in export prices and earnings during the first half of the 1980s coincided with a sharp rise in international interest rates. The average interest payable on outstanding commercial debt rose from 8.4 per cent in the 1970s to 11.4 per cent because an increasing part of long-term loans had been contracted at variable interest rates, and the ratio of interest payments to export earnings rose from less than 2 per cent to more than 8 per cent. Simultaneously, new private lending collapsed, and this was responsible for the decline in the net new long-term borrowing by SSA from $10.8 billion in 1980 to about $7 billion per annum in the three years that followed. The region in fact started making net negative transfers to private lenders as interest payments exceeded net new lending.

However, aggregate net resource flows and aggregate net transfers to SSA as a whole remained positive as a result of the response of the international community to increasing payments difficulties in the region. Since 1980 SSA's external financing has increasingly been from official sources. ODA and official lending both rose, the latter in large part in the context of stabilization and adjustment programmes (chart 5), and there was a marked shift in total ODA flows in the 1980s in favour of SSA.

However, for the region as a whole and for most SSA countries individually, the additional resource flows were not sufficient to offset the impact of terms-of-trade losses on foreign exchange earnings, let alone the increased debt service. According to one estimate, between 1980 and 1990 only six out of 21 countries for which data are available were able to cover their terms-of-trade losses with net ODA inflows.[9] There was a GDP loss in SSA of $16.4 billion due to the terms of trade, and an ODA net inflow of $2.4 billion, which shows that less than 15 per cent of the terms-of-trade losses were compensated by ODA.[10]

The burden fell on imports and investment. Imports were reduced drastically during the first half of the 1980s. Although they recovered slowly from 1987 onwards, in per capita terms import volumes were still one third lower in 1993 than in 1980. The impact of the worsened terms of trade on import compression was particularly severe. Indeed, if the terms of trade had remained at their 1976-1978 levels, SSA imports could have been higher by one quarter of their actual value in every year between 1981 and 1993 even without any increase in export volumes. Additional ODA during that period made up for only one quarter of the loss in export purchasing power.

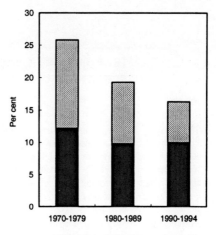

Chart 6

PUBLIC AND PRIVATE INVESTMENT IN SUB-SAHARAN AFRICA, 1970-1994

(Per cent of GDP, weighted averages)

■ Private investment ▨ Public investment

Source: F.Z. Jaspersen et al., *Trends in Private Investment in Developing Countries - Statistics for 1970-1994,* IFC Discussion Paper, No. 28 (Washington, D.C.: World Bank, 1996).

Import compression inevitably led to a lower utilization of existing capacity and a fall in new investment. Part of that capacity became unusable, giving rise to the phenomenon of "de-industrialization". Investment fell continuously throughout the period and failed to recover. For 1980-1994 the average decline amounted to 0.5 per cent per annum, and in per capita terms it was much greater. The share of investment in GDP, which had averaged around 26 per cent in the 1970s, fell to below 20 per cent in the 1980s and to 16 per cent in the first half of the 1990s (chart 6). Public investment was cut by more than half, while private investment fell from over 12 per cent of GDP in the 1970s to around 10 per cent.

The decline in investment had a major influence on the pace of structural change. It meant that SSA was unable to make a positive adjustment to the changed global environment and shifts in key prices affecting its economic performance. Such adjustment would have required a restructuring of agriculture and industry, but the region was caught in a vicious circle whereby the existing accumulation and production structures were unable to generate the growth in export earnings needed to maintain imports, which in turn constrained investment and income growth. The dilemma was further accentuated by the downward trend in the terms of trade and insufficient aid flows to compensate the loss of purchasing power of exports.

D. Adjustment, recovery and prospects

The recovery that began in 1994 and continued during the subsequent three years has given grounds for renewed optimism. Indeed, in 1995 the African region as a whole achieved positive per capita income growth for the first time in many years, a performance that was repeated in 1996 and again, although to a lesser extent, in 1997. The recovery was greatly helped by much better weather conditions as well as by diminished civil strife in a number of countries. It was underpinned by strong growth in export earnings, and a consequent improvement in the trade and current account balances as well as in debt and debt servicing ratios. After a drop in 1993 and an increase of around 3 per cent in 1994, the export earnings of SSA rose by 16 per cent in 1995 and 10 per cent in 1996. Although export volumes improved, particularly in 1996, much of the increase in export earnings resulted from a sharp turnaround in non-oil commodity prices, which rose by 25 per cent between 1993 and 1996 and accounted for much of the 13 per cent improvement in SSA's terms of trade in that period.

In assessing whether the present recovery constitutes a turning point in Africa it is essential to examine the underlying economic conditions. These conditions have been influenced significantly by the structural adjustment programmes (SAPs) that many African countries have been pursuing since the early 1980s with the help of the Bretton Woods institutions. The main policy elements of the SAPs were discussed in *TDR 1993* and an assessment was made of their impact on economic performance. It was noted that despite a decade-long adjustment hardly any country had successfully completed its SAP with a return to sustained growth. The high frequency and persistence of SAPs suggested that SSA countries were locked into adjustment programmes, unable to restore self-sustained growth. A main shortcoming of these programmes was their failure to restore investment. Indeed, in many instances, application of SAPs was associated with declines in investment. However, this feature was considered at the time by the World Bank as the reflection of an "investment pause" resulting from stabilization measures and changes in key relative prices associated with the removal of distortions, rather than as an inherent weakness of the policies promoted.[11]

There can be little doubt that an improved policy environment and, in particular, greater macroeconomic stability have made an important contribution to economic recovery in a number of countries. Nevertheless, it is not clear whether the structural adjustment policies adopted so far have been able to reduce sufficiently the major structural and institutional impediments to the accumulation and structural change needed to initiate rapid and sustained growth. As pointed out in *TDR 1993*, assessing the impact of SAPs on economic performance is a tricky exercise involving a number of methodological difficulties. Nevertheless, experience strongly suggests that the link between adjustment and performance has been weak.

In 1993 the World Bank introduced a four-way classification of SSA countries in order to assess the adjustment experience; it identified 15 countries as a core group of adjusters that accounted for the bulk of Africa's population and income and were thought to have been able to put in place fairly good economic policies and to have introduced some significant institutional changes.[12] However, the subsequent economic performance of this group as a whole and, in particular, their contribution to the current recovery in SSA appear to have fallen short of expectations. Indeed, of these 15 countries, only three are among what IMF now classifies as "recent strong performers" (table 1). In other words, the large majority of countries that account for much of the recent faster growth in SSA were not among the World Bank "core group of adjusters" five years ago, and most of the countries that were thought to be pursuing relatively sound policies at the time are not among the strong performers today.[13]

Indeed, the rapid growth among some of the "recent strong performers" can largely be explained by some special circumstances that are of a one-off nature and unrelated to SAPs. Angola and Ethiopia certainly benefited greatly from the ending of civil strife, which had seriously disrupted economic activity. In Equatorial Guinea the exploitation of newly discovered oil reserves has been the main factor responsible for recent expansion.

These considerations once again highlight the problem of discontinuity of economic performance in SSA noted above. Since independence, there have always been countries that have performed reasonably well for a few years, but surges of growth have rarely been sustained.

The recent recovery in SSA appears to have been due primarily to increasing utilization of the existing capacity made possible by a relaxation of the foreign-exchange constraint, rather than to new investment. Indeed, evidence suggests that "the investment pause" has not come to a halt and the private investment response to SAPs continues to be weak. For SSA as a whole, the average ratio of private investment to GDP during 1995-1997 was only slightly above the rate achieved during the early 1990s, despite an acceleration of growth.[14] At around 17 per cent of GDP total investment in SSA remains below the average rate not only in the newly industrialized economies of Asia (about one third of GDP) but also in Latin America (slightly above 20 per cent).[15]

According to one view, the problem is not just the level of investment but its distribution. On this view the share of public investment in total investment in Africa is very high compared with other regions, constituting a major impediment to growth, since private investment tends to be much more efficient than public investment.[16] This view, however, not only ignores the mounting evidence regarding the complementarity between public and private investments, but also

Table 1

ADJUSTMENT AND PERFORMANCE IN AFRICAN COUNTRIES

Core group of adjusters[a]	Recent strong performers[b]
Burundi	Angola
Gambia	Benin
Ghana	Botswana[c]
Guinea	Côte d'Ivoire
Kenya	Equatorial Guinea
Lesotho	Ethiopia
Madagascar	Guinea-Bissau
Malawi	*Lesotho*
Mauritania	Mauritius[c]
Namibia	*Nigeria*
Nigeria	South Africa
Uganda	Togo
United Rep. of Tanzania	*Uganda*
Zambia	
Zimbabwe	

a E.V.K. Jaycox, *Africa: From Stagnation to Recovery* (Washington, D.C.: World Bank, February 1993).
b IMF, *World Economic Outlook*, April 1998 (Washington, D.C.: IMF), Vol. I, table 12.
c In the 1993 grouping by the World Bank Botswana and Mauritius were excluded as outliers.

is misleading when absolute levels of investment are compared. According to a recent study of 53 developing countries, including 10 in SSA, in the 1980s public investment appears to have been generally more productive than private investment. This was explained by a shift of public investment projects to more productive uses as well as by a reduction in the productivity of private investment resulting from insufficient complementary public investment.[17] Moreover, the high share of the public sector in SSA is not due to excessive public investment. Indeed, as the figures in table 2 show, as a proportion of GDP the SSA governments invest less than any other region, in particular the Asian countries. It is also notable that the average share of public investment in the "recent strong performers" during 1990-1996 was greater than in other SSA countries by about one percentage point of GDP.

Table 2

PUBLIC INVESTMENT RATIOS, BY REGION, 1990-1996

(Percentages)

| Region | Public investment as a share of | |
	Total investment	GDP
Sub-Saharan Africa	28.9	4.8
Western Hemisphere	24.1	4.9
Asia (excluding Japan)	31.1	8.6
NIEs	22.0	6.8

Source: S. Fischer, E. Hernández-Catá and M. S. Khan, "Africa: Is this the turning point?", IMF Paper on Policy Analysis and Assessment 98/6 (Washington, D.C., 1998), table 3.

The need for public investment is much greater in SSA, where human and physical infrastructure is extremely inadequate, than in countries with higher levels of industrialization and development. Moreover, given the rudimentary state of the entrepreneurial class, the public sector may still find it necessary to invest in a number of areas which elsewhere are normally in the domain of the private sector. Certainly, there are serious problems in the allocation and efficiency of public investment in many countries in SSA, the resolution of which could provide significant one-off productivity gains, but there can be little doubt that a public investment rate of 5 per cent of GDP is barely adequate to ensure the improvement in the physical and human infrastructure needed for sustained growth.

It thus appears that at the current rate of aggregate investment it would be very difficult to accelerate long-term growth in SSA regardless of how efficiently it is allocated and used. Current forecasts by the World Bank for the next 10 years give an average rate of growth of about 4 per cent per annum, i.e. maintenance of the average growth rate of the last three years. Even if this is realized, per capita income in the region would increase, on average, by 1 per cent per annum, so that "the coming decade would only represent the recovery of ground lost over 20 years".[18] But even

achieving this performance is far from being assured. Since 1990 ODA has been declining both in real terms (chart 7) and in relation to the GDP of the recipient countries. Moreover, commodity prices have levelled off and turned downwards, a movement which has been accentuated by the weakening of global demand due to the East Asian financial crisis. In these conditions, and given the weak supply response to adjustment policies, even these modest growth projections may prove to be over-optimistic, as they have done in the past.[19]

It is generally agreed that greater policy effort is needed to translate the current recovery into stronger and sustained growth in Africa. There can be little doubt that an important reason for the continuing poor performance of countries undertaking SAPs is slippage in programme implementation. However, programme compliance has not always resulted in strong economic performance, a fact which suggests that there are also serious problems in programme design. In particular, there

Chart 7

FLOWS OF OFFICIAL DEVELOPMENT ASSISTANCE TO NON-OIL EXPORTING COUNTRIES IN SSA, 1970-1996

(Index numbers, 1970 = 100)

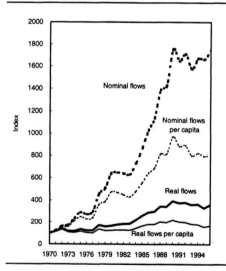

Source: World Bank, *Global Development Finance 1997.*
Note: ODA flows exclude technical cooperation grants; real flows are at 1970 import prices.

are reasons to believe that the emphasis on removing price distortions is not necessarily the best way to bring about a strong supply response and growth performance. The following chapters take a closer look at the question of incentives and supply response, seek to identify the main constraints and opportunities in agriculture, industry and trade, and discuss the policies needed to remove the constraints and to realize the opportunities.

There is also a consensus that restoration of economic growth in SSA is unlikely without a solution to the problem of external debt overhang. Indeed, the failure to address the debt problem and to provide adequate external financing is often seen as a major weakness in programme design. While the international community has recognized the need to support greater policy efforts with increased debt relief and net transfer of resources to most SSA countries through the HIPC Initiative, a number of issues remain unresolved. Past *TDRs* discussed many of these issues in detail. What follows provides a brief review, focusing on the link between debt relief and capital accumulation.

E. Improving the prospects: The role of debt relief

Debt overhang describes a situation in which creditors' demand for full debt servicing can reduce the present value of debt servicing in the future by depressing investment and growth. This would damage the interests not only of the debtor countries but also of the creditors. Such a situation could not be rectified by provision of liquidity (new debt) in order to overcome current debt-servicing difficulties. Rather, it calls for a reduction in the stock of debt and debt servicing.

Various debt indicators illustrate the extent and nature of the problem in SSA (table 3). Ninety-three per cent of SSA's external debt is public and publicly guaranteed, and almost 80 per cent of this amount is owed to official creditors, including a substantial and growing part to multilateral financial institutions (chart 8). The debt problem in SSA is therefore essentially one of official debt. Although its external debt is only a small part of the total debt of developing countries, as a proportion of exports and GDP it is the highest of any developing region (table 3). Moreover, unlike in other developing regions, these ratios have exhibited a rising trend since 1988, when creditors first recognized the need to introduce debt reduction as a central element of an international debt strategy dealing with the debt of poor countries.

The relatively low debt service ratio in SSA compared with other regions is not always explained by greater concessionality of the debt. For instance, concessional debt is relatively higher in South Asia, where the debt service ratio is also higher. Rather, it is explained by a continuous growth of arrears, which is perhaps the best indicator of the extent of the debt overhang. Accumulated arrears, on interest and principal payments, reached $64 billion in 1996, amounting to about 27.4 per cent of the total debt. More worrying, two thirds of the increase in debt since 1988 has been due to arrears (table 3).

There is ample evidence of the adverse effects of the debt overhang on investment and growth in Africa.[20] Since the external debt is mainly owed by governments, the debt overhang deters public investment in physical and human infrastructure as well as growth-enhancing current spending on health and education. Also, it creates a problem of policy credibility and considerable uncertainty for private investors, who run the risk that gains from investment could be taxed away to service external debt. This is true not only for domestic investors but also for foreign investors; the latter tend to stay out of countries with serious debt-servicing difficulties. Indeed, it is almost impossible for a country suffering from debt overhang to have access to private capital markets:

> All creditworthiness and ratings analyses on which foreign investors rely include strong negative debt elements. Those running

Table 3

EXTERNAL DEBT INDICATORS FOR DEVELOPING COUNTRIES, 1988 AND 1996, BY REGION

(Percentages)

	Debt/exports		Debt/GNP		Debt service/ exports		Interest and principal arrears as a share of			Share of official debt in total debt
							Total debt		New debt since 1988	
	1988	*1996*	*1988*	*1996*	*1988*	*1996*	*1988*	*1996*	*1996*	*1996*
Sub-Saharan Africa	244.2	236.9	67.7	76.2	20.8	12.4	11.8	27.4	64.8	75.6
North Africa/Middle East	175.4	126.8	41.7	34.0	19.7	12.1	6.8	5.5	0.1	72.4
East Asia	136.7	98.9	33.7	30.8	21.2	12.2	0.5	3.6	5.6	44.5
South Asia	294.6	208.8	28.2	28.3	26.2	23.1	0.0	0.1	0.1	76.3
Latin America	308.0	202.8	56.4	41.4	36.8	30.0	5.2	1.8	-0.1	33.0
All developing countries	175.6	146.2	35.7	37.0	22.0	16.4	5.4	6.1	1.1	50.2

Source: World Bank, *Global Development Finance 1997* (Washington, D.C., 1997).

portfolio investment funds in Africa or attempting to promote investor interest in HIPC privatizations assess the existence of debt overhang as a key negative influence. Some incentives, such as export-credit guarantees, are directly cut off as a consequence of a debt overhang.[21]

A factor that has played a key role in the persistence of debt overhang in SSA is the short-leash approach adopted by the international community since the start of the debt-servicing difficulties in the early 1980s. While, as repeatedly urged by the UNCTAD secretariat, significant amounts of debt reduction would have been needed to eliminate the debt overhang, to restore growth and to reduce the debt ratios to sustainable levels, in much of the 1980s efforts to deal with the debt problem of low-income countries sought to ensure that debt forgiveness was the exception rather than the norm.[22] This approach started to change with recognition of the need for genuine concessionality in Paris Club reschedulings for poorer countries. The first major step was taken at the Toronto Summit in 1988, where creditor governments recognized the need to reduce the non-concessional official debt owed by low-income countries. However, the debt reduction operations have gone through

many incremental steps, from Toronto terms to London terms (or enhanced Toronto terms) to Naples terms and to Lyon terms, as improvements made in each step proved inadequate in dealing with the problem.

A major shortcoming of these steps was the exclusion of multilateral debt from debt reduction. Multilateral debt accounted for an increasing proportion of the total debt of the poorer countries as a result of the international debt strategy pursued in the 1980s, when lending was increased by the multilateral financial institutions with a view to avoiding a global financial crisis. Moreover, in most cases adjustment policies failed to restore external financial viability:

Following the initial onset of the developing country debt crisis in the early 1980s, many developing countries borrowed heavily from multilateral sources in order to finance debt servicing to private creditors, thereby shifting the balance of debt from private to public creditors. In addition, many countries borrowed heavily in the context of IMF/WB structural adjustment programmes. The poor performance of countries under these adjustment pro-

Chart 8

COMPOSITION OF PUBLIC AND PUBLICLY GUARANTEED EXTERNAL DEBT OF SUB-SAHARAN AFRICA, 1980, 1990 AND 1997

(Per cent shares)

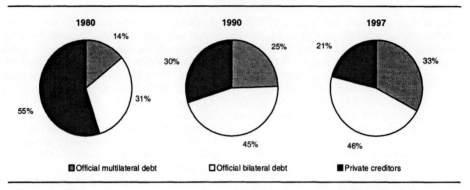

Source: World Bank, *Global Development Finance 1998, Analysis and Summary Tables* (Washington, D.C., 1998).

grammes ... has left much of the borrowing simply unpayable.[23]

The HIPC Initiative has thus received widespread support in the international community, not only as a comprehensive and coordinated approach, but also as a crucial step in recognizing that losses on bad loans should not be borne by the debtors alone, but shared also by the creditors, particularly in view of the key role that the multilateral financial institutions played in setting the policies in debtor countries. Moreover, the Initiative has been formulated in recognition of the need to reach a sustainable debt position in the context of growth and development.

However, the view is gaining strength in the international community that the HIPC Initiative needs a significant adjustment to become a decisive move to help re-establish the conditions for sustained economic growth. The basic issues relate to eligibility and the adequacy of the debt reduction to be granted, as well as the speed with which countries in need will actually benefit from relief.

There can be little doubt that, since all the debt has to be paid in foreign currency, export earnings are an important determinant of debt-servicing capacity. However, as a very large proportion of debt is owed by the public sector, the debt burden relative to government revenues is at least equally relevant in determining debt-servicing capacity. Even when the economy generates sufficient export earnings and faces no external financing gap, servicing of external sovereign debt could pose serious difficulties. It would necessitate a transfer from the private to the public sector through either cuts in public spending or increases in taxation, both of which might have serious consequences for stability and growth.[24]

Responding to the concern of the countries with high export-GDP ratios and low debt-servicing ratios, the Executive Boards of IMF and the World Bank approved in April 1997 the introduction of an additional sustainability criterion which would allow debt reduction if the debtor country has, *inter alia*, an export-to-GDP ratio of at least 40 per cent and a minimum threshold ratio of fiscal revenue to GDP of 20 per cent.[25] By mid-1998 two countries (Côte d'Ivoire and Guyana) had qualified on the basis of this additional criterion.

While, according to this criterion, eligibility will depend on having a minimum fiscal revenue ratio, one of the arguments advanced in favour of debt relief is that it would allow debtor governments to reduce high taxes, which "tend to undermine growth by introducing serious distortions in the economy, including heightened barriers to trade (via trade taxes), capital flight, tax evasion and reduced work effort".[26] More importantly, while the addition of the fiscal burden criterion has somewhat broadened the range of eligibility and the scope for debt relief, it does not appear to go far enough in restoring the financial viability of the public sector, which holds the key to restoring stability and growth. For instance, a non-eligible country with an export-to-GDP ratio of less than 40 per cent and a debt service ratio of less than 20-25 per cent can still face a considerable fiscal burden, of up to 10 per cent of GDP. The kind of problems this would create is illustrated by the following:

> For example, a well-designed budget might include current expenditures on education (mostly at the primary and secondary level) of some 5 per cent of GDP; public health outlays of some 3 per cent of GDP; costs of public administration of 2 per cent of GDP; and expenses on police and defence of some 3 per cent of GDP. Infrastructure spending is sure to require at least 5 per cent of GDP, even if the government leaves much of the infrastructure finance to the private sector (e.g. for power, telecommunications and ports) and focuses its attention on items (e.g. rural roads) that are much harder to finance through the market. The total outlays in this illustration total 18 per cent of GDP. Evidently, there is virtually no room for debt-servicing, nor for subsidies to households and firms or income transfer programmes other than in health and education. As experience has shown, attempts to collect more than a minimum in external debt servicing result in (a) serious budget deficits; (b) unacceptable cuts in education, public health, or basic infrastructure; or (c) tax rates at levels that jeopardize economic growth.[27]

These considerations suggest that greater attention should be paid to the fiscal burden of debt (e.g. by setting limits to the amount of debt servicing from the budget expressed as a proportion of GDP) in assessing debt sustainability, independently of the degree of export orientation of the economy and the extent to which debt servicing cuts into export earnings.

There are also more fundamental questions raised by the implementation of the HIPC Initiative. They can be illustrated by reference to the considerations set out in *TDR 1998*, Part One, chapter IV, on the relevance of the principles of bankruptcy codes to international debt workouts. The Initiative is addressed to countries which are unable to service their debts fully. Such a situation corresponds to the notion of insolvency under bankruptcy codes, which enables debtors to benefit from a number of arrangements, including debt standstill, debtor-in-possession financing and debt reduction. Judicial procedures would not permit practices such as requiring debtors to maintain debt servicing and forcing a long delay between the recognition of insolvency and debt reduction. Such procedures would also avoid a situation requiring unanimity among creditors as regards the debt-restructuring plan – a requirement which allows a minority of creditors to block a deal. Moreover, under insolvency procedures, the amount of debt reduction needed and the conditions attached would not be determined by the creditors, and the same principles would apply to all creditors in order to ensure comparability of settlements.

As discussed in *TDR 1998*, Part One, chapter IV, there are serious difficulties in replicating the insolvency procedures for international debt through an international bankruptcy court, not only for sovereign debtors but also for private debtors. Nevertheless, it is possible to establish the key insolvency principles and apply them within the existing international framework. The application of these principles would dictate an immediate write-off of all unpayable debt in SSA, determined on the basis of an independent assessment of debt sustainability.

Experience so far demonstrates that the approach to debt reduction used so far has been inadequate. Not only has it perpetuated aid dependency, but it has also failed to promote "sound policies" and commitment to and ownership of the programmes. Resolving the crisis in SSA requires a bolder approach in order to secure the rapid and adequate debt reduction needed to restore the financial viability of the public sector and economic growth, and in order to ensure that the operation will never have to be repeated.

Notes

1   Here, in tracing post-independence performance, 1965 is taken as the cut-off date. Of the British and French colonies, Ghana (1957) and Guinea (1958), respectively, were the first to gain independence. Territories that gained independence after the mid-1960s include Botswana (1966), Mauritius (1968), Guinea-Bissau (1974), Angola (1975), Cape Verde (1975), Mozambique (1975), Sao Tome and Principe (1975) and Zimbabwe (first in 1965, with the Unilateral Declaration of Independence by Southern Rhodesia, and subsequently in 1980, when independence was formally granted by the British Parliament).

2   See J. Dunning, "Changes in the level and structure of international production: The last one hundred years", in M. Cassen (ed.), *The Growth of International Business* (London: Allen and Unwin, 1983), table 5.2. In 1970, FDI was equivalent to 0.52 per cent of GDP in SSA, versus 0.26 per cent in East and South-East Asia, and 0.74 per cent in Latin America and the Caribbean; see UNCTAD, *Foreign Direct Investment in Africa* (United Nations publication, Sales No. E.95.II.A.6), New York and Geneva, 1995, table 18.

3   See B. van Arkadie, "The State and economic change in Africa", in H. J. Chang and R. Rowthorn (eds.), *The Role of the State in Economic Change* (Oxford: Clarendon Press, 1995).

4   In the early 1970s Western Europe was the destination of 55 per cent of African exports, and the origin of 65 per cent of all African imports. In the first half of the 1990s more than 60 per cent of African exports went to Western Europe and about 55 per cent of African imports originated there. The share of intra-African trade in total imports of African countries fell to 3.1 per cent by 1980. It then doubled during the 1980s and had risen to 8.6 per cent by 1995. The issue of intraregional trade is discussed in greater detail in chapter IV below.

5   The issue of commodity diversification is discussed in greater detail in chapter IV.

6   See D. Ben-David and D. Papell, "Slowdowns and meltdowns: Postwar growth evidence from 74 countries", CEPR Discussion Paper No. 1111 (London: Centre for Economic Policy Research, 1995).

7   Moreover, the decline in commodity prices made a major contribution to disinflation in OECD countries; see *TDR 1987*, Part One, chapter II.

8   For a detailed discussion of the fallacy-of-composition problem see *TDR 1993*, Part Two, chapter II, p. 101.

9   See *TDR 1993*, Part Two, chapter II, pp. 97-99.

10   See G. Helleiner, "Trade, aid and relative price changes in sub-Saharan Africa in the 1980s", paper presented at the conference "From Stabilization to Growth in Africa", Marstrand, Sweden, 6-7 September 1992. See also *Adjustment in Africa. Reforms, Results and the Road Ahead*, World Bank Policy Research Paper (New York: Oxford University Press for the World Bank, 1994), p. 29; and for more recent years R. Faruqee and I. Husain, "Adjustment in seven African countries", in I. Husain and R. Faruqee (eds.), *Adjustment in Africa. Lessons from Country Case Studies* (Washington, D.C.: World Bank, 1994).

11   See *TDR 1993*, Part Two, chapter II, pp. 109-110.

12   E. V. K. Jaycox, *Africa: From Stagnation to Recovery* (Washington, D.C.: World Bank, February 1993).

13   This is also confirmed by the results of the World Bank's own assessment of adjustment programmes in Africa. Only one country (Nigeria) classified by IMF as a "recent strong performer" in 1998 was among the six countries which the World Bank had found in 1994 to have made "large improvements in macroeconomic policies"; and another recent strong performer (Uganda) was among those nine countries that had been found to have made "small improvements" *(Adjustment in Africa: Reforms, Results, and the Road Ahead, op. cit.*, pp. 57-59). The listing of Nigeria as a "recent strong performer" is somewhat surprising since GDP growth was, on average, below 3 per cent in 1990-1996 and only slightly above 3 per cent in 1997. Moreover, Nigeria benefited from the strength of oil prices; average prices in 1996 were almost a third higher than two years earlier, but with current trends in oil markets this performance may not be repeated.

14   IMF, *World Economic Outlook*, April 1998 (Washington, D.C.: IMF), table 12.

15   For a discussion of recent savings and investment performance in SSA, see S. Fischer, E. Hernández-Catá and M.S. Khan, "Africa: Is this the turning point?", IMF Paper on Policy Analysis and Assessment 98/6 (Washington, D.C., 1998).

16   *Ibid.*, p. 12 and IMF, *World Economic Outlook*, April 1998, *op. cit.*, p. 72.

17   R. Ram, "Productivity of public and private investment in developing countries: A broad international perspective", *World Development*, Vol.24, No.8, 1996.

18   World Bank, *Global Economic Prospects and the Developing Countries* (Washington D.C.: World Bank, 1997), Appendix I, p. 86.

19   In 1992 the World Bank growth projection for SSA for the 1990s was an average rate of 3.8 per cent per

annum; see *Global Economic Prospects and the Developing Countries* (Washington, D.C.: World Bank, 1992), annex. The actual rate until 1997 was about 2.5 per cent per annum. Thus, to achieve 3.8 per cent for the whole decade, the region would need to grow at a rate of no less than 6 per cent per annum during the rest of the 1990s. But the growth rate now projected for the remainder of the 1990s is in the order of 4 per cent. Even if this growth rate were realized, this would mean some 2.8 per cent growth per annum for the decade as a whole, i.e. one percentage point less than the original World Bank projections. The same considerations are broadly valid for the projections for 1992-2002 in the 1993 issue of *Global Economic Prospects and the Developing Countries* (see table 7.4).

20   For a survey of these studies and the underlying mechanisms see M. Martin, "A multilateral debt facility – global and national", in UNCTAD, *International Monetary and Financial Issues for the 1990s*, Vol. VIII (United Nations publication, Sales No. E.97.II.D.5), New York and Geneva, 1997.

21   *Ibid.*, p. 150.

22   See in particular *TDR 1988*, Part One, chap. IV.

23   J. D. Sachs, "External debt, structural adjustment and economic growth", in UNCTAD, *International Monetary and Financial Issues for the 1990s*, Vol. IX (United Nations publication, Sales No. E.98.II.D.3) New York and Geneva, 1998, p. 53.

24   This is, in effect, similar to the domestic budgetary transfer problem that faced a number of countries in Latin America in the 1980s when the public sector lacked the resources needed to service debt even though the private sector generated adequate foreign exchange earnings to make such payments; see *TDR 1989*, Part One, chapter IV.

25   See *TDR 1997*, box 2.

26   Sachs, *op. cit.*, p. 46. This criterion is indeed a reflection of donor concern that aid reduces tax effort and hence leads to aid dependency. However, if an extra dollar of aid indeed reduces taxation, this would mean that the aid is partly transferred to the private sector. It has been argued that "not only is there no evidence for this effect, but that had it happened it would have been desirable"; see P. Collier, "Aid and economic development in Africa" (Oxford University: Centre for the Study of African Economies, October 1997), mimeo, p. 1.

27   Sachs, *op. cit.*, p. 49. The above does not necessarily imply net negative transfers by the country. As the author points out (p.54, note 1), "overall foreign assistance may exceed 5 per cent of GDP, but much of it will go directly to enterprises and households, and thus will not be available as a source of revenue support for budgetary outlays".

Chapter II

THE ROLE, STRUCTURE AND PERFORMANCE OF AGRICULTURE

A. Introduction

Agriculture is the key sector in many African countries, particularly in low-income countries in SSA. Analysts with very different perspectives agree that the generally weak performance of the sector in the 1970s contributed to the economic crisis which developed in the region at the end of the decade.[1] But there is little consensus about the causes of this weak performance, why it has persisted in many countries despite policy reforms, and what should be done to end it. Promoting agricultural development in Africa has proved to be a complex matter and has given rise to different views on both the role of agriculture in economic development and the tasks which governments should undertake.

Two main issues recur in policy debates, the first being the mix of private incentives and public goods that can best support agricultural development. The second issue is the pattern and processes of resource flows and linkages between agriculture and other sectors of the economy that best promote overall economic development, and what government needs to do to facilitate them.

Agricultural policy reform in Africa has been based on the view that poor performance is due to policies designed to extract resources from farmers in order to promote industrialization and to serve urban interests at the expense of agriculture. The alignment of producer prices to world prices and the fostering of private input and output mar-

kets were expected to provide the necessary incentives to farmers to increase output. However, many have argued that "getting the prices right" is not sufficient, because agricultural supply response is constrained by structural factors, including infrastructure, technology and various agrarian institutions such as the gender division of labour and land tenure patterns. There is now increasing agreement on the importance of such non-price constraints on production and productivity growth.[2] But which ones are critical, how they are to be removed, and whether there are trade-offs between policies which support the achievement of price and non-price conditions for agricultural growth are still open questions. Moreover, despite greater understanding in some of these areas, policy is still geared to reducing the fiscal burden of the agricultural sector, and wedded to privatization and market liberalization rather than to pragmatic solutions tailored to the level of development.[3]

The issue of price incentives is embedded within a broader issue relating to intersectoral transfers between agriculture and industry, urban bias, and the contribution of agriculture to the overall growth process. Since the initiation of the reform process, this broader issue has been neglected as the idea that sustained growth in Africa depends on industrialization has fallen out of favour. But this does not mean that the effects of agricultural policy on other sectors, and vice versa, can be ignored. The basic policy problem of all predominantly agrarian economies, including those in Africa, is how to manage the relations between agriculture and the rest of the economy in a way that promotes agricultural growth and thus enables a structural transformation in which the relative importance of the agricultural sector declines as other sectors, and particularly manufacturing, move onto a dynamic growth path. Thus, policy issues in agriculture need to be addressed in terms of multiple intersectoral linkages which often involve complex policy choices.[4]

The central theme of this and the next chapter is the role of government in promoting agricultural development, focusing in particular on how policy affects incentives and investment. This chapter discusses the role, structure and performance of the agricultural sector in Africa. It starts with the main ways in which agriculture can contribute to economic growth in that region. This is followed by a discussion of its main structural characteristics, including ownership patterns, infrastructure and production structure. Finally, the chapter examines agricultural performance since the 1970s, focusing on total production and food output, exports and productivity growth. It is shown that there have been some improvements in agricultural growth since the mid-1980s. Nevertheless, productivity growth is sluggish, food production still lags behind population growth and the agricultural trade balance continues to deteriorate. The next chapter examines the role of policy in this situation, in particular its impact on incentives, and the influence of structural constraints on investment behaviour and supply response.

B. The role of agriculture in economic growth

Although the economic importance of agriculture has been declining over the last 25 years, the sector still accounts for a large share of GDP and employment in many African countries (table 4). In 16 SSA countries the agricultural sector employs more than two thirds of the labour force and generates more than one third of GDP. In 14 countries more than 80 per cent of the labour force are still in agriculture. Economies in which agriculture contributes less than one third of total GDP and less than two-thirds of the total labour force include the North African and South African Customs Union (SACU) countries, three oil exporters – Congo, Gabon and Nigeria – as well as Cape Verde, Côte d'Ivoire, Mauritania and Mauritius. All the middle-income economies in Africa except Cameroon are in this group. There are only 15 countries in Africa as a whole in which the sector's share in GDP is less than 15 per cent, and in only eight of these (Algeria, Botswana, Cape Verde, Lesotho, Mauritius, South Africa, Swaziland and Tunisia) agriculture absorbs less than 40 per cent of the labour force.

In such predominantly agricultural economies there are two main ways in which output per head can be increased: by shifting employment from agriculture to the industrial sector, where labour productivity is typically higher; and by increasing sectoral labour productivities while maintaining or raising the level of employment. As international comparisons show, there are ample opportunities for enhancing productivity within agriculture in low-income countries. But the scope for sustaining a high rate of productivity growth is much greater in manufacturing. Agriculture is "innately a slow-growing sector"[5], and accelerating agricultural growth normally entails moving from a growth rate of 2-3 per cent to one of 4-6 per cent. By contrast, in manufacturing, because of the greater potential for productivity gains and also because of higher income elasticity of demand, growth rates of 8-10 per cent can be sustained over long periods.

The realization of such growth potentials is an extremely complex process. It depends on an appropriate structure of incentives for private investment in both the agricultural and the industrial sectors, as well as on public investment in physical and social infrastructure. Also, it requires the attainment of key macroeconomic balances: be-

Table 4

AFRICA: CHANGES IN THE SHARE OF AGRICULTURE IN THE LABOUR FORCE AND GDP SINCE 1970, BY REGION

(Percentages)

	Share in			
	Total labour force		GDP	
Region	1970	1990	1970	1995
Low-income countries in:				
West Africa*ª*	83.7	75.4	41.5	38.2
East and Southern Africa*ᵇ*	80.9	78.5	39.1	35.4
Middle-income countries in:				
West Africa*ᶜ*	79.1	67.9	32.2	25.2
East and Southern Africa*ᵈ*	59.5	33.4	27.5	7.8
South Africa	31.0	13.5	7.9	4.7
North Africa*ᵉ*	49.6	35.4	19.3	14.7
Oil exporters*ᶠ*	75.6	55.3	27.3	21.4

Source: UNCTAD secretariat calculations, based on World Bank, *World Development Indicators, 1997* (CD-Rom).
Note: Shares are simple averages of individual country shares.
  a Benin, Burkina Faso, Central African Republic, Chad, Gambia, Ghana, Mali, Mauritania, Niger, Sierra Leone, Togo.
  b Burundi, Democratic Republic of the Congo, Kenya, Lesotho, Madagascar, Malawi, Rwanda, Somalia, Sudan, Uganda, Zambia, Zimbabwe.
  c Côte d'Ivoire, Senegal.
  d Botswana, Mauritius, Swaziland.
  e Algeria, Egypt, Morocco, Tunisia.
  f Cameroon, Congo, Gabon, Nigeria.

tween foreign exchange requirements and foreign exchange availability; between the rate of growth of real wages and the availability of wage goods; between public sector investment needs and non-inflationary means of financing such investment; and broadly between savings and investment. In the early stages of development the growth of agriculture is itself a major component of overall economic growth. But in addition, there are linkages through which agricultural growth can also stimulate growth in other sectors.

In Africa, overall economic growth depends critically on the performance of agriculture.[6] Firstly, except in a small number of countries with rich mineral resources, significant earnings from tourism or workers' remittances, agriculture is the most important source of foreign exchange earnings, con-tributing over 50 per cent of total exports in recent years in 20 countries (chart 9). Such earnings are needed to finance the import not only of interme-diate and capital goods for local industries, but also of the manufactured consumer goods that must be made available to farmers if incentives to increase output are to have any impact. There is evidence from the early 1980s that a shortage of such incentive goods can create a vicious cir-cle by prompting a reduction in the production of cash crops which in turn deepens the payments cri-sis, thereby aggravating the shortage of manufactured goods and causing further cutbacks in production.[7]

A second key contribution by agriculture is the provision of food supplies. This is particu-larly important in view of very high levels of food deprivation in SSA. A number of estimates sug-

Chart 9

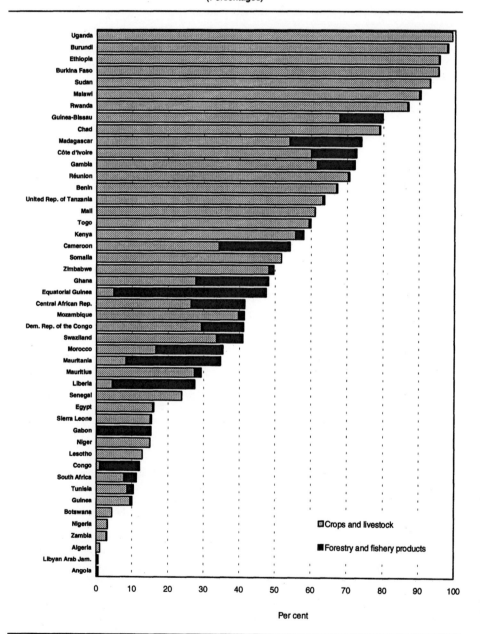

SHARE OF AGRICULTURAL PRODUCTS IN TOTAL EXPORTS FROM AFRICAN ECONOMIES, 1995

(Percentages)

Per cent

☒Crops and livestock

■Forestry and fishery products

Source: UNCTAD secretariat calculations, based on FAO, *FAOSTAT* database.

gest that during 1990-1992 about 43 per cent of the population of SSA – some 215 million people – had inadequate access to food, double the number in 1969-1971.[8] Reducing this deprivation is not only a moral and political priority for governments, but also a critical economic objective since poor nutrition tends to reduce labour productivity.[9] Another reason why food supplies are important is that lower real food prices have important growth-enhancing ramifications throughout the economy, as they allow real wages to rise without impeding accumulation.

Agriculture's third contribution to overall growth is through the supply of raw materials to industry. These forward linkages from agriculture are important because high productivity in agriculture and cheap agricultural raw materials tend to increase profitability and investment in agro-processing industries, thereby enhancing international competitiveness. It has been estimated that between one third and two thirds of manufacturing value added in sub-Saharan Africa depends on agricultural raw materials.[10] For Zimbabwe, one of the economies with a more diversified industrial structure, agriculture provides 40 per cent of all manufacturing inputs. In Kenya, nearly half of micro-enterprises (almost two thirds if forestry and textiles are included) rely directly on agricultural supplies.[11]

Fourthly, being the dominant sector, agriculture can provide, directly or indirectly, resources for public or private investment both within and outside agriculture by generating what is technically known as the "net agricultural surplus", which is simply defined as the total value added in the sector minus the consumption of direct agricultural producers. During the immediate post-colonial period, attempts were made to mobilize the available agricultural surplus of farm households producing export crops through the marketing boards which had been established during the colonial period. Estimates suggest that before the 1980s, export crops contributed from 20 per cent to 40 per cent to government revenue.[12]

Another of agriculture's contributions is the provision of a domestic market for manufacturing. This was historically important for economies which managed to build up a small, inward-looking manufacturing sector. According to a study of seven countries for 1965-1986, "a major cause of manufacturing growth in SSA has been rooted in the establishment of an environment conducive

to steady expansive growth outside the sector itself and principally primary-product related".[13] For all except two countries (Côte d'Ivoire and Zambia) the predominant source of growth was increasing domestic demand, which accounted for 54 per cent of manufacturing growth in Botswana, 55 per cent in Cameroon, 69 per cent in Kenya, 76 per cent in Nigeria and 72 per cent in Zimbabwe. As urban incomes grow and manufacturing becomes internationally competitive, the dependence on rural demand is weakened. Nevertheless, as experience shows, including in East Asia, this source of demand is particularly important in the early stages of import substitution when manufacturers rely on the domestic market before they can compete with more efficient producers in world markets.[14] In Africa, too, manufacturing export success has almost invariably been developed on the basis of import-substitution activities.

Lastly, agricultural policy has been used in Africa to promote a pattern of income distribution which is regarded as legitimate and which therefore does not threaten political stability. This is an extremely delicate problem in nation-state building in Africa. Some aspects of agricultural pricing policy, particularly the practice of providing uniform guaranteed prices countrywide, have been part of an implicit social contract designed to redress colonial imbalances and ensure that certain ethnic groups with less fertile land and limited access to markets are not totally excluded.[15]

A major dilemma in agrarian economies is that policies designed to increase the contribution of the agricultural sector to the rest of the economy can impede agricultural growth, thereby failing to attain their original objectives. Thus, attempts to provide fiscal revenues through taxation of agricultural exports may reduce incentives for agricultural producers and cut foreign exchange earnings. Again, policies designed to provide cheap food for the urban population or cheap supplies to industry can reduce agricultural incentives, thereby creating shortages. Similarly, the system of agricultural pricing can be abused to reward political support or punish opposition, or favour urban against rural interests.[16] Experience shows that the countries of SSA have not always been able to strike a balance between such conflicting objectives. This has not only impeded agricultural growth and depressed the living conditions of a large proportion of the population, but also reduced significantly the contribution of agriculture to the rest of the economy.

C. Main features of African agriculture

Policies designed for agricultural development and their effects on the overall performance of the economy are circumscribed by certain structural features of African agriculture. These include specific forms of production and a historical legacy of intersectoral dualism between agriculture and non-agriculture. Equally important is the nature of agricultural production, particularly its tradability. These issues are taken up in the following sections.

1. Forms of production

Agrarian production relations and institutions are very diverse in Africa, but in general it is possible to identify three forms of production. The first is "smallholder production", in which work is organized by households around a gender division of labour. Men and women have responsibilities for different crops, or for specific tasks at different stages of production of the same crops, but women, who provide a major part of the labour input, often do not have full control over the product of their labour. Access to land is mediated through indigenous systems of tenure in which membership of the local community is the primary basis for various land-use rights, although there are also land markets for buying and selling user rights, but not outright ownership of parcels of land.[17] Very little of the arable land area is irrigated and thus most producers are subject to the vagaries of the weather.[18] Owing to the dependence on rainfall there is strong seasonality in labour use, particularly in semi-arid areas, where about 70 per cent of labour is expended in a four-month period. In such areas labour shortages in critical periods of planting and harvesting can be particularly acute and coexist with underemployment during the rest of the year.

The second form of production is large-scale capitalist farming. Some farms are foreign-owned plantations, generally export-oriented; some are old colonial settler estates oriented to export or domestic markets; and some are new African estates, often set up by the newly emerging elites. There has been an expansion of this last type in the domestic cereals sector since the mid-1970s, but in some countries such African agribusinesses are also export-oriented.[19]

The third form of production – large-scale state-owned farms – was most strongly developed in the post-colonial period in the few African countries engaged in effecting a transition to socialism (for example, Algeria, Ethiopia, Guinea-Bissau and Mozambique). Following the privatization drive, public ownership of farms is now quite unimportant.

Although smallholder production is the dominant form of production in Africa, it coexists with large-scale capitalist farming. This coexistence has generally not been benign, though it has the potential for positive linkages in forms of contract farming where smallholders act as outgrowers for large agribusinesses. Large settler farms were generally established through measures which sought to reduce the profitability of more efficient smallholder production, constraining competition and ensuring the availability of a workforce. These measures restricted the access of smallholders to land, markets and infrastructure services, which eventually could result in soil erosion, the drying up of wells and exhaustion of pasture.[20]

Today smallholders include both small and medium-sized farm units. Although often described as "subsistence farmers", small units are often enmeshed in product markets, both selling and buying foodstuffs through the year on a seasonal basis and even producing cash crops for export. Larger units produce primarily for sale, hire labour and use manufactured inputs. Farmers in this category, who have variously been called "progressive", "commercial" or even "capitalist" farmers, are responsible for a large proportion of marketed output in many African countries. Those who are mainly involved in export crops are concentrated in areas of relatively high and regular rainfall where infrastructure is also generally better. The commercially oriented food crop farmers have developed as a result of growing urban demand and with state support, particularly through the integrated rural development programmes of the 1970s which sought to provide seed, fertilizer, pesticides and low-cost credit, and to guarantee market outlets. It is these farmers which form the basis of what is now being described as Africa's maize revolution.[21] They are found in areas closer to major urban centres and with better agro-ecological conditions, but with less favourable rainfall than areas of export crop production.

A significant feature of both small and medium-sized farm units making up the "smallholders" is that an important part of their incomes is derived from non-farm employment in formal or informal activities. This, it is now realized, is widespread throughout Africa (see table 5). Indeed, recent estimates suggest that on average as much as 42 per cent of rural household incomes is derived from non-farm employment, as compared with 40 per cent in Latin America and 32 per cent in Asia.[22] This involves some rural employment, but it often entails the migration of male household members to urban centres. For rich farmers, who occupy the more lucrative niches in the labour market, off-farm earnings provide a source of investment in agriculture, while for the poor they mainly supplement consumption.

Selling labour time to other farmers does not appear to be a major source of earnings for smallholders. This reflects the relative underdevelopment of rural labour markets outside those countries in which capitalist agribusinesses are important. However, evidence suggests that non-monetized labour exchanges are an important form of interaction between rich and poor smallholders.[23] Moreover, the situation is changing, as with rising population densities some farmers are becoming land-poor with use rights over a plot of land not large enough to meet their subsistence needs. A process of concentration of control over different rights in land is occurring as land becomes scarce and commercially valuable. Moreover, some smallholders have become simply "too poor to farm" in the sense that, despite access to land, they cannot mobilize sufficient amounts of labour and other inputs to make a living.[24] Despite these trends, the intensity of landlessness in Africa is still less than in Asia or Latin America. Indeed, in most of rural Africa where indigenous systems of land tenure prevail, it is difficult even to speak of

Table 5

NON-FARM INCOME OF RURAL HOUSEHOLDS IN AFRICA: CASE STUDY EVIDENCE

Country	Period	Share of non-farm income in total income (Per cent)
Botswana	1974-1975	54
Botswana	1985-1986	77
Burkina Faso (fav.)	1978-1979	22
Burkina Faso (unfav.)	1981-1984	37
Burkina Faso (fav.)	1981-1984	40
Ethiopia (overall)	1989-1990	36
Ethiopia (lowland, fav.)	1989-1990	44
Ethiopia (highland, unfav.)	1989-1990	38
Ethiopia (pastoral)	1989-1990	38
Gambia	1985-1986	23
Kenya (central)	1974-1975	42
Kenya (western)	1987-1989	80
Kenya	1984	52
Lesotho	1976	78
Malawi	1990-1991	34
Mali	1988-1989	59
Mozambique	1991	15
Namibia (fav.)	1992-1993	56
Namibia (unfav.)	1992-1993	93
Niger (fav.)	1989-1990	43
Niger (unfav.)	1989-1990	52
Nigeria (northern)	1974-1975	30
Nigeria (northern)	1966-1967	23
Rwanda	1990	30
Senegal (northern, unfav.)	1988-1989	60
Senegal (central)	1988-1990	24
Senegal (southern)	1988-1990	41
South Africa[a]	1982-1986	75
Sudan	1988	38
United Rep. of Tanzania	1980	25
Zimbabwe	1988-1989	35
Zimbabwe (overall)	1990-1991	38
Zimbabwe (poor)	1990-1991	31

Source: T. Reardon, "Using evidence of household income diversification to inform study of the rural nonfarm labour market in Africa", *World Development*, Vol. 25, No. 5, May 1997.

Note: Non-farm income is income from local non-farm wage employment, local non-farm self-employment and migrants' remittances. The abbreviations "fav." and "unfav." denote favourable and unfavourable agroclimatic zones, respectively.

a Former homelands.

"landlessness" since members of the community have direct or indirect access to community land.[25]

2.   Intersectoral dualism

There is a large gap in income per head between the agricultural and non-agricultural sectors in Africa. Value-added per worker in the latter sectors is between 7 and 8 times higher than in agriculture; in Asia and Latin America it is only between 2.5 and 3.5 times higher (table 6).

Table 6

INTERSECTORAL DUALISM: A REGIONAL COMPARISON

	Income ratio[a]			
	1950-1960	1960-1970	1970-1980	1980-1990
Africa	7.05	8.33	8.74	7.79
Asia	1.87	3.37	3.31	3.57
Latin America	2.42	3.00	2.81	2.51
Other	1.88	2.17	2.15	2.25

Source: D. Larson and Y. Mundlak, "On the intersectoral migration of agricultural labour", *Economic Development and Cultural Change*, Vol. 45, No. 2, 1997.
a Ratio of non-agricultural value-added per worker to that in agriculture.

This differential is one of the key indicators of "urban bias"in Africa, but this bias cannot be simply attributed to post-colonial pricing policies.[26] Intersectoral dualism has historical and geographical roots in colonial policies that sought to set up institutional barriers to rural-urban interaction, and in poor agro-ecological conditions. But it is ultimately based on lack of investment in African agriculture and the persistence of low agricultural labour productivity, features which will be examined below.

Intersectoral dualism has important implications for agrarian production relations and structural change. It implies that earnings potentials outside agriculture can be much higher, and it is this differential which, in general terms, underlies the attractiveness to farm households of "straddling"

between the agricultural and non-agricultural sectors. Such straddling can have positive effects on agriculture because, as noted, non-farm incomes can provide an important source of farm investment. However, to the extent that off-farm employment opportunities are available, there is continual pressure for productive labour to be diverted from agriculture. Under these conditions, there may be little incentive to adopt high-yielding crop varieties, which can require greater labour inputs. Rather, the types of innovation which are attractive are those which save household labour time and thus enable the diversion of labour from the farm.

The implications of this situation depend on whether there is surplus agricultural labour, i.e. whether the withdrawal of labour will reduce output. In East Asia, at an early stage of industrialization, a combination of widespread surplus labour in agriculture with employment opportunities in the urban economy led to strong dynamic complementarities between agricultural and industrial growth. In such conditions, rapid growth of urban employment can reduce population pressure on land and increase agricultural labour productivity. But where population densities are low, land is not fertile and there are labour shortages in agriculture, the withdrawal of labour can lead to a decline in agricultural output.

The picture in Africa varies from place to place. But a number of astute observers have identified the absence of surplus labour as characteristic of African agriculture in the past, except perhaps in areas concentrating on exports.[27] Moreover, despite high rates of population growth, widespread labour shortages are still identified as a key constraint. Household studies in Southern Africa suggest that "contrary to orthodox thinking, withdrawal of labour from the African countryside tends to result in residual farm work forces which have a lower productive potential than they otherwise would have had".[28] Also, it is estimated that as many as 30 per cent of farm households in Southern Africa are female-headed households with limited productive assets.[29]

3.   Export and food crops, and tradability

Whether governments should give priority to export or food crops has been a perennial issue in the debate on agricultural policy in Africa. In the 1970s both African governments and donors laid emphasis on increasing food production. When export promotion became a central goal of policy reforms in the 1980s, priorities shifted in favour of export crops. It has been argued that the goal of national food self-sufficiency, to which many African governments were committed, was wrongheaded since rising food demand could be met through imports.

Three factors have been increasing the rate of growth of food demand in Africa. The first is the extremely rapid growth of population, which is estimated to have risen from 2.5 per cent per annum in 1960 to 3.2 per cent in the late 1980s. This is the fastest growth rate recorded in human history and contrasts with downward trends both in South Asia, where the rate dropped from 2.5 per cent to 2.1 per cent over the same period, and in Latin America, where it dropped from 2.9 per cent to 2.5 per cent.[30] Second, Africa is experiencing the most rapid rate of urbanization in the world, and it is estimated that the share of the urban population will reach 41 per cent by the year 2000. Third, in view of the prevailing low income levels, improvements in income tend to be spent on food. Estimates show that the overall income elasticity of expenditure on food is close to unity. As income increases, consumption of main staple coarse grains (sorghum, millet and maize) and roots and tubers also rises, but their share in expenditure falls, while for wheat, wheat products and livestock products both the level and the share of expenditure increase with income.

There are a number of difficulties in meeting this rapid growth of food demand through imports, the most important of which is that a major part of staple food in SSA consists of crops which are non-tradable internationally outside Africa. This problem is usually overlooked and agriculture is typically described as a fully tradable sector.[31] However, major domestic food staples over much of Africa, notably cassava, plantain, yams, millet and sorghum in West and Central Africa, and white maize in Southern and East Africa, are not traded internationally outside the region. There is little external demand for them and there are few other international sources of supply.

The extent to which national food demands are met through such non-tradable crops varies from country to country, but traditional food staples are very important in most countries. The major exception is North Africa, where the main source of dietary energy is tradable wheat. Trad-

able rice is also significant in a few West African countries (Gambia, Liberia and Sierra Leone) and also in Madagascar and (along with wheat) in Mauritius. But non-tradable roots and tubers provide an important part of total dietary energy supply in much of West and Central Africa, making up over 33 per cent of the total in 13 countries (Angola, Benin, Burundi, Congo, Côte d'Ivoire, Democratic Republic of the Congo, Ghana, Mozambique, Nigeria, Rwanda, Togo, Uganda and United Republic of Tanzania). Of the other cereal crops, sorghum and millet are the key staples in some Sahelian countries and also Sudan, while white maize is consumed widely in Africa and is the main staple in East and Southern Africa (table 7). Yellow maize is widely traded internationally and can be substituted in diets for white maize, but it is considered inferior and its consumption is mainly a function of poverty levels. Moreover, transport costs for cereals are high, given current infrastructure and marketing systems, and this means that local prices in the cities of the landlocked countries (Burkina Faso, Chad, Malawi, Mali, Niger, Zambia and Zimbabwe) generally fluctuate in a range discouraging trade outside the region and sometimes even within the region.[32]

Another problem in shifting production to exports and relying on food imports relates to the volatility of export prices and the downward trend in the terms of trade. Indeed, foreign exchange shortages have often limited the ability of SSA countries to import food in adequate quantities, and swings in export earnings have been a major factor in large yearly fluctuations in food consumption.[33]

There is no simple answer to the choice between food crops and export crops. On the one hand, there is constant upward pressure on food prices because of rising demand. On the other hand, export crops face declining terms of trade and unstable prices. The development of the food sector has implications for poverty, and also has the political dimensions of food security and economic self-reliance. But, more importantly, it is a critical economic issue, with serious implications for overall growth and macroeconomic balances. Indeed, the competitiveness of exports is often conditioned by the factors which influence the domestic supply of and demand for food. In this respect, increasing productivity and food supply is crucial in improving international competitiveness, both in agriculture and in industry, because it helps to keep down wage costs without lowering workers' living standards.[34]

Table 7

SHARE OF MAJOR FOOD GROUPS IN TOTAL DIETARY ENERGY SUPPLY IN AFRICA, BY COUNTRY, 1990-1992

(Percentages)

Country	Roots and tubers	Main cereals			
		Maize	Sorghum and millet	Rice	Wheat
Total Africa	**14.9**	**14.6**	**10.2**	**6.8**	**15.2**
Dem. Rep. of the Congo	**56.2**	9.5	0.7	3.4	1.8
Ghana	**40.7**	15.0	5.4	5.3	4.1
Mozambique	**39.5**	23.5	4.2	4.2	4.1
Benin	**38.2**	20.0	6.8	5.2	3.0
Congo	**38.1**	4.5	0.0	3.8	13.5
Central African Rep.	**36.0**	9.0	3.8	1.9	3.9
Angola	**29.8**	16.1	2.6	6.0	6.5
Togo	**28.8**	22.0	14.0	5.0	6.6
Burundi	**28.4**	12.3	3.7	1.8	2.0
Rwanda	**28.2**	7.0	10.3	0.7	1.1
Uganda	**27.8**	7.8	9.5	0.9	0.4
Côte d'Ivoire	**27.2**	9.3	1.4	21.3	5.2
Nigeria	**26.0**	5.2	22.4	8.8	1.7
Gabon	**21.9**	8.6	0.0	6.9	9.8
Cameroon	**18.0**	14.3	13.0	4.8	6.1
Malawi	3.8	**67.5**	0.7	1.4	0.3
Zambia	9.9	**64.6**	1.3	0.4	4.0
Lesotho	0.7	**56.4**	2.9	0.5	16.4
Zimbabwe	1.6	**41.5**	5.9	0.5	10.9
Kenya	8.0	**40.4**	1.4	2.1	5.8
South Africa	1.7	**32.4**	2.1	3.1	15.9
United Rep. of Tanzania	24.6	**31.8**	4.9	7.0	1.9
Somalia	0.9	**23.5**	15.4	7.6	8.6
Ethiopia	4.2	**18.7**	11.4	0.1	16.1
Namibia	15.6	**16.9**	10.9	0.0	6.0
Botswana	1.5	**16.8**	12.0	2.5	12.6
Niger	3.6	0.3	**65.9**	4.7	3.4
Burkina Faso	0.9	12.3	**56.1**	5.8	1.4
Mali	1.9	8.6	**48.8**	12.7	1.8
Sudan	0.6	1.0	**38.4**	0.7	18.4
Chad	15.2	2.4	**35.3**	4.8	3.2
Madagascar	21.0	3.9	0.0	**48.9**	1.7
Sierra Leone	4.4	1.2	3.8	**45.2**	3.3
Liberia	22.3	0.0	0.0	**42.8**	1.7
Gambia	1.0	3.8	18.3	**38.1**	4.6
Guinea	13.9	3.1	2.7	**33.9**	5.0
Senegal	1.0	5.4	22.6	**27.2**	8.4
Mauritius	1.3	0.4	0.0	**22.5**	21.7
Tunisia	1.4	0.0	0.1	0.3	**52.0**
Algeria	2.2	0.2	0.1	0.4	**50.2**
Morocco	1.9	3.7	0.3	0.4	**44.2**
Libyan Arab Jamahiriya	1.7	0.2	0.0	4.2	**37.9**
Egypt	1.7	17.3	1.1	9.6	**36.4**
Mauritania	0.5	0.6	6.9	17.6	**30.0**
Swaziland	1.4	11.7	0.0	3.6	**26.4**

Source: FAO, *The Sixth World Food Survey* (Rome: FAO, 1996).

D. Trends in agricultural production, trade and productivity

1. Production

As noted in the previous chapter, agricultural growth in Africa has generally been unsatisfactory. FAO statistics, which indicate the volume of agricultural and food output, suggest that this was particularly so in SSA during the 1970s and early 1980s, when output per capita fell. After 1984 agricultural growth accelerated: from 1970 to 1984, total agricultural output rose by 1.2 per cent per annum, and thereafter by 3.1 per cent. However, the recovery only halted the decline in per capita output (chart 10).

Chart 10

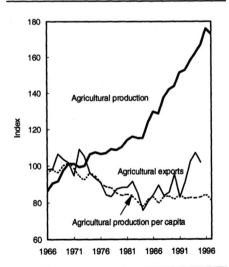

VOLUME OF AGRICULTURAL PRODUCTION AND EXPORTS IN SUB-SAHARAN AFRICA, 1966-1997

(1969-1971 = 100)

Source: UNCTAD secretariat calculations, based on FAO, FAOSTAT database.

This general trend conceals many differences between countries, regions and commodities. Table 8 compares the growth of agricultural production in the 1970s with growth since 1984. In a sample of 44 countries post-1984 agricultural growth performance was better in 22 and worse in 15 than in the 1970s. Whereas in the 1970s a total of 11 countries had growth rates in excess of 3 per cent, in the post-1984 period there was a total of 13 countries. During the 1970s in six of these 13 countries – Algeria, Chad, Ghana, Nigeria, Togo and Uganda – agricultural growth was less than 1 per cent per annum or negative. All the West African Sahelian countries improved their performance after 1984 compared with the 1970s. In contrast, there is a clear tendency for the countries whose performance worsened to be located in Southern or East Africa.

Overall trends in food production are similar to those for agricultural production. There was some recovery in the rate of growth of output after 1984 for the region as a whole, but again only enough to halt the decline in per capita food production. Regional disaggregation shows that in North Africa a rapid upward trend that had emerged in the mid-1980s was reversed in the early 1990s. In West and Central Africa, the trend since 1984 has been upward but weak, whilst in Southern and East Africa it has been downward (table 9). In the latter regions the downward trend is observed in countries both with and without civil unrest. Table 9 shows that within SSA the growth rate of food production was higher since 1985 than in the 1970s in 18 countries, and of these countries Benin, Burkina Faso, Chad, Ghana, Guinea, Mali, Niger, Nigeria, Togo and Uganda all achieved growth rates higher than 3 per cent per annum.[35]

2. Trade

Focusing on SSA, figures for the volume of agricultural exports indicate a similar post-1984 improvement. The volume of agricultural exports was actually declining from 1972 to 1984, but since

Table 8

COMPARISON OF TRENDS IN AGRICULTURAL PRODUCTION IN AFRICAN COUNTRIES DURING 1970-1980 AND 1985-1996

(Average annual growth of output)

		1970-1980					
		More than 4 per cent	**3-4 per cent**	**2-3 per cent**	**1-2 per cent**	**0-1 per cent**	**Negative**
1985-1996	**More than 4 per cent**			Benin Mali	Burkina Faso Niger	Togo	**Ghana Nigeria**
	3-4 per cent	Tunisia			**Egypt Guinea SSA average**	**Algeria Chad**	Uganda
	2-3 per cent	Côte d'Ivoire	Gabon Kenya	Central African Republic Guinea-Bissau	**Dem. Rep. of the Congo Ethiopia* Morocco**		Angola Namibia
	1-2 per cent		Malawi Sudan Zambia		Cameroon Congo Madagascar	**Lesotho Mauritania Senegal**	
	0-1 per cent	Libyan Arab Jam.	United Rep. of Tanzania	South Africa Zimbabwe	Burundi Sierra Leone	Mauritius	**Botswana Mozambique**
	Negative	Rwanda	Swaziland				Gambia

Source: UNCTAD secretariat calculations, based on FAO, *The State of Food and Agriculture* (Rome: FAO, 1997).
Note: Growth was higher in 1985-1996 than in the earlier period for countries shown in bold.
  a   1985-1992.

then it has recovered, though with great variability and at a rate slower than that of the growth in the volume of agricultural production (chart 10). An important feature of the agricultural export trends is that during the first half of the 1970s there was actually a steep rise in unit value, which was more marked or more prolonged than in either Latin America or Asia. As a consequence, agricultural export earnings grew rapidly until 1977, even though the volume fell. But from 1977 to 1982 both the unit value and the total value of agricultural exports fell. Because of the continued decline in unit values from 1986 to 1993, a resumption in the growth of export volumes did not result in any increase in agricultural export revenue. However,

the situation changed after 1993 owing to a steep increase in the unit value of agricultural exports and a continued rise in export volumes.

As in agricultural production, there have been marked differences in export performance among countries (table 10). In 24 countries out of a sample of 46 the growth in the volume of agricultural exports was higher during the post-1984 period than in the 1970s. In 13 countries the volume of agricultural exports continued to decline.

For individual export crops, it is difficult to identify a clear general pattern. For cotton and coffee, two main traditional agricultural exports,

Table 9

COMPARISON OF TRENDS IN FOOD PRODUCTION IN AFRICAN COUNTRIES DURING 1970-1980 AND 1985-1996

(Average annual growth of output)

		1970-1980					
		More than 4 per cent	**3-4 per cent**	**2-3 per cent**	**1-2 per cent**	**0-1 per cent**	**Negative**
1985-1996	**More than 4 per cent**			Benin	Niger	Burkina Faso	Ghana Nigeria
	3-4 per cent	Côte d'Ivoire Tunisia		Egypt	Guinea Mali Morocco SSA average	Algeria Chad Togo Uganda	
	2-3 per cent	Sudan	Central African Republic Gabon Kenya	Guinea-Bissau	Cameroon Dem. Rep. of the Congo Ethiopia[a]		
	1-2 per cent		Zambia		Congo Madagascar	Mauritania Mauritius Senegal	Angola Namibia
	0-1 per cent	Libyan Arab Jam. U. R. of Tanzania	Swaziland	Malawi South Africa	Sierra Leone Lesotho	Burundi	Botswana Mozambique
	Negative		Rwanda		Zimbabwe		Gambia

Source: See table 8.
Note: See table 8.
  a 1985-1992.

the export volumes of the largest producers in SSA were about the same in 1995 as in 1970. For cotton, declines in export volumes in the 1970s were reversed during 1981-1989; for coffee there was no clear tendency. The volume of cocoa exports decreased in the 1970s, with an upturn in 1979. In contrast, tea and tobacco, which are of less importance, show an upward trend from 1970 which continued in the 1980s. For all traditional export commodities except tea, the world market share of SSA was lower in 1995 than in 1970.

Agricultural imports have also been growing, in large part on account of cereals. The increase was particularly rapid after 1976. With regard to crops and livestock, the trade performance ratio, i.e. the ratio of the agricultural trade balance (X-M) to total agricultural trade (X+M), fell from 0.51 in 1966-1968 to 0.44 in 1972-1974 and 0.18 in 1979-1981 (table 11). Subsequently, agricultural exports generally rose more slowly than imports. Consequently, net agricultural exports fell in all groups of countries; out of the seven subregions covered in table 11, four registered deficits in agricultural trade during 1993-1995. This worsening of the net agricultural export position of Africa was due to a rapid increase in food imports, exceeding the growth in earnings from export crops.

Table 10

COMPARISON OF TRENDS IN AGRICULTURAL EXPORTS IN AFRICAN COUNTRIES DURING 1970-1980 AND 1985-1996

(Annual average growth of export volume)

		1970-1980					
		More than 4 per cent	3-4 per cent	2-3 per cent	1-2 per cent	0-1 per cent	Negative
1985-1996	More than 4 per cent	Gabon		Sudan		Cameroon	Benin Namibia Burkina Faso Nigeria Egypt Somaliaᵃ Ghana Togo Guinea-Bissau Uganda Kenya U.R.ofTanzania Libyan Arab Jam.ᵃ
	3-4 per cent	Côte d'Ivoire		Zimbabwe			Tunisia
	2-3 per cent						Botswana Mozambique Zambiaᵃ
	1-2 per cent			Chad			Madagascar Morocco
	0-1 per cent	South Africa		Mali		Mauritius	Central African Rep. Guinea
	Negative			Malawi Swaziland		Rwanda	Algeria Gambia Angola Lesotho Burundi Liberiaᵃ Congo Mauritania D. Rep. of Niger the Congo Senegal Ethiopiaᵇ Sierra Leone

Source: UNCTAD secretariat calculations, based on data from FAO Statistics Division.
  Note: See table 8.
   a   1985-1995.
   b   1985-1992.

3. Productivity levels and trends

Post-1970 trends in land and labour productivity are shown in chart 11, using wheat units as a measure of output. For sub-Saharan Africa as a whole, there was a dramatic decline in labour productivity during 1975-1984. A temporary improvement in the mid-1980s was followed by fluctuating but generally stagnant levels of productivity. On the other hand, output per hectare has continued to grow more or less at a constant rate from the 1970s onwards, with a slight acceleration in the mid-1980s.[36]

Different regional and country performances lie behind these average trends. The main contrast is between West and Central Africa, on the one hand, where an improvement in both yields and labour productivity has taken place since 1983, and the southern, Sudano-Sahel and eastern regions, on the other hand, where labour productivity has

Table 11

AGRICULTURAL TRADE PERFORMANCE, BY REGION, 1966-1995

Region	Ratio of trade balance to total trade in agricultural products[a]			
	1966-1968	*1972-1974*	*1979-1981*	*1993-1995*
Sub-Saharan Africa	0.51	0.44	0.18	0.10
Low-income countries in:				
West Africa[b]	0.34	0.18	0.09	-0.21
East and Southern Africa[c]	0.47	0.43	0.30	0.05
Middle-income countries in:				
West Africa[d]	0.38	0.26	0.13	0.08
East and Southern Africa[e]	0.27	0.31	0.11	-0.10
South Africa	0.42	0.49	0.50	0.09
Oil exporters[f]	0.25	0.08	-0.35	-0.56
North Africa[g]	-0.16	-0.23	-0.64	-0.65

Source: See table 8.
a The balance of the region's trade with agricultural products (X-M) divided by the sum of its agricultural exports and imports (X+M); forestry and fishery products are not included.
b Benin, Burkina Faso, Central African Republic, Chad, Equatorial Guinea, Gambia, Ghana, Guinea, Guinea-Bissau, Liberia, Mali, Mauritania, Niger, Sao Tome and Principe, Sierra Leone, Togo.
c Burundi, Democratic Republic of the Congo, Ethiopia, Kenya, Lesotho, Madagascar, Malawi, Mozambique, Rwanda, Somalia, Sudan, Uganda, United Republic of Tanzania, Zambia, Zimbabwe.
d Côte d'Ivoire, Senegal.
e Botswana, Mauritius, Namibia, Seychelles, Swaziland.
f Angola, Cameroon, Congo, Gabon, Nigeria.
g Algeria, Egypt, Libyan Arab Jamahiriya, Morocco, Tunisia.

either been declining from the mid-1970s onwards or, at best, has remained stagnant. These regions register a much more modest improvement of yields.

Other studies show that the overall growth of total factor productivity in agriculture in 47 African countries was 1.3 per cent per annum between 1961 and 1991. But about one quarter of the countries experienced negative productivity growth, and another quarter positive growth but of less than 1 per cent. Examining countries in different regions and comparing differences in their performance in terms of total factor productivity provides evidence of convergence, in the sense that the countries with the lowest productivity within regional sets have higher rates of productivity growth. But this does not hold for the continent as a whole.[37]

How far are African productivity levels and trends determined by policy choices and how far by natural conditions? It will be useful to start addressing this question by means of a comparative intercontinental investigation of land, labour and capital use and of productivity differentials in agriculture.

The indicators in table 12 show that during the early 1990s average labour and land productivities in cereal production in Africa were much lower than in Asia and Latin America. There is, of course, considerable variation among countries in all regions. But even low-income Asian countries had higher cereal yields per unit of agricultural land than all African countries except Malawi; in some cases the yield differential was as much as one to four. Moreover, yields in Africa are sub-

Chart 11

LAND AND LABOUR PRODUCTIVITY IN SUB-SAHARAN AFRICA, BY REGION, 1969-1994

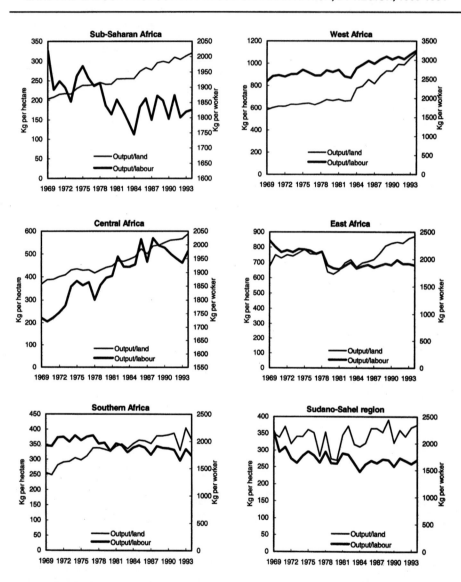

Source: M. Karshenas, "World agricultural output in wheat equivalent units" (London: School of Oriental and African Studies, 1998), mimeo.

Note: *Output* is measured in wheat equivalent units in 1980 world relative prices. *Land* covers arable land, land under permanent crops, and permanent meadows and pastures. *Labour* refers to the economically active population in agriculture. Regional groupings are as follows: *Sub-Saharan Africa:* all of the following; *West:* Benin, Côte d'Ivoire, Ghana, Sierra Leone; *Central:* Cameroon, Central African Republic, Congo, Democratic Republic of the Congo; *East:* Kenya, Madagascar, Uganda; *Southern:* Botswana, Lesotho, Malawi, Mozambique, United Republic of Tanzania, Zambia, Zimbabwe; *Sudano-Sahel:* Burkina Faso, Chad, Gambia, Mali, Mauritania, Niger, Senegal, Sudan.

Table 12

AGRICULTURAL PRODUCTIVITY AND ITS DETERMINANTS IN AFRICA, ASIA AND LATIN AMERICA, 1994

	Africa	Asia[a]	Latin America
Cereal yield (kg/hectare)	1 230	2 943	2 477
Cereal output per capita[b] (kg)	159	274	280
Land/labour[c]	5.9	1.3	24.8
Fertilizer/arable land (kg/hectare)[d]	19	126	63
Irrigated area/arable land (per cent)[d]	6.6	33.3	9.2
Tractors/arable land (no./1,000 hectares)[d]	290	804	1 165

Source: UNCTAD secretariat estimates, based on FAO, *Production Yearbook 1995*, and *Fertilizer Yearbook 1995*.
a Including China and Asian economies in transition, excluding Japan.
b Of total population.
c Ratio of the agricultural area (land under temporary and permanent crops and under permanent pasture) to economically active population in agriculture.
d Arable land includes land under temporary and permanent crops.

ject to much greater annual variation than in Asia (see chart 12).

These differences reflect natural and technical endowments of agriculture. Agro-ecological conditions in Africa are difficult. In general terms it is estimated that 46 per cent of the continental land mass is unsuitable for direct rain-fed cultivation because the growing period is too short, in large part because of aridity. Of the land which is suitable for rain-fed cultivation, about half has been classified as marginal in the sense that, for a representative range of crops, yields are only between 20 and 40 per cent of the maximum attainable on the best land. As farmers move on to new areas there is a constant downward pressure on average yields. Also, there is a high risk of drought over 60 per cent of the land area of Africa. In particular, the Sahel, the Horn of Africa and the countries in Southern Africa around the Kalahari desert are characterized by high inter-annual and intra-seasonal rainfall variability. The shift into marginal land is also associated with increasing farming risks. In addition, many African soils are fragile, and inappropriate land use, poor management and lack of inputs can quickly lead to land degradation.[38]

Differing land/labour ratios, which measure the degree to which extensive production methods are used, also affect productivity indicators.

Intensive and extensive production methods require different patterns of input use and capitalization. Intensive methods require fertilizers, insecticides, irrigation and improved varieties in order to improve yields per hectare. Extensive methods, on the other hand, allow investment in labour-saving machinery, and therefore tend to increase labour productivity.

Asian and Latin American indicators in table 12 are consistent with these propositions. But for Africa this is only part of the story. The land/labour ratios in Africa are lower than in Latin America but higher than in Asia. Disregarding ecological differences, *ceteris paribus*, the relatively more intensive African agriculture should be expected to achieve higher yields than in Latin America. However, African cereal yields are about one half of those in Latin America, mainly because of undercapitalization. The use of fertilizers and tractors is much more limited and irrigation less widespread in Africa than in other developing regions. Agricultural capital stock per hectare of agricultural land in sub-Saharan Africa in 1988-1992 appears to have been one sixth of the Asian level and less than a quarter of that of Latin America. The scope for economically viable small- and medium-scale irrigation is smaller in Africa and it has been used only to a very limited extent: only 28 per cent of the "irrigable" land is actually irri-

Chart 12

CEREAL YIELDS AND THEIR VARIATION IN SUB-SAHARAN AFRICA AND ASIA

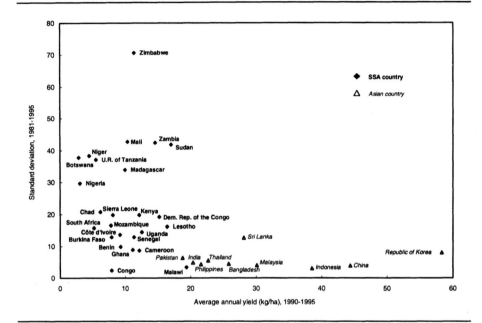

Average annual yield (kg/ha), 1990-1995

Source: M. Karshenas, "Capital accumulation and agricultural surplus in sub-Saharan Africa and Asia", UNCTAD/GDS/MDPB/Misc. 1 (Geneva, 1998).

gated in Africa as a whole, and this proportion is less than 10 per cent in Central, East and West Africa.[39]

The undercapitalization of African agriculture is becoming increasingly serious because with rapid population growth land reserves of whatever quality, are being exhausted. This is occurring to different degrees in different parts of Africa. In the Mediterranean and arid North African region there is virtually no remaining land reserve. In Sudano-Sahelian Africa and humid and sub-humid West Africa, there are land reserves which are approximately equal in extent to the area under existing cultivation, but the reserves are of marginal quality and 75 per cent of the land reserve in the Sudano-Sahelian zone is concentrated in one country – Sudan. The main land reserves in Africa are located in humid Central Africa and sub-humid and semi-arid Southern Africa. In both these regions there is unused land considered very or moderately suitable for cultivation (with yields

over 40 per cent of the maximum attainable). But a further problem in such regions is infestation by tsetse flies and thus the prevalence of trypanosomiasis.

Projections of land/labour ratios suggest that by 2025 over 50 per cent of SSA will be in high-density conditions similar to those in South Asia.[40] This transition from land abundance to land scarcity has important implications. During the post-colonial era, the overall orientation in Africa has been towards extensive patterns of agriculture. Much of the expansion of production has been effected by bringing in new areas of land rather than by adopting yield-increasing technologies. Thus, for example, between 1961 and 1990, 47 per cent of the increase in cereal output in SSA was due to an increase in cultivated area, whilst 53 per cent was attributable to increasing average yields. In contrast, just 6 per cent and 14 per cent of the increase in East Asia and South Asia, respectively, was attributable to area increases, whilst the rest was due to higher yields.[41] Already in the 1960s, expansion of cultivated area meant moving on to increasingly marginal land in many countries, something that partly explains the adverse labour productivity trends noted above. But as land reserves are exhausted it becomes necessary to shift from a pattern of agricultural growth based on area expansion to one based on intensification. A shift to more intensive agriculture requires significant investment by farmers and governments; otherwise, there will be strong pressures for a further acceleration of environmental degradation. Such new investment and resource use in favour of intensification involve irrigation as well as the implementation of new technologies (e.g. for the cultivation of high-yielding varieties) and higher levels of input utilization (e.g. fertilizers).

E. Conclusions

Poor agricultural performance in Africa is often portrayed as the outcome of the self-interested policy decisions of urban elites acting against the interests of the majority of farmers. But this view fails to recognize the difficult dilemmas faced by African governments in formulating agricultural policy. These are rooted in the trade-offs between the various important contributions which the agricultural sector makes to the overall growth process in low-income countries. All predominantly agricultural countries face these dilemmas, but they are particularly acute in sub-Saharan Africa for three reasons. First, an important part of agricultural output consists of goods which are non-tradable internationally outside the region. Second, agricultural production takes place in a difficult, risky and fragile natural environment and is seriously undercapitalized, particularly in the context of a transition from land abundance to land scarcity. Third, there is persistent and historically founded intersectoral dualism with very high differentials between output per worker in agriculture and other sectors.

The period since the middle of the last decade has witnessed intense policy efforts to reverse the poor performance during the 1970s. Indeed, in terms of a number of key indicators, including productivity, output and export volumes, the post-1984 period has generally been better than the 1970s and early 1980s. But the improvement has not been sufficient to increase per capita food production and net agricultural exports, or to sustain productivity growth. Moreover, the improvement has been patchy, with many countries faring worse in the later period while a few countries apparently turned their agriculture around. Only a few countries have managed to achieve rates of growth of agricultural value added in excess of 4 per cent. This continued weak performance of agriculture in Africa thus raises the question of the effectiveness of policies in removing impediments to agricultural development, including lack of incentives and structural bottlenecks. The next chapter takes up this question.

Notes

---

1   See, for example, World Bank, *Accelerated Development in Sub-Saharan Africa: An Agenda for Action* (Washington, D.C.: World Bank, 1981) – the so-called Berg Report; and A. Singh and H. Tabatabai, "The world economic crisis and Third World agriculture in the 1980s", chapter 2 in A. Singh and H. Tabatabai (eds.), *Economic Crisis and Third World Agriculture* (Cambridge: Cambridge University Press, 1993).

2   See U.J. Lele, "Agricultural growth, domestic policies, the external environment and assistance to Africa: Lessons of a quarter century", MADIA Discussion Paper 1 (Washington, D.C.: World Bank, 1989).

3   For the latest approach to policy reform see J. Meerman, *Reforming Agriculture: The World Bank Goes to Market* (Washington D.C.: World Bank, 1997). For another view of the current official approach to agriculture and its relationship with earlier donor and African government strategies, see K. Cleaver, *Rural Development Strategies for Poverty Reduction and Environmental Protection in Sub-Saharan Africa* (Washington, D.C.: World Bank, 1997).

4   See C.P.Timmer, "Getting agriculture moving: Do markets provide the right signals?", *Food Policy*, Vol.20, No.5, 1995. The different priorities attached by aid donors and African governments to food and export crop production are just one indication of such policy complexity; see, in particular, OAU, *Lagos Plan of Action for the Implementation of the Monrovia Strategy for the Economic Development of Africa*, Addis Ababa, 1980; and Economic Commission for Africa, *African Alternative Framework to Structural Adjustment Programmes for Socio-Economic Recovery and Transformation (AAF-SAP)* (E/ECA/CM.15/6/Rev.3), Addis Ababa, 1989.

5   J. W. Mellor, *Agriculture on the Road to Industrialization* (Baltimore and London: Johns Hopkins University Press, 1995), p. 5.

6   For agricultural growth linkages in Africa, see S. Block and C.P. Timmer, *Agriculture and Economic Growth in Africa: Progress and Issues*, Agricultural Policy Analysis Project Phase III Research Report No.1016 (Bethesda, Maryland, March 1997).

7   See J.C. Berthélemy and C. Morrisson, *Agricultural Development in Africa and the Supply of Manufactured Goods* (Paris: OECD Development Centre, 1989). For the role of such a vicious circle in an assessment of the breakdown in accumulation in the United Republic of Tanzania at the end of the 1970s, see M. Wuyts, "Accumulation, industrialization and the peasantry: A Reinterpretation of the Tanzanian Experience", *Journal of Peasant Studies*, Vol. 21, No. 2, 1994, pp. 159-193.

8   See FAO, *The Sixth World Food Survey* (Rome: FAO, 1996).

9   It has been estimated that 10-20 per cent of people in poor countries, mostly smallholders in Africa and labourers in South Asia, are too undernourished and unhealthy to work more, even if incentives are provided for them to do so. See World Bank, *Poverty and Hunger: Issues and Options for Food Security in Developing Countries* (Washington, D.C.: World Bank, 1986).

10 See S. Jaffee, "Enhancing agricultural growth through diversification in sub-Saharan Africa", in S. Barghouti, S. Garbus and D. Umali (eds.), *Trends in Agricultural Diversification: Regional Perspectives*, Technical Paper No.180 (Washington, D.C.: World Bank, 1992).

11 Block and Timmer, *op. cit.*

12 R.H. Bates, *Markets and States in Tropical Africa: The Political Basis of Agricultural Policies* (Berkeley: University of California Press, 1981). In

some cases, such as Uganda in the 1950s, the contribution was as high as 90 per cent, whilst in others, such as Kenya in the 1960s, it was as low as 10 per cent.

13 R.C. Riddell, *Manufacturing Africa: Performance and Prospects in Seven Countries in Sub-Saharan Africa* (London: James Currey, 1990), pp.34-35.

14 See *TDR 1997*, Part Two, chapter VI, pp. 182-183. For the relationship between import-substitution industrialization and the development of manufactured exports in Africa, see S. Wangwe, *Exporting Africa: Technology, Trade and Industrialization in Sub-Saharan Africa*, UNU/Intech Studies in New Technology (London and New York: Routledge,1995).

15 For the use of agricultural policy as part of an implicit distributional social contract, see T.S. Jayne and S. Jones, "Food marketing and pricing policy in Eastern and Southern Africa: A survey", *World Development*, Vol. 25, No. 9, pp. 1505-1527. For a discussion of the politics of inclusion in Africa see D. Rothschild and W. Foley, "African States and the politics of inclusive coalitions", in D. Rothschild and N. Chazan (eds.), *The Precarious Balance: State and Society in Africa* (Boulder, Colorado: Westview Press, 1988).

16 See Bates, *op. cit.*

17 A penetrating discussion of African land tenure is to be found in H.W.O. Okoth-Ogendo, "Some issues of theory in the study of tenure relations in African agriculture", *Africa*, Vol. 59, No. 1, 1989, pp. 6-12. A balanced account of gender relations is provided by A. Whitehead, "Rural women and food production in sub-Saharan Africa", in J. Dreze and A. Sen (eds.), *The Political Economy of Hunger* (Oxford: Clarendon Press, 1990). See also A. Tibaijuka, "The cost of differential gender roles in African agriculture: A case study of smallholder banana-coffee farms in Kagera Region, Tanzania", *Journal of Agricultural Economics*, Vol. 45, No. 1, 1994.

18 At present only 7.5 per cent of arable land is irrigated, and six countries (Egypt, Madagascar, Morocco, Nigeria, South Africa and Sudan) account for 75 per cent of total irrigated land. See FAO, "Food production and the critical role of water", Technical Background Document No. 7 for the World Food Summit, Rome, 13-17 November 1996.

19 For a discussion of the estate sector in Malawi and Kenya, see U.J. Lele and M. Agarwal, "Smallholder and large-scale agriculture in Africa: Are there tradeoffs between growth and equity?", MADIA Discussion Paper 6 (Washington, D.C.: World Bank, 1989).

20 See K. Deininger and H. Binswanger, "Rent-seeking and the development of large-scale agriculture in Kenya, South Africa, and Zimbabwe", *Economic Development and Cultural Change*, Vol. 43, 1995, pp. 493-522. On contract farming, which has been important in the expansion of non-traditional agricultural exports, see G. Porter and K. Phillips-Howard, "Comparing contracts: An evaluation of

contract farming schemes in Africa", *World Development*, Vol. 25, No. 2, 1997, pp. 227-238.

21   See D. Byerlee and C. K. Eicher, *Africa's Emerging Maize Revolution* (London and Boulder, Colorado: Lynne Rienner, 1997).

22   T. Reardon et al., "The importance and nature of rural nonfarm income in developing countries with policy implications for agriculturalists", in *The State of Food and Agriculture 1998* (Rome: FAO, 1998). These estimates are based on a review of about 100 farm household surveys undertaken from the 1970s to the 1990s.

23   See, for example, M. Mamdani, "Extreme but not exceptional: towards an analysis of the agrarian question in Uganda", *Journal of Peasant Studies*, Vol. 14, No. 2, 1987, pp. 191-225.

24   In Malawi, which has a large population in relation to the area of cultivable land and where the development strategy of the 1970s was founded on African estate production, it was estimated that at the end of the 1980s, 56 per cent of households on customary land (approximately 3.6 million people) were working less than one hectare of land and that their holdings were insufficient to meet their basic food needs. The phrase " too poor to farm" is taken from A. Whitehead, *Poverty in Northern Ghana*, Report to ESCOR (London: Overseas Development Agency, 1986). See also P. Hill, *Rural Hausa: A Village and a Setting* (Cambridge: Cambridge University Press, 1972).

25   For countries such as Kenya, where ownership of land is individually registered, it is possible to speak of the emergence of a landless population, and estimates of rural landless in the early 1980s range from 200,000 to 410,000 households, some 12 per cent of households in some provinces. Women and young men may not have direct access to land under the indigenous communal system, and on this basis it has been estimated, for example, that the number of landless men between the ages of 16 and 30 is 40 per cent in some areas of Zimbabwe. See J. Testerink, "Land relations and conflict in Eastern and Southern Africa", Occasional Paper No.4 (Perth, University of West Australia: Indian Ocean Centre for Peace Studies, 1991).

26   An extended argument regarding the relationship between agrarian conditions and wage rates in Africa and Asia, and their consequences for intersectoral dualism, is to be found in M. Karshenas, "Capital accumulation and agricultural surplus in sub-Saharan Africa and Asia", UNCTAD/GDS/MDPB/Misc. 1 (Geneva, 1998). For mineral economies, "Dutch disease" phenomena have been identified – see T.A. Oyejide, "Food Policy and the Choice of Trade Regime", and T. B. Tshibaka, "Commentary on the trade regime", in J.W.Mellor, C.L.Delgado, and M.J. Blackie (eds.), *Accelerating Food Production in Sub-Saharan Africa* (Baltimore: Johns Hopkins University Press, 1987).

27   See, in particular, J.W. Mellor, "Determinants of rural poverty: The dynamics of production, technol-ogy, and price", chap. 4 in J.W. Mellor and G.M. Desai (eds.), *Agricultural Change and Rural Poverty: Variations on a Theme by Dharm Narain* (Baltimore: Johns Hopkins University Press, 1986). Even W. Arthur Lewis, who first explained how economic development could take place with unlimited supplies of labour, excluded Africa from his discussion of the labour-surplus economy. J. Stiglitz argued that labour was not in surplus in most African economies, but sought to identify various conditions in which the withdrawal of labour did not result in falling output. See "Rural-urban migration, surplus labour, and the relationship between urban and rural wages", *East African Economic Review*, Vol.1, No.2, 1969. S. Berry argued that the labour-surplus model of development was not relevant for Africa, and focused on the absence of automatic reinvestment of profits in the nascent capitalist sector, and on the role of government; see "Economic development with surplus labour: Further complications suggested by contemporary African experience", *Oxford Economic Papers*, Vol. 22, No.2, July 1970, pp.275-287. For a recent assessment of the labour constraint in African agriculture see K. Saito, "Raising the productivity of women farmers in sub-Saharan Africa", World Bank Discussion Papers, Africa Technical Department Series, No.230, 1994, chap. 6.

28   A. Low, *Agricultural Development in Southern Africa: Farm-Household Economics and the Food Crisis* (London: James Currey, 1986), p.188.

29   R. Bush, L. Cliffe and V. Jansen, "The crisis in the reproduction of migrant labour in southern Africa", in P. Lawrence (ed.), *World Recession and the Food Crisis in Africa* (London: James Currey, 1986).

30   The increasing death rates associated with the spread of AIDS lend some uncertainty to population projections. However, it is estimated that the African population will double in the next 20 years if the current trend persists. With a fertility decline of 2.75 per cent a year over the period 1990-2020, the projected increase is from about 500 million in 1990 to 1,100 million in 2020. There are, of course, differences between countries, but one classification of countries according to their population growth rates over the period 1980-2000 indicates that 34 per cent of the 1980 African population were living in countries with very high population growth rates (over 3.5 per cent per year) and only 16 per cent in countries with rates of under 2.5 per cent a year.

31   The importance of the non-tradability of agriculture has, however, been particularly stressed by C.L. Delgado in his "Why domestic food prices matter to growth strategy in semi-open West African economies", *Journal of African Economies*, Vol.1, No.3, 1992, pp. 446-471; and "Agricultural diversification and export promotion in sub-Saharan Africa", *Food Policy*, Vol. 20, No.3, 1995, pp. 225-243. For an analysis of the reasons for non-tradability, see S.C. Kyle and J. Swinnen, "The theory of contested markets and the degree of tradeability of agricultural

commodities: An empirical test in Zaire", *Journal of African Economies*, Vol. 3, No. 1,1994, pp. 93-113.

32   See, for example, Delgado, 1995, *op. cit.*.

33   This has been analysed in C. Kirkpatrick and D. Diakosavva, "Food insecurity and foreign-exchange constraints in sub-Saharan Africa", *Journal of Modern African Studies*, Vol. 23, No. 2, 1985, pp. 239-250.

34   The economic importance of increasing the productivity of food producers is emphasized by O. Aboyade, "Growth strategy and the agricultural sector", in Mellor, Delgado and Blackie (eds.), *op. cit.*, and also by Delgado, 1995, *op. cit.*

35   See S. A. Salih, *Food Security in Africa*, UNU/ WIDER World Development Studies, No. 3 (Helsinki, 1995).

36   The use of "wheat units" allows cross-country and inter-temporal comparisons of productivity without reference to prices. For an earlier application of this approach in Africa see S. Block, "The recovery of agricultural productivity in sub-Saharan Africa", *Food Policy*, Vol. 20, No. 5, 1995, pp. 385-405. This study covered the period 1963-1988, and identified a recovery in agricultural productivity in the period 1983-1988, which was particularly marked in West Africa, though not necessarily sustainable. The present results, which are based on a new data set on wheat units, indicate that there was a similar recovery in labour productivity in the mid-1980s and that it has not been sustained.

37   See A. Lusigi and C. Thirtle, "Total factor productivity and the effects of R&D in African agriculture", *Journal of International Development*, Vol. 9, No. 4,1997, pp. 529-538; and A. Lusigi, J. Piesse and C. Thirtle, "Convergence of per capita incomes and agricultural productivity in Africa, *Journal of International Development*, Vol. 10, No. 1, 1998, pp. 105-116.

38   FAO, *African Agriculture: The Next Twenty-Five Years* (Rome: FAO, 1986), annex II: "The land resource base".

39   The estimates of irrigation potential are taken from FAO, 1996, *op. cit.* Aggregate capital stock estimates for 1988-1992 are from FAO, *Investment in Agriculture*, Technical Background Document No.10 for the World Food Summit, Rome, 13-19 November 1996, table 3. They cover investment in land development for arable cropping, planting tree crops, irrigation, building up and housing livestock, and mechanization and farm implements. Expressed in relation to area of agricultural land, they are as follows: sub-Saharan Africa: $157 per hectare; Latin America and the Caribbean: $665 per hectare; and Asia: $913 per hectare.

40   Estimates of land reserves are from FAO, 1986, *op. cit.* Projections of land/labour ratios are those of H. Binswanger and P. Pingali in "Technological priorities for farming in sub-Saharan Africa", *World Bank Economic Research Observer*, Vol. 3, No. 1, 1988, pp. 81-98.

41   Saito, *op. cit.*, table 2.3.

Chapter III

AGRICULTURAL POLICIES, PRICES AND PRODUCTION

A. Introduction

Throughout the early post-colonial period in Africa there were two basic approaches to the development of agriculture. The first aimed at "modernizing" smallholder agriculture through the promotion of specialization, standardization and increased use of productivity-enhancing inputs and quality control, particularly by means of integrated rural development projects. The second aimed at channelling resources into highly capitalized indigenous private agribusinesses and state farms. Both these approaches sought to address undercapitalization and structural constraints in African agriculture, but had serious shortcomings in their design and implementation.

At the beginning of the past decade policy reforms were initiated in line with the view that what mattered most for agricultural development were market incentives. It was argued that much of the poor performance of agriculture in SSA was due to excessive taxation of farmers by governments. According to this view, policies designed to extract resources from agriculture in order to promote industrial development and to provide subsidized goods and services to the urban economy undermined agricultural development by reducing the attractiveness of farming:

African farmers have faced the world's heaviest rates of agricultural taxation ... explicitly through producer price fixing, export taxes, and taxes on agricultural inputs. They

were also taxed implicitly through overvalued exchange rates, and through high levels of industrial protection ... The high rates of taxation contributed to sub-Saharan Africa's alarming decline in ... agricultural growth.[1]

Reforms have accordingly aimed at removing distortions in the incentive structure. The initial thrust of reforms was to realign producer prices with world prices through marketing boards and to correct overvalued exchange rates. From the late 1980s onwards there was wider recognition of the importance of structural constraints,[2] but in reality greater attention has been paid to deregulating agricultural markets by dismantling the marketing boards and allowing a greater role for private actors in both product and input markets. Current best practice in agricultural policy is now regarded as including unsubsidized market-determined prices for both inputs and outputs, prices at border parity determined on the basis of "adequate" exchange rates, and economically neutral taxation of agriculture and other sectors. On this view, governments' responsibility is to maintain access to markets, ensure dissemination of information, and provide adequate legal and regulatory frameworks, rather than to intervene in prices.[3]

However, despite intensive reforms over a number of years, the supply response to price liberalization has been much less than expected, raising several questions about the underlying rationale of the reforms. First, have governments in SSA really taxed agriculture excessively, especially compared with the rest of the developing world? Second, how far have price reforms removed taxation and resulted in greater incentives for farmers? Lastly, are price incentives the only, or even the most important, component of agricultural growth and development?[4] Addressing these questions is essential for greater understanding of the factors affecting agricultural development, including the role of price and non-price incentives, the provision of public goods, and structural and institutional impediments to supply response. That is the purpose of this chapter.

The next section enlarges on the brief analysis of the behaviour of agricultural prices presented in *TDR 1997*, covering a wider range of prices, using a broader sample of countries and products, and making international comparisons.[5] This is followed by a discussion of various factors affecting supply behaviour in SSA, and of the role of public investment in removing structural impediments.

The analysis shows that export crops were not always taxed through price-fixing much more in African than in other major producing countries and that subsequent liberalization of agricultural markets has not always reduced the margin between export prices and producer prices. Secondly, the domestic terms of trade for agriculture in SSA were generally kept above the world terms of trade

between agricultural commodities and manufactures. This was partly due to price and subsidy policies in favour of food crops. Since reforms began, agricultural terms of trade and real producer prices have generally performed better in those countries that have continued with interventionist policies in agricultural marketing than in those with more liberal policies.

The behaviour of production and exports noted in the last chapter has been influenced by a number of factors, including the policy reforms. In the context of falling world prices, incentives provided through pricing and exchange rate reforms have been weak. Recovery in production in the mid-1980s coincided with the turnaround in net resource flows (chapter I, chart 5) and the recovery in imports. Increased availability of consumer goods in rural areas in some cases, and pressure to satisfy basic consumption needs in others, appear to have contributed to a positive short-run supply response in some countries. Where devaluations have corrected major exchange rate misalignments, exports recovered, partly because they were diverted into official channels. But adjustment policies have failed to address a number of institutional and structural impediments to increasing agricultural productivity and output. Removing such impediments would have called for increased public investment in agricultural infrastructure and research, but this has not been possible under fiscal retrenchment characteristic of adjustment programmes.

B. Agricultural prices

1. Taxation of export crops

One way of addressing the question of "taxation" of agriculture is to examine the margin between export prices (in national currency) and prices received by farmers for major export crops, and to compare the margins between major African and non-African exporters of these crops.[6] Chart 13 presents estimates of the evolution of the ratio of prices received by farmers to border (unit ex-

port) prices for coffee, cocoa, tea, cotton and tobacco since 1970. This relative magnitude, which is a non-adjusted nominal protection coefficient (NPC), gives a measure of the rate of surplus extraction from farmers by exporters.

Clearly, the margin between export and producer prices indicates a surplus extraction only when producers and exporters are different entities, and not when producers export directly, as in

Chart 13

**RATIO OF PRODUCER PRICES TO BORDER PRICES ª FOR FIVE MAJOR EXPORT CROPS:
COMPARISON BETWEEN AFRICAN AND OTHER DEVELOPING COUNTRIES, 1970-1994**

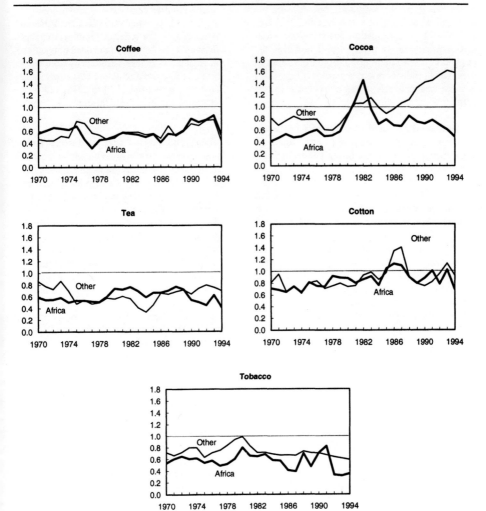

Source: UNCTAD secretariat calculations, based on FAO, *FAOSTAT* database; and IMF, *International Financial Statistics* (tapes).
Note: The country samples are as follows: *Coffee exporters: African:* Burundi, Cameroon, Côte d'Ivoire, Ethiopia, Guinea, Kenya, Madagascar, Malawi, Rwanda, Uganda, United Republic of Tanzania. *Other:* Colombia, Costa Rica, Guatemala, Indonesia. *Cocoa exporters: African:* Côte d'Ivoire, Ghana, Guinea, Nigeria. *Other:* Dominican Republic, Ecuador, Malaysia, Indonesia, Papua New Guinea. *Tea exporters: African:* Burundi, Cameroon, Kenya, Malawi, Rwanda, United Republic of Tanzania, Uganda. *Other:* India, Indonesia, Sri Lanka, Turkey. *Cotton exporters: African:* Burkina Faso, Burundi, Cameroon, Chad, Mali, Sudan, Uganda, United Republic of Tanzania, Zimbabwe. *Other:* Egypt, India, Pakistan, Paraguay, Syria, Turkey. *Tobacco exporters: African:* Malawi, Zambia, Zimbabwe. *Other:* India, Indonesia, Republic of Korea, Thailand, Turkey.
 ª Unit value of exports.

the case of plantation- and TNC-based agribusiness. Moreover, it does not necessarily represent explicit taxation by governments in the sense used in conventional analysis. Such a margin also exists in the case of private traders and exporters. Nevertheless, public marketing boards were the principal exporting agents in Africa until the early 1990s, while similar institutions were less widespread elsewhere. In what follows, however, the term "tax" is used to describe the margin between export and producer prices regardless of the institutional arrangements in the markets for export crops.

It should be noted that this is a crude approximation of the degree of taxation since no allowance is made for marketing and transportation costs and any other value added between the initial (on-farm) and export stages of the marketing chain. However, since domestic transaction costs are generally higher in African countries than in most other developing countries, the observed NPC values may overstate the extent of taxation of farmers in SSA countries compared with other developing countries. Nevertheless, there may also be greater value added between the farm and the export stages among non-African exporters, accounting for part of the margin between the border and producer prices.

The rate of taxation is not independent of the exchange rate. The border price is determined by the nominal exchange rate and dollar prices received by exporters in international markets. A lower exchange rate would thus raise the domestic currency prices received by exporters. If prices paid to farmers remain unchanged, or are raised by less than the rate of devaluation of the currency, the tax rate will rise. Indeed, such behaviour was observed after the post-1986 devaluations in a number of countries in SSA when prices received by farmers declined relative to unit export values. However, even when devaluations lead to a widening of the margin, they tend to raise real producer prices of export crops vis-à-vis non-tradables, thus providing incentives for exports.

It is generally agreed that the currencies of many SSA countries were overvalued during the period from the mid-1970s to the mid-1980s. However, the evidence presented in chart 15 does not support the conventional view that African producers have always been more heavily taxed than those in other developing countries through crop pricing policies. Indeed, it suggests that this claim

is a gross oversimplification. A commodity-specific comparison of African and non-African exporters presents a much more complex picture:

- For *coffee*, on average the ratio of producer prices to border (unit export) prices does not appear to have been very different between African and non-African producers except during 1975-1977, when the level of taxation in Africa was higher. Producer prices were around 50 per cent of actual border prices in both instances from 1979 to 1988, and then increased sharply before falling back to their previous levels.

- *Cocoa* producers in Africa were always more heavily taxed than in other developing countries, except for a brief interlude in the early 1980s. Producer prices in Africa were on average 55 per cent below actual border prices throughout the 1970s, against 60-80 per cent for their competitors. The situation improved in Africa briefly after 1980, but soon deteriorated significantly when the benefits of devaluations were retained primarily by exporters. Paradoxically, taxation appears to have risen during the reform period in Africa. By contrast, since the late 1980s, prices received by non-African cocoa producers appear to have exceeded the export unit values, which suggests that exports were subsidized.

- For *tea*, taxation was higher in Africa at the beginning and the end of the period under consideration. However, unlike in the case of cocoa, Africa had lower rates of taxation of producers for roughly half of the period covered. During most of the 1980s, African producer prices averaged around 70 per cent of border prices, whereas the ratio was generally below 50 per cent for other developing country producers.

- Taxation of *cotton* appears to have been more moderate and stable than that of tree crops, among both African and non-African producers, and no major difference emerges between the two groups of countries in this respect. The moderate downward trend of the tax rates in the 1980s was reversed subsequently in both groups of countries.

- For *tobacco*, the proportion of border prices received by African producers has consistently been lower than that received by non-African producers, particularly since the late 1970s. A rising rate of taxation set in after 1980.

Therefore, while in some cases African farmers have indeed faced very heavy taxation compared with other major exportering countries, in other cases they have not.[7] Of the five export crops studied, it is only for cocoa and tobacco that the ratio of producer prices to border prices before the reform process was significantly lower in Africa than in the other major exporters. For coffee and cotton there appears to be no significant difference in the ratio of producer to border prices between African and non-African countries during the pre-reform era. The findings of earlier research – to the effect that the African producers faced higher rates of taxation – were based on a sample of three countries, two of which were major cocoa exporters, and also reflect the adverse effects of exchange rate overvaluation.[8]

Chart 13 also suggests that price reforms in Africa have not always led to lower rates of taxation of export crop producers. Since the mid-1980s, the ratio between producer and export prices has declined for all products considered here except coffee. This implies that the benefits of devaluations during that period accrued to traders more than to farmers. Nevertheless, it should be noted that not all SSA countries in the chart are "reformers". An analysis of price movements differentiating between reformers and non-reformers is contained in subsection 3 below.

The relevant comparison for traded (importable) food crops such as cereals is between the prices received by farmers and import costs in domestic currency. The latter are determined by world prices and exchange rates, while the former are influenced by pricing and subsidy policies. A positive margin between the prices received by farmers and unit import costs indicates protection of food crop farmers. By raising import costs, devaluations permit reduction of direct price supports of food crops and/or subsidies.

Chart 14 shows the evolution of average ratios of producer prices to world prices (expressed in domestic currencies) for cereals between 1970 and 1994 in a number of countries in SSA. It is apparent that prices received by farmers progressed faster than world prices until the mid-1980s, a fact which indicates high rates of implicit subsidization. Again, market-based reforms and devaluations are possible reasons for the subsequent reversal.

Chart 14

RATIO OF PRODUCER PRICES TO WORLD MARKET PRICES FOR THREE MAJOR CEREALS IN SSA, 1970-1994

(Index numbers, 1973 = 100)

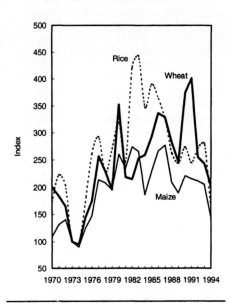

Source: UNCTAD secretariat calculations, based on UNCTAD, *Commodity Price Statistics;* and FAO, *FAOSTAT* database.

Note: Ratios are calculated on the basis of prices received by farmers and world prices expressed in domestic currencies at current exchange rates. Averages are for the following countries: *wheat:* Burundi, Chad, Ethiopia, Kenya, Malawi, Niger, Sudan, Uganda, United Republic of Tanzania, Zambia; *maize:* Burkina Faso, Burundi, Cameroon, Chad, Côte d'Ivoire, Ethiopia, Ghana, Guinea, Kenya, Madagascar, Malawi, Mali, Niger, Nigeria, Senegal, Sudan, Uganda, United Republic of Tanzania, Zambia; *rice:* Burkina Faso, Burundi, Cameroon, Chad, Côte d'Ivoire, Ghana, Guinea, Kenya, Madagascar, Malawi, Mali, Niger, Nigeria, Uganda, United Republic of Tanzania, Zambia.

2. Terms of trade and real producer prices

The analysis above is a simplified version of the conventional approach to the taxation of export crops. It focuses on output prices alone and ignores the prices paid for the products purchased by farmers. It is indeed the prices of output relative to inputs and to consumer goods purchased by producers that determine the latter's real incomes and consumption, and hence influence their production and investment decisions. The broadest measure of this relative price is the domestic terms of trade of agriculture.

This subsection concentrates on trends in the agricultural terms of trade in SSA for a sample of 20 countries, using two measures. The first refers to agriculture as a whole and is measured as the ratio of the implicit agricultural GDP deflator to the implicit non-agricultural (or manufacturing) GDP deflator. These domestic terms of trade are contrasted with world terms of trade, obtained by deflating the world prices of agricultural products with unit export values of manufactures. The second indicator – real producer prices – refers to specific agricultural products and is measured by the ratio of producers' prices to the domestic consumer price index.[9]

Chart 15 presents trends in agricultural terms of trade in world markets and SSA. There is almost an uninterrupted decline in world terms of trade for agricultural products from 1973 to 1995. Although the decline was somewhat moderate after 1986, and there was an upturn during 1994-1995, the average indices for 1987-1995 were about 60 per cent and 40 per cent below the 1973 levels for "all food" and "raw materials", respectively.

However, the domestic terms of trade of agriculture in SSA show quite different behaviour. After rising during the first half of the 1970s, they remain broadly stable until the early 1990s before rising again; the average index for 1987-1995 is 13 per cent above the 1973 level. Hence, in general, farmers in SSA appear to have been protected from adverse trends in world terms of trade for agricultural commodities.

Again, there is a need for caution in interpreting this evidence because of differences between the commodity compositions of the two terms of trade series. This could reduce the reliability of comparisons, particularly when price dynamics are different for different commodities. Indeed, prices of non-tradable food appear to have been an important factor in the better performance of the domestic terms of trade. However, this alone does not account for the large disparity in the movements of agricultural terms of trade between world markets and SSA. The evidence regarding

Chart 15

COMPARISON OF DOMESTIC TERMS OF TRADE OF AGRICULTURE WITHIN SSA WITH WORLD TERMS OF TRADE, 1970-1995

(Index numbers, 1973 = 100)

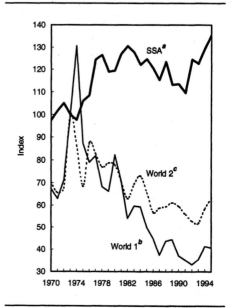

Source: UNCTAD secretariat calculations, based on UNCTAD, *Commodity Price Statistics;* and World Bank, *World Development Indicators 1997* (CD-Rom).

a   Unweighted average of the domestic terms of trade of agriculture for Burkina Faso (except for 1995), Burundi, Cameroon, Côte d'Ivoire, Ghana, Kenya, Madagascar, Malawi, Mali, Nigeria, Senegal and Zambia. The domestic terms of trade of agriculture are measured by the ratios of the implicit sectoral deflator for agriculture to the implicit sectoral deflator for industry.

b   Ratio of world free market price index for "all food" (tropical beverages, food, vegetable oilseeds and oil) to the unit value index of exports of manufactures from developed market economies.

c   Ratio of world free market price index for agricultural raw materials to unit value index of exports of manufactures from developed market economies.

real producer prices suggests that SSA pricing policies, particularly with respect to tradable food crops, played an important role in stabilizing domestic terms of trade for agriculture.

Chart 16 shows trends in real producer prices from 1970 to 1994 for four major export crops

SUB-SAHARAN AFRICA: REAL PRODUCER PRICES FOR SELECTED EXPORT AND FOOD CROPS, 1970-1994

(Index numbers, 1973 = 100)

Export crops

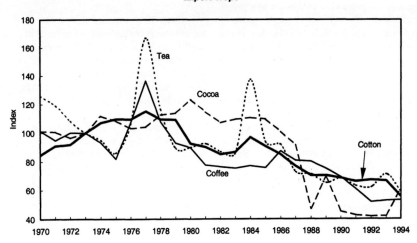

Food crops

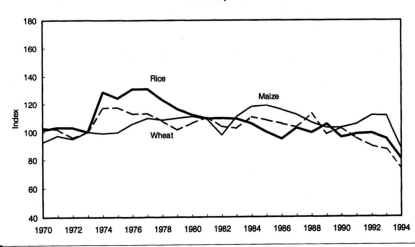

Source: UNCTAD secretariat calculations, based on FAO, *FAOSTAT* database; and IMF, *International Financial Statistics.*
Note: Real producer prices are nominal prices received by farmers divided by the consumer price index. Data are unweighted averages for the following countries: *cocoa:* Cameroon, Côte d'Ivoire; *coffee:* Burundi, Côte d'Ivoire, Ethiopia, Kenya, Madagascar, United Republic of Tanzania; *cotton:* Burkina Faso, United Republic of Tanzania; *tea:* Burundi, Kenya; *wheat:* Burundi, Ethiopia, Kenya, Niger, Sudan, United Republic of Tanzania, Zambia; *maize:* Burkina Faso, Burundi, Cameroon, Côte d'Ivoire, Ethiopia, Ghana, Kenya, Madagascar, Niger, Nigeria, Senegal, United Republic of Tanzania, Zambia; *rice:* Burkina Faso, Burundi, Cameroon, Côte d'Ivoire, Ghana, Kenya, Madagascar, Niger, Nigeria, United Republic of Tanzania, Zambia.

and three food crops in SSA countries. Overall, the contrast between the sharp deterioration for export crops and a high degree of stability for food crops is striking. Real producer prices of cocoa, coffee, cotton and tea in the early 1990s were 40-50 per cent lower than their average levels during the 1970s. For cereals, real domestic prices in SSA were relatively stable over the same period, with some modest declines after the mid-1980s. A comparison between domestic and international prices shows that while in real terms, domestic prices of export crops generally followed the downward trend in international prices, for cereals those prices were higher and more stable (chart 17).

Movements in domestic terms of trade and real producer prices are influenced by a host of factors, including developments in world markets for agricultural commodities and manufactures, government intervention in national output and/ or input markets, and exchange rate policies. Generally, in most African countries government intervention until recently favoured food crops over export crops through price supports and subsidies. This, together with overvalued exchange rates, kept food prices high relative to export crops. With market liberalization, the prices of both food crops and export crops have been linked more closely to world prices, but more so for export crops. Devaluations only partly compensated for the downward trend in real prices of export crops in world markets while, as noted above, at the same time widening the rate of taxation. Consequently, in general, real producer prices for export crops fell throughout the 1980s while those for cereals rose or fell less. These differing trends are shown in chart 18 for changes between the average prices in 1981-1983 and in 1992-1994 for a number of food and export crops in various countries. Nevertheless, despite this broad tendency, there are important differences in the behaviour of real prices of the same food and export crops in different countries, reflecting in large part differences in exchange rate policies and the extent and type of intervention in agricultural product markets.

3. Policy reforms and agricultural prices

The findings discussed above show that despite widespread market-oriented agricultural price reforms, the past ten years have not produced significant improvements in relative prices and terms of trade for agriculture or lowered the rates of taxation of farmers. A more direct way of studying the impact of these reforms is to compare the price movements between "reforming" countries and those that continued with "interventionist" policies. Here, this exercise is carried out for the same set of prices examined above, with countries classified on the basis of their policy regimes as evaluated by the World Bank in its study *Adjustment in Africa* cited above.[10]

Chart 19 shows that since 1984 the overall domestic terms of trade for agriculture have moved much more favourably in the "heavy intervention" countries than in the "light intervention" ones. As of 1993, the former group had achieved an improvement of 24 per cent compared with a 7 per cent decline in the latter.

The impact of policy regimes on real producer prices is examined here by classifying major African producers of cocoa, coffee, cotton, tea and cereals into groups with "continued interventionist", "continued liberal" and "newly liberalized" policy regimes vis-à-vis agricultural markets as defined by the World Bank. For export crops, with the exception of coffee until 1992, real producer prices have performed better since 1984 in those countries which have continued with interventionist policies in the markets for the specified commodities than in those with more liberal policy regimes (chart 20). This is consistent with the findings reported in the World Bank study,[11] which show that in those countries which had continued with centralized producer pricing, there was an increase of 4.8 per cent in the domestic real producer prices for export crops, whereas there was a fall of 18.8 per cent in countries which had shifted from centralized pricing to indicative pricing or total deregulation. For food crops, it appears that farmers in countries with a high degree of intervention in agricultural markets enjoyed significantly better relative prices than the average, particularly during more recent years.

The picture is much the same regarding the taxation of export crops, as measured by the ratio of prices received by farmers to border prices (chart 21). In countries with ongoing or newly liberalized marketing arrangements this ratio fell faster or rose much less rapidly than in countries with continued government intervention, with once again the single exception of cocoa. The impact of the policy regime on relative movements between import and producer prices of cereals is more ambiguous.

Chart 17

REAL WORLD MARKET PRICES AND REAL PRODUCER PRICES IN AFRICA FOR SELECTED PRIMARY COMMODITIES, 1970-1995

(Index numbers, 1973 = 100)

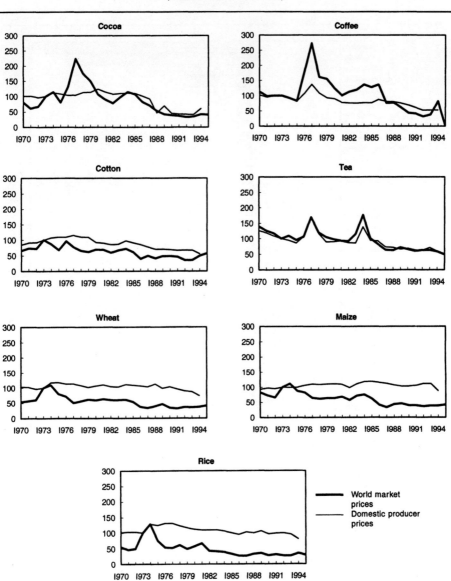

Source: UNCTAD secretariat calculations, based on UNCTAD, *Commodity Price Statistics* (tapes); FAO, *FAOSTAT*; and IMF, *International Financial Statistics* (tapes).

Note: Real world market prices are nominal prices deflated by the unit value index of exports of manufactures from developed market economies. Real producer prices are nominal prices received by farmers deflated by the consumer price index. Averages of real producer prices relate to the countries specified in chart 16.

Chart 18

CHANGE IN REAL PRODUCER PRICES OF MAJOR EXPORT AND FOOD CROPS IN SELECTED SUB-SAHARAN AFRICAN COUNTRIES BETWEEN 1981-1983 AND 1992-1994

(Percentages)

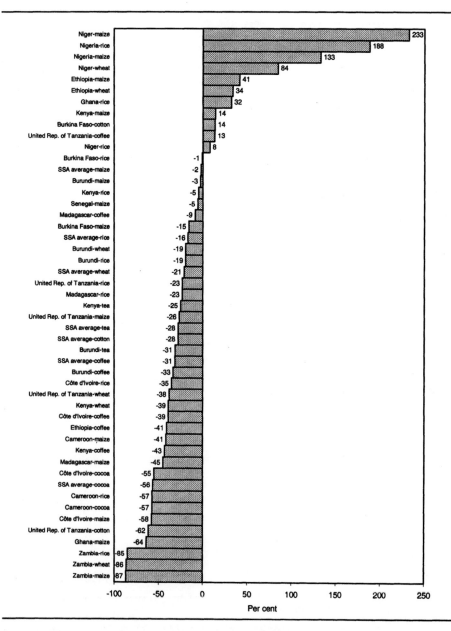

Niger-maize	233
Nigeria-rice	188
Nigeria-maize	133
Niger-wheat	84
Ethiopia-maize	41
Ethiopia-wheat	34
Ghana-rice	32
Kenya-maize	14
Burkina Faso-cotton	14
United Rep. of Tanzania-coffee	13
Niger-rice	8
Burkina Faso-rice	-1
SSA average-maize	-2
Burundi-maize	-3
Kenya-rice	-5
Senegal-maize	-5
Madagascar-coffee	-9
Burkina Faso-maize	-15
SSA average-rice	-16
Burundi-wheat	-19
Burundi-rice	-19
SSA average-wheat	-21
United Rep. of Tanzania-rice	-23
Madagascar-rice	-23
Kenya-tea	-25
United Rep. of Tanzania-maize	-26
SSA average-tea	-28
SSA average-cotton	-28
Burundi-tea	-31
SSA average-coffee	-31
Burundi-coffee	-33
Côte d'Ivoire-rice	-35
United Rep. of Tanzania-wheat	-38
Kenya-wheat	-39
Côte d'Ivoire-coffee	-39
Ethiopia-coffee	-41
Cameroon-maize	-41
Kenya-coffee	-43
Madagascar-maize	-45
Côte d'Ivoire-cocoa	-55
SSA average-cocoa	-56
Cameroon-rice	-57
Cameroon-cocoa	-57
Côte d'Ivoire-maize	-58
United Rep. of Tanzania-cotton	-62
Ghana-maize	-64
Zambia-rice	-85
Zambia-wheat	-86
Zambia-maize	-87

Per cent

Source: UNCTAD secretariat calculations, based on data from FAO, *FAOSTAT* database; and IMF, *International Financial Statistics*.

Chart 19

DOMESTIC TERMS OF TRADE OF AGRICULTURE AND POLICY ORIENTATION OF SSA COUNTRIES BY COUNTRY GROUPING, 1984-1993

(Index numbers, 1984 = 100)

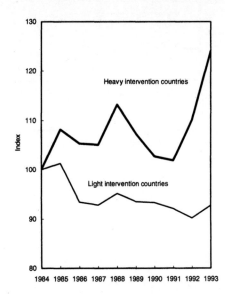

Source: UNCTAD calculations, based on World Bank, *World Development Indicators 1997* (CD-Rom).

Note: Data are unweighted averages of countries classified according to their degree of market intervention (see text). Heavy intervention countries are Burkina Faso, Cameroon, Côte d'Ivoire, Ghana, Kenya, Madagascar, Senegal, United Republic of Tanzania and Zambia; light intervention countries are Burundi, Chad, Malawi, Mali, Nigeria, Rwanda and Uganda. The domestic terms of trade of agriculture are measured as the ratio of the implicit sectoral deflator for agriculture to that for manufacturing or industry.

4. Implications

The findings of the foregoing subsections are cause for concern. First of all, they suggest that the assumptions about agricultural pricing policies in the 1970s which underlie the subsequent reforms are not entirely valid. It is true that the African governments which depended on export crops allowed their currencies to appreciate in the 1970s, and this was a handicap for African agriculture. However, while producers of certain export crops indeed faced heavy taxation, the margins between export prices and producer prices were not always higher for African than for non-African producers. Nor is it true that the entire agricultural sector was always subject to falling real prices, either for food crops or for export crops.[12]

The findings also suggest that the pricing reforms of the 1980s and the market liberalization and privatization of the 1990s have generally been associated with falling real producer prices for export crops. The domestic terms of trade have apparently turned against farmers more in those countries which have sought to link domestic and world prices. The shift from public to private marketing agents has not increased the proportion of export prices passed on to producers.

Local studies of prices of specific commodities can no doubt refine the general features identified here. However, the dynamics of agricultural price formation and the problems facing reformers and export crop farmers cannot be properly understood in the national context alone. When world prices and real producer prices for agricultural commodities are rising, there is scope for surplus extraction without undermining incentives and production. When international prices and real producer prices for agricultural commodities are falling, it would be difficult for public marketing agencies to impose an additional squeeze on farmers through forward market linkages, i.e. by higher margins between border and producer prices. In a sense, low taxation may have been an inevitable response to adverse global conditions.

Competition among traders should limit the scope of surplus extraction from farmers. In particular, the lifting of institutional restrictions on marketing can benefit farmers in more accessible and high population density areas. However, whether liberalization is an appropriate approach to agricultural development in a situation of missing and imperfect markets, adverse global conditions and poor infrastructure is very questionable. One close observer of African agriculture has argued that "donor emphasis on precipitating market liberalization in the short run may well set back the cause of market development".[13] Policies formulated without paying attention to the characteristics of domestic market structures and constraints and global conditions court failure.

Chart 20

REAL PRODUCER PRICES FOR SELECTED COMMODITIES, AND POLICY ORIENTATION OF SSA COUNTRIES BY COUNTRY GROUPING, 1984-1994

(Index numbers, 1984 = 100)

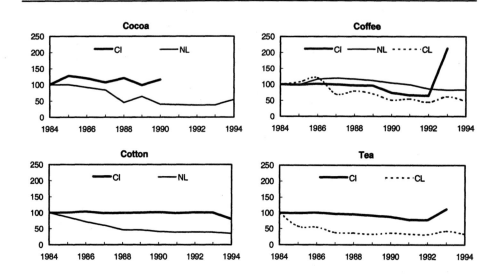

Source: UNCTAD secretariat calculations, based on FAO, *FAOSTAT* database; and IMF, *International Financial Statistics* (tapes).
Note: Real producer prices are nominal prices received by farmers deflated by the consumer price index. Countries are classified according to their degree and history of market intervention (see text). The country groupings are: NL = newly liberalized; CI = continued intervention; CL = continued liberalization. Averages are unweighted and include the following countries: *Cocoa:* CI: Ghana; NL: Cameroon, Côte d'Ivoire. *Coffee:* CI: Rwanda; CL: Kenya; NL: Burundi, Côte d'Ivoire, Madagascar, United Republic of Tanzania. *Cotton:* CI: Burkina Faso; NL: United Republic of Tanzania. *Tea:* CI: Burundi, Rwanda; CL: Kenya. A rise in the index indicates an improvement in real producer prices.

C. Agricultural supply behaviour: Sources and constraints

The response of agricultural production to price incentives depends on a host of structural and institutional factors influencing productivity and profitability. Empirical analyses generally suggest that the aggregate supply response of producers to price incentives is weaker in low-income countries, and show that:

... the magnitude of supply response to economic reforms depends on the degree to which

the agricultural economy is developed. Adequate rural infrastructure (irrigation, roads and transport, power, telecommunications), credit, market information, recurrent inputs, research, extension and farmer education and health are necessary for agricultural development. If these are seriously deficient, even getting the prices right in an ideal enabling environment will not suffice to develop agriculture.[14]

Chart 21

RATIO OF PRODUCER PRICES TO BORDER PRICES [a] FOR SELECTED COMMODITIES, AND POLICY ORIENTATION OF SSA COUNTRIES BY COUNTRY GROUPING, 1984-1994

(Index numbers, 1984 = 100)

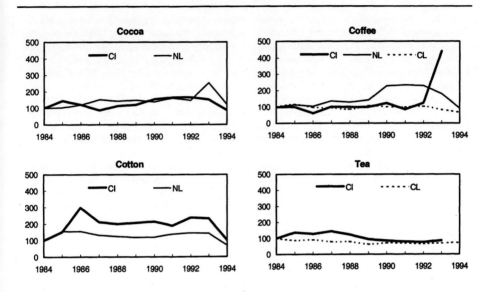

Source: See chart 20.
Note: See chart 20. The country grouping is as in that chart, with the addition of Uganda (coffee, NL), Chad and Mali (cotton in both cases NL). A rise in the index indicates that producers receive an increased share of the border price.
  [a] Export unit value.

In SSA weak supply response to price incentives used to be attributed to a lack of motivation and the allegedly perverse economic rationality of African farmers, particularly smallholders. These colonial stereotypes have been swept away by research which has shown that African producers have the same keen sense of costs and returns as farmers throughout the world.[15] But at the same time, it has become increasingly evident that structural and institutional constraints are particularly tight for African producers.[16] These constraints include inadequate basic infrastructure; missing or imperfect markets for output, land, labour and credit; supply problems for agricultural inputs and basic consumer goods purchased by farmers; lack of appropriate technological packages; gender relations; and high levels of risk.

1. Short-run supply response

The way in which these constraints work can best be understood by isolating the main agricultural supply processes. In the short run, aggregate supply response to price incentives can occur through three basic processes. First, idle land and labour can be brought into use, leading to an expansion in output through a "vent for surplus" mechanism.[17] Second, price incentives may lead to efficiency gains resulting from reallocation of resources and changes in the output mix. Third, intensification of production can occur through the application of more variable inputs and through greater care and attention at all stages of the production cycle. Different factors enhance or constrain the efficacy of each of these processes.

(a) "Vent for surplus"

Production may be expanded when farm households make a greater effort and bring idle land into use in response to price incentives or greater availability of incentive goods. This mechanism is of historical importance in Africa, and has been widely used to explain the initial surge in newly introduced export crops – coffee, cotton, cocoa, groundnuts and palm nuts – which occurred with the first wave of globalization at the turn of this century. It is likely that part of the short-run supply response to policy reforms was due to "vent for surplus" effects. There was a widespread tendency among commercially oriented smallholders in a number of SSA countries in the early 1980s to reduce their marketed output because of the unavailability of such consumer goods as soap, textiles, matches, tea, coffee, sugar, cooking oil, tinned milk, fish, cement, metal roof sheeting, radios and bicycles, due to foreign exchange shortages and the collapse of the domestic manufacturing industry. The negative effects of such shortages on recorded market output have been extensively studied in Ghana, Madagascar, Mozambique and the United Republic of Tanzania.[18] When trade liberalization, import expansion, reform of the exchange rate policy and the dismantling of price controls made incentive goods less scarce in rural areas, productive capacity was brought back into use.

However, there are limits to such expansion. First, it is a one-off response. As a World Bank report on the United Republic of Tanzania remarked, agricultural growth during 1983-1990 was "a one-time phenomenon associated with a return to a market-clearing situation in the rural economy that cannot be expected to sustain growth in the 1990s".[19] Secondly, there may not always be unutilized resources. In both high and low population density countries, the land tenure system means that there are pockets of high-density settlement alongside low-density areas where the entry of outsiders into the local community can be limited or fraught with social problems. Even where there are community land resources available, poorer farmers simply cannot farm extra land because they cannot mobilize the necessary complementary inputs. High levels of poverty mean that "farmers in most of SSA cannot afford to keep either their labour or land idle even at very unattractive prices".[20] Nevertheless, because part of their basic consumption needs are market-mediated, falling real producer prices can cause already hard-working farmers to work even longer hours simply to sustain minimal subsistence. For the richer farmers, what is important is the thinness of rural markets for wage labour, which makes it difficult to hire extra labour.

An important part of the total labour in agriculture is provided by women, and time allocation studies show a strong gender dimension to household labour constraints. Women, who are responsible for directly productive agricultural work as well as for maintaining the household and reproduction, have heavy work burdens. This situation is not simply due to cultural norms, but is closely associated with lack of infrastructure and transport means, with much time being spent in fetching water and firewood, and carrying goods.[21] Also, both men and women are affected by morbidity (sickness), which reduces production and productivity; and evidence shows that the distance of the rural population from health facilities reduces their use and leads to increases in the number of days lost through illness.[22] When there has been a switch from food crops to export crops, inadequate nutrition can constrain supply response. As a World Bank report on Malawi observed, the "nutritional implications of extensive switching of production away from non-tradable food crops into export crops have impeded adjustment".[23]

(b) Output mix adjustment

Three main factors influence the ability of farmers to achieve efficiency gains through a reallocation of resources. The first is the level of capitalization of farm operations. In semi-arid Africa the key element for farmers is animal traction (oxen or a donkey with a plough), which allows households not only to cultivate more land and enhance yields, but also to have greater flexibility in reorienting production. Micro-analysis of recent supply behaviour in Burkina Faso shows that farm households responded positively to increases in the prices of cotton and maize, two key cash crops. By contrast, increased prices for these crops led to a decrease in aggregate supply for farmers limited to hoe cultivation, because cotton and maize demand more labour than millet and sorghum.[24]

The second factor, which limits changes in output mix, is the commitment of households to meet part of their subsistence needs through their own production. This behaviour results from the fact that the rural food markets are thin, food prices in rural markets are highly volatile, and there are large margins between rural producer prices and consumer prices. The opportunity cost of export crop production is thus the retail price of food in rural markets. As a consequence, poor farmers tend to grow food crops with low risks and low returns. It makes economic sense to meet household food needs through one's own production, even though shifting to export crops appears to be more rational. Evidence shows that "consumer prices for staple food must fall by 5-30 per cent to stimulate cash cropping incentives in most grain deficit areas of Zimbabwe".[25]

The third factor is gender relationships, which can reduce the flexibility of household units to reallocate resources. The rigidity of the gender division of labour in Africa is now perhaps over-accentuated, but it is certainly true that asymmetries in the provision of household labour and the control of income from specific crops and plots of land significantly reduce flexibility. A typical example is the adoption of rice production in northern Cameroon, where income from rice sales is controlled by men. It has been shown that many women preferred to work on subsistence crops even though returns from rice cultivation were higher.[26]

(c) Agricultural intensification

Another form of response to price incentives – agricultural intensification – can either be labour-based or involve both additional labour and other variable inputs such as organic and chemical fertilizer on a given unit of land. The observation that the transition from extensive slash-and-burn production methods to intensive farming techniques occurs with rising population density has led to the suggestion that intensification is constrained by low population density and the consequent lack of inducement to intensify production. But although this process of intensification promoted by high population density may be relevant in a subsistence economy, in most current African conditions sustainable intensification requires additional capital and hence depends on assessment of profitability and risk, as well as on the availability of credit, skills and appropriate intensification packages. All of the latter can be influenced by policy and, whether market-driven or state-administered, are characterized by gender biases.

An important trend which has been observed in many African countries during the policy reform is the decline in the use of purchased inputs,

particularly fertilizers. Firstly, input prices have risen sharply with the removal of subsidies;[27] and secondly, fertilizer distribution systems have broken down as private traders have not adequately replaced marketing boards, particularly in supplying farmers in need of small quantities of fertilizer in remote areas. Once again infrastructure is a key constraint. There are also problems related to credit markets. The marketing boards had offered an institutional response to the problem of missing private credit markets. As they had a legal monopsony over marketed output, they could provide seasonal inputs on credit against the potential crop as collateral. Through the interlocking of input supply and output marketing a larger number of small farmers had access to both inputs and working capital. With privatization, this system of seasonal credit has broken down.[28]

These factors have had adverse consequences so far for the maize revolution which was developing in East and Southern Africa. In the 1980s major increases in food grain production were achieved in Kenya, Zambia and Zimbabwe through pricing and market support policies which encouraged farmers to adopt hybrid maize seed, resulting from decades of agricultural research, and to increase fertilizer use. Policies included the expansion of marketing board buying stations in smallholder areas, expansion of state credit disbursed to smallholders, and subsidies on inputs. In the 1990s, however, this approach came to be regarded as fiscally unsustainable. With the dismantling of state marketing services, reduced availability of credit and rising real fertilizer prices, yields and production per capita stagnated, even when allowance is made for the adverse effects of drought. Remoter areas of large, low population density countries can be particularly affected by the policy change. The transition from pan-territorial to market pricing has reduced grain prices received by smallholders in the more remote grain-surplus areas in the United Republic of Tanzania and Zambia. In Madagascar food market liberalization has been associated with an increase in price volatility and greater regional and seasonal price dispersions.[29]

In high-density areas, declining use of purchased inputs raises questions about the sustainability of intensification. Evidence from the Senegalese groundnut basin, for example, shows that with the abolition of fertilizer subsidies and the increasingly difficult access to fertilizer credit, aggregate annual use of fertilizer has declined from a high of 80,000 tons in the mid-1970s to a range of 20-30,000 tons during the 1980s and 1990s. Farmers have compensated by increasing the seed per hectare, a solution that may make sense in the short term, given prevailing prices of groundnuts and fertilizer, but that will have adverse ecological consequences over the longer term.[30]

2. Investment and productivity growth

Both the removal of various structural obstacles to agricultural supply response and long-run trends in productivity and output depend on the pace of investment and technological progress. In predominantly agricultural economies, the net agricultural surplus (i.e. the agricultural value-added minus agricultural producers' total consumption) is the major source of funding for investment both within agriculture and outside. In extreme conditions where productivity is very low, the value-added of the sector is barely sufficient to meet the basic subsistence and simple reproduction needs of agricultural producers, and there may even be insufficient surplus to maintain the natural resource base. Because of the undercapitalization of African agriculture, many African farmers are in this low-productivity, hand-to-mouth situation. In such situations there can be no agricultural growth without an external injection of resources to increase productivity.

Greater understanding of how more successful African farmers have been able to create an agricultural surplus, and of what they do with that surplus, is vital to successful agricultural policies in Africa. There is unfortunately a general lack of knowledge of private farm investment behaviour, and the general omission of this issue in policy analysis which underpins agricultural reforms has been highlighted in a recent report by the World Bank Operations Evaluation Department with regard to its own agricultural sector studies:

> There is no analysis of the constraints on private sector investment in any of the reports. Nevertheless all the reports stress the need to develop an effective enabling environment that would help to induce private investment. Unlike the old public production paradigm, the new market friendly policy line depends on private investment to achieve rapid growth, in agriculture as in other sectors. In many countries, achieving the needed rate of private investment in agriculture is a problem the Bank has not addressed in its sector work on agriculture.[31]

Smallholder farm investment is primarily founded on the surplus generated by both on-farm and off-farm activities. The absence of individual rights to land has meant that few farm households have collateral for loans from formal banking institutions. Private traders provide seasonal credit, tying their loans to purchase of crops, but this usually entails high implicit rates of interest and is likely to be avoided unless a farmer is desperate and seeking a "hungry season" loan to guarantee the survival of the household.[32] Small farmers in the past had access to credit provided by marketing boards or special directed credit agencies, but with the implementation of reforms these sources started to disappear. What is more, special directed credit arrangements, which were an important component of donor lending, particularly by the World Bank, have been replaced by liberalized financial intermediation and market-based interest rates. The previous arrangements did not reach the poorest smallholders for whom they were often designed. However, available evidence on financial liberalization suggests that these reforms have also been unable to increase the volume of savings or access to credit in rural areas except by those who can offer collateral.[33]

Under these conditions non-farm income has become an even more important source for on-farm investment, directly or as collateral. How non-farm earnings derived from the public and private sector wage bill can propel agrarian capital accumulation has been shown historically for Kenya.[34] But where urban unemployment is on the increase, such opportunities are diminishing. Moreover, whether non-farm income is reinvested in agriculture depends on a delicate balance of incentives and capital requirements. These are affected by the physical and economic environment, including infrastructure and market structures, the scale and timing of non-farm income flows in relation to farm investment needs, and intra-household distribution and control of both non-farm and on-farm incomes. The persistence of a high degree of intersectoral dualism, which is rooted in low agricultural productivity, has been only marginally affected by agricultural price reforms.[35]

An important tendency observed in Africa amongst successful farmers is the diversification of their portfolios, using net incomes from farming to invest in trade and urban real estate, or in their children's education, rather than for expansion of agricultural production. This behaviour reflects both the relative profitability and the riskiness of investment in different sectors. Diversification of activities in different sectors results from high levels of risks associated with each of them, while shifting resources out of agriculture reflects the higher risks of agricultural operations based on climate, markets and public policy. Moreover, market price risks of agricultural activity appear to have increased as a result of deregulation of crop markets.[36]

How customary land tenure arrangements affect incentives for private farm investment is a critical issue. According to one view, since tenure insecurity undermines investment incentives and diverts resources into unproductive litigation costs, land registration and freehold titles are necessary in order to unleash agricultural investment. However, other analyses of the effects of such land reforms indicate that "in the absence of profitable technological options, registration will have little effect on investment and productivity in agriculture"[37] and suggest that investments to improve land are actually increased under the indigenous tenure system because they can increase security of use rights. This debate is still open, but it is certain that the tenure system does affect the operation of rural labour and capital markets, and one legacy of the multiplication of land rights which occurred in the colonial period is that agricultural surplus and entrepreneurial energies are deployed to build up access to, and command over, land and labour resources rather than to increase their productivity.[38]

The profitability of private investment in agriculture depends on public investment in infrastructure. This includes institutional support for specific crops (see box 2), as well as location-specific investments in safe water, electricity, health and education facilities, and also transport. The rural transport bottleneck is a particularly important constraint on private farm investment because it reduces real returns and is also a source of product market imperfections. The density of rural roads in Africa is very low, particularly when compared with Asia.[39] Moreover, many of the roads are in a poor state of repair because of lack of proper maintenance, motorized transport services are often in short supply and expensive, and there is a dearth of non-motorized off-road trans-

port equipment, which is particularly important for delivering produce to the first point of sale. The experience of the Northern Guinea Savanna of Nigeria, a country where the rural road network expanded by 45 per cent between 1985 and 1992, shows how rural road investment can, in association with the discovery of locally adapted hybrid varieties of maize and demonstration effects of rural development projects, facilitate expansion of food production.[40]

Because of lack of data, it is not always possible to gauge how public expenditure supporting farm investment has developed under adjustment programmes. However, in many SSA countries, much of public investment expenditure in agriculture was externally financed, often in the form of integrated rural development projects, but such expenditure has been declining. From available evidence it appears that the proportion of government expenditure going to agriculture has remained under 10 per cent of total expenditure on average.[41] This is a better indicator of urban bias in Africa than agricultural pricing policy.

The rate of technological change in agriculture depends ultimately on agricultural research. Most of the problems with that research, pointed out a decade ago, are still unsolved: costs of R&D in Africa are higher than elsewhere, owing in part to the fact that programmes are still largely foreign-funded, and the small size of countries and research stations, dispersion and high staff turnover impede the attainment of a "critical mass". As a result, with the notable exception of maize, "most of SSA now offers smallholders no dramatic, immediately applicable new technology that might (with adequate price incentives) safely and substantially increase the profitability of food farming over large areas. While this is so, the elasticity of total farm output to currently recommended policy changes, including price changes, can seldom be very large".[42] These observations are probably as true to a large extent now as they were ten years ago. Evidence for 19 countries in SSA shows that real agricultural expenditures, which had been growing rapidly in the 1960s and moderately in the 1970s, ceased to grow in the 1980s and early 1990s. In 1991, the research expenditure in these countries was 0.7 per cent of agricultural GDP. However, estimates of the returns to investment in maize research indicate high annual rates of return, usually in excess of 40 per cent.[43]

Box 2

PRICE AND NON-PRICE FACTORS IN COTTON DEVELOPMENT IN SSA

A comparative analysis of cotton production and exports in SSA was carried out in the late 1980s for Cameroon, Kenya, Malawi, Nigeria, Senegal and the United Republic of Tanzania.[1] It illustrated the role of price and non-price factors in agricultural development, starting from the observation that there had been a clear tendency since the early 1970s for francophone African countries to perform better in cotton production and exports than anglophone countries (with the exception of Zimbabwe).

In two countries (Nigeria and the United Republic of Tanzania) price factors were found to have played a major role in determining the volume of cotton production. In both countries abnormally low relative prices of tradables favoured the production of food crops. The Dutch-disease-induced increase in labour cost in Nigeria and the dearth of consumer goods in the United Republic of Tanzania acted as further disincentives for the production of agricultural exportables.

However, apart from these extreme cases, differences in cotton production performance could not be explained by differences in the evolution of real producer prices. Rather, and particularly in the more successful countries (Cameroon and Senegal), non-price factors (including research, credit and subsidized inputs) explained most of the production increase. In Senegal, they more than compensated for the negative effect of declining producer prices.

The analysis also found that much of the difference in performance amongst the sample countries was due to institutional factors. In general, francophone countries appeared to benefit from better coordination between upstream and downstream agents in the cotton industry, thanks to the presence of the Compagnie Française pour le Développement des Fibres Textiles (CFDT). The CFDT improved vertical integration in the countries where it operated, and provided positive inputs in terms of professionalism, know-how and experience with technological, market and finance conditions.

As a result of this key institutional difference, a distinct high-input/high-yield technological pattern prevailed in cotton production in the francophone countries, while the anglophone ones were stuck in a low-input/low-yield pattern. Despite the relative success of the former, the CFDT-inspired approach was not immune to criticism, because it led to high production and administrative costs and to an excessive and even monopolistic focus on cotton. In the anglophone countries, on the other hand, lack of technological progress was making cotton cultivation increasingly unattractive, except as a diversification and risk-minimization strategy.

The main conclusion of the analysis was that, notwithstanding the relevance of macroeconomic and sectoral pricing policies, institutional factors had been paramount in explaining inter-country differences in cotton production growth. The unsatisfactory performance of cotton in an otherwise relatively successful economy such as Kenya underlined the importance of crop- and sector-specific institutional arrangements, often rooted in part in the colonial legacy of the various countries. The political influence of cotton producers was also important. Future priorities for cotton development were identified as follows: to strengthen research and extension systems; to eliminate input supply and finance bottlenecks; and to build institutions, including through regional cooperation and coordination.

---

[1]   U. J. Lele, N. van de Walle and M. Gbetibouo, "Cotton in Africa: An analysis of differences in performance", MADIA Discussion Paper No. 7 (Washington, D.C.: World Bank, 1989).

D. Adjustment policies and agricultural performance

As noted in the previous chapter, agricultural production grew so slowly in the 1970s and early 1980s that output per capita was falling. For many countries, there was also a dip in agricultural export volumes. In the mid-1980s, output picked up and the downward trend in exports was reversed, but despite these improvements, agricultural production per capita has stagnated and export volumes have not yet recovered to their 1970 levels in most countries.

How these trends are related to various policies pursued under structural adjustment programmes introduced in the 1980s is difficult to ascertain since these programmes combine three elements (financing, policy design and implementation). While the reduction of agricultural taxation through output pricing and market deregulation has been at the centre of adjustment policies, the reforms have also involved a wider range of measures which have affected not only output prices, but also a host of other elements such as: prices and the availability of agricultural inputs, incentive goods and rural credit; the quantity and quality of rural transport infrastructure and transport means; the quality and costs of health and education services for farmers; agricultural research and extension systems; opportunities for and remuneration of off-farm employment; and the level of food demand. The performance of African agriculture reflects the influence of this package of measures, as well as of the external financing associated with adjustment programmes, on incentives and structural constraints on agricultural production, investment and productivity growth.

Agricultural performance is also affected by the weather, changes in international prices and external demand. It is notable that the acceleration in the growth of agricultural output and the recovery of export volumes in the mid-1980s co-incided with a reversal in the downward trend in net resource transfers, in large part on account of substantial increases in ODA (see chapter I, chart 5). This was also associated with a shift from declining to rising import volumes.

As already discussed, reforms have not always succeeded in altering price structures as intended. They have often failed to reduce the taxation of export crops or to improve the agricultural terms of trade and real producer prices. Moreover, reforms have not effectively tackled key structural constraints which impede the acceleration of agricultural growth in many countries. It has been suggested that "SSA suffers from structural handicaps that are impossible to remove or reduce through the standard policy reform programs".[44] There are indications that some ingredients of reforms have actually aggravated constraints on the growth of smallholder production. Major exceptions to this situation are those countries where, in the past, attempts were being made to foster domestic capitalist agribusinesses or state farms. In such cases, important restrictions on smallholder choices and access to resources were removed. But elsewhere access to inputs and credit has not improved because input subsidies and public agricultural services (input provision, product distribution, credit and extension) have been reduced, and the private sector has not adequately taken over these functions. Moreover "the decline in donor support to rural development projects and integrated commodity projects was accompanied by a decline in investment in rural health, education and infrastructure facilities",[45] the more so because governments have been unwilling or unable to provide the operation and maintenance funds required to sustain investment. The decline in external aid to sub-Saharan African agriculture was very steep during 1987-1994, when it dropped from \$4,609 million to \$1,322 million (at constant 1990 prices).[46]

The upturn in agricultural production and export volumes reflects greater utilization of existing resources rather than an acceleration of investment and productivity growth. Production and export expansion in the mid-1980s coincided with a recovery in external resource flows and imports. Exchange rate adjustments and trade liberalization also appear to have contributed by shifting the incentives towards exports and reducing shortages of incentive goods in the countryside. Moreover, given the declines in real producer prices and per capita incomes, it is possible that there has been a more intensive utilization of household labour.[47]

Currency depreciations can be expected to cause a shift from food crops to export crops since many food crops are not tradable. Again, incentives for food production vis-à-vis export crops are weakened by the removal of subsidies and by depressed food demand due to contractionary monetary and fiscal policies. However, higher food import costs associated with devaluations at the same time encourage consumers to substitute local food for imports. The effects of devaluations on output mix between export and food crops for domestic consumption thus depend on the degree of tradability of food crops and reliance on food imports. It appears that where a currency was grossly overvalued and parallel currency markets were pervasive, exports either declined or were diverted into unofficial channels. In such cases, exchange rate adjustments supported by export promotion measures have achieved positive results in spite of the downward trend in real producer prices.[48]

Table 13 compares post-1984 trends in total agricultural production, export volume and food production with average growth rates in the 1970s for three groups of countries defined according to the degree of compliance with adjustment programmes. These groups are not defined simply on the basis of pricing policies, but of their overall compliance with conditionality with regard to macroeconomic policy (fiscal deficit reduction, public expenditure levels, exchange rates, etc.), of their public sector management (including civil service reform, public expenditure reform and public enterprise restructuring and privatization), and of their private sector development (including financial sector reform, trade policy reform, regulatory environment, and pricing and incentives).[49] Three generalizations can be made from the table:

- First, it is apparent that for all groups of countries, the most significant change is in the volume of agricultural exports. This reflects the partial recovery from the dip of the 1970s and early 1980s and the return of exports to official marketing channels. However, the improvement in export performance is actually weakest for the good compliers.

- Second, there is little difference between the groups in terms of improvements they achieved in growth rates of total agricultural and total food production. However, this result changes when low population density countries (which are not found amongst the good compliers) are excluded. There is a clear tendency for the aggregate agricultural growth rates to be lower in the post-1985 period than in the 1970s in these countries.[50] When the sample is limited to high and medium population density countries, weak and poor compliers have a better overall performance in terms of agricultural growth.

- Third, there is a major divide between Southern and East African countries, on the one hand, and West and Central African countries on the other. In the former, the growth of agricultural output is lower in the post-1984 period than in the 1970s in both good and poor compliers, but it is markedly lower in the good compliers. For West and Central Africa it is faster in all cases, but particularly so in the good compliers. Also, in Southern and East Africa, the recovery of agricultural exports appears to be associated with a decline in the rate of growth of food production. Although drought may be part of the reason, the decline also reflects, as noted above, the immediate impact of the dismantling of the state-centred approach to expanding food grain production.

As with all exercises of this type, these results must be interpreted with caution. However, they do not provide much support to the idea that adjustment programmes have generally brought a better policy mix for tackling incentives and structural and institutional constraints across Africa.

Table 13

AGRICULTURAL PERFORMANCE AND COMPLIANCE WITH
ADJUSTMENT PROGRAMMES IN SSA

	Average annual volume increase					
	Agricultural production		Agricultural exports		Food production	
	1970-1980	1985-1995	1970-1980	1985-1995	1970-1980	1985-1995
Country group	*(Per cent)*					
Country with good compliance	1.0	2.2	-2.0	1.0	1.0	1.9
West and Central Africa *a*	0.0	3.0	-2.8	1.7	-0.0	2.6
Southern and Eastern Africa *b*	2.6	1.0	-0.7	-0.2	2.5	0.9
Country with weak compliance	1.6	2.7	-3.3	3.4	1.7	2.6
	(0.9)	*(3.2)*	*(-3.4)*	*(3.7)*	*(1.0)*	*(2.9)*
West and Central Africa *c*	1.8	3.4	-1.4	2.8	1.8	3.3
Southern and Eastern Africa *d*	1.4	1.4	-6.5	4.4	1.6	1.4
Country with poor compliance	1.8	2.6	-4.9	2.3	1.9	2.7
	(1.2)	*(3.7)*	*(-4.0)*	*(4.8)*	*(1.0)*	*(3.4)*
West and Central Africa *e*	1.6	3.0	-5.8	3.5	1.7	3.1
Southern and Eastern Africa *f*	2.2	2.0	-3.4	0.4	2.1	1.9

Source: UNCTAD secretariat calculations, based on FAO, *FAOSTAT* database. The classification of countries is that of World Bank, *Adjustment Lending in Sub-Saharan Africa: An Update,* Report No. 16594 (Washington, D.C., May 1997).
Note: Group averages are unweighted. Those shown in brackets exclude low population density countries (see text), asterisked below.
  a Benin, Gambia, Ghana, Mali, Mauritania.
  b Malawi, Mauritius, United Republic of Tanzania.
  c Burkina Faso, Guinea, Côte d'Ivoire*, Niger, Togo, Guinea-Bissau*, Senegal.
  d Uganda, Madagascar*, Zambia*, Zimbabwe.
  e Central African Republic*, Congo*, Gabon*, Nigeria, Cameroon*.
  f Kenya, Burundi, Democratic Republic of the Congo*.

E. Conclusions

Comparative analysis shows that a particularly effective agricultural development strategy in the early stages of development is a two-sided approach in which the State taxes agriculture, but at the same time counterbalances this resource outflow by making adequate investment in basic infrastructure for agricultural production, and helping to introduce a stream of innovations needed to enhance productivity and profitability of private investment. This pattern has been identified as the main characteristic of East Asian agricultural development.[51]

In Africa too, before the agricultural marketing reforms, public policy aimed at a two-sided approach. But, as in the case of import-substitution strategy in industry, there were serious problems of policy design and implementation. Many governments sought to raise revenue by taxing export crops without ploughing part of the money back into the sector to increase productivity. Instead, they concentrated on the promotion of food crop production, often subsidizing marginal areas through pan-territorial price support. A significant proportion of public expenditure in agriculture went into financial subsidies, particularly for inputs (e.g. fertilizers), credit and marketing, rather than into infrastructure investment and agricultural research to enhance agrarian capital formation and productivity growth. More important, a large share of revenues obtained from export crops went into urban consumption.

The success of market-based agricultural development in Africa requires on-farm private investment. This can occur only through a policy which increases the profitability of investment and lowers risks by providing a stable environment and removing technical and financial constraints on the capacity and willingness to invest. Agricultural reforms have not succeeded in this respect. They have sought to improve profitability through action on one side of the equation, namely through higher output prices. But in practice, because they have been implemented in the context of imperfect private markets and falling international commodity prices, they have failed to reverse the downward trend in real producer prices. The bias of agricultural policy reforms in favour of export production has also ignored the fact that for many farmers it is lower food prices and improved food distribution systems that would encourage them to grow high-value crops.

Farmers have also been squeezed because key production and marketing costs – the other side of the profitability equation – have risen rapidly: prices of fertilizers and transport costs have soared with devaluations and removal of subsidies. Lower wages have not been much help because hired labour generally accounts for less than 20 per cent of the total labour force. The dismantling of marketing boards has increased price risks, adding to the uncertainties of rain-fed agriculture. The interlocking marketing systems centred on marketing boards which provided inputs and credit have been only partially replaced by private sector arrangements.

Analysis of supply behaviour has identified many institutional and structural constraints. Some of these, such as low population density and agro-climatic conditions, are legacies of geography and history, and out of reach of policy, at least in the short to medium term. Some, notably the gender division of labour and control of resources, can be quite intractable and give rise to complex policy decisions. But other structural constraints can be reduced through public investment in agricultural research and infrastructure, and through measures designed to increase farmers' skills, access to finance and capacity to invest. The importance of tackling these policy-based constraints is now well established by analysis and empirical evidence. Reorienting development policy in this direction will require a shift from an approach based on ideology to one governed by pragmatism.

Notes

1   *Adjustment in Africa* (Washington, D.C.: World Bank, 1994), p. 76. For an earlier formulation of this view see *Accelerated Development in Sub-Saharan Africa: An Agenda for Action* (Washington, D.C.: World Bank, 1982) and *World Development Report 1986* (Washington, D.C.: World Bank, 1986).

2   See, in particular, H. Binswanger, "The policy response of agriculture", in *Proceedings of the World Bank Annual Conference on Development Economics* (Washington, D.C.: World Bank, 1989), pp. 231-

258, together with comments by A. Braverman and A. Valdes and the floor discussion of the paper, pp. 259-271.

3   See J. Meerman, *Reforming Agriculture: The World Bank Goes to Market*, World Bank Operations Evaluation Department Study (Washington, D.C.: World Bank, 1997), p. 70.

4   These are indeed old questions raised as part of the criticism of the reform process described as "pricist", i.e. something that proceeds "as if correct pricing

policy – for farm inputs, outputs, and foreign exchange – were (a) readily definable and attainable, (b) in general best approached by reducing state involvement in agricultural markets, (c) at least the most important component in, probably in most cases necessary and sufficient for, rapid and equitable agricultural growth" (M. Lipton, "Limits of price policy for agriculture: Which way for the World Bank?", *Development Policy Review*, Vol. 5, 1987, p. 201).

5   Part of the empirical results discussed in this section are from K. Boratav, "Movements in relative prices in sub-Saharan Africa" UNCTAD/GDS/MDPB/ Misc. 12 (Geneva, 1998). Detailed information on the methodology and the data used can be obtained from the UNCTAD secretariat.

6   For some of the more complex ways of making cross-country comparisons of agricultural taxation and problems associated with them, see M. J. Westlake, "The measurement of agricultural price distortion in developing countries", *Journal of Development Studies*, Vol. 23, 1987; D. Byerlee and M. L. Morris, "Calculating levels of protection: Is it always appropriate to use world reference prices based on current trading status?, *World Development*, Vol. 21, No. 5, 1993; and M. Karshenas, "Dynamic economies and the critique of urban bias", *Journal of Peasant Studies*, Vol. 24, No. 1/2, 1996.

7   The conventional claim of excessive taxation of agriculture in Africa has been questioned by J. G. Beynon, "Pricism v. structuralism in sub-Saharan African agriculture", *Journal of Agricultural Economics*, Vol. 40, No. 1.

8   See A.O. Krueger, M. Schiff and A. Valdes (eds.), *The Political Economy of Agricultural Pricing Policy*, Vol. 4, *A Synthesis of the Economics in Developing Countries* (Baltimore: Johns Hopkins University Press for the World Bank, 1991-1992).

9   Both indicators have shortcomings which warrant caution in their interpretation. When GDP deflators at market prices rather than factor costs are used in estimating the overall terms of trade of agriculture, there may be inter-temporal inconsistencies in the measure of relative agricultural prices. For instance, a country may have dismantled its marketing boards and introduced explicit taxes on agricultural exports. Under those circumstances the market price measure of the agricultural GDP deflator can show an increase without any change in the prices received by producers. The estimates of real producer prices use FAO producer prices, but once again caution is needed in interpreting the data. Past FAO price series for SSA refer mostly to official prices paid by marketing boards to farmers, or to government support prices. When prices in parallel markets are higher, the official prices underestimate the prices actually received by farmers. By contrast, after liberalization, reported prices usually refer to average prices received by farmers. This may result in an overestimation of the effect of liberalization on producer prices.

10   Chart 19 classifies countries into those with "heavy" and "light" intervention using an overall score of 15 in table A13 of *Adjustment in Africa* as the breakpoint, whilst charts 20 and 21 use crop-specific information in table A9 of that study to classify countries as "continued interventionist", "continued liberal" or "newly liberalized". For other recent classifications see *Adjustment Lending in Sub-Saharan Africa: An Update*, Operations Evaluation Department Report No. 16594 (Washington, D.C.: World Bank, 1997); and K. Cleaver, *Rural Development Strategies for Poverty Reduction and Environmental Protection in Sub-Saharan Africa* (Washington, D.C.: World Bank, 1997); the latter uses a qualitative rating based on recent World Bank evaluations. To examine how different classifications can affect results, table 1 of the latter study has been taken as a check-list of the country classifications used in this section for comparing the terms of trade of agriculture under different policy regimes. The listing in that study produces three countries which fall into the market-oriented group in the present chapter (Malawi, Mali and Uganda) and three countries (Cameroon, Madagascar and Senegal) which fall into the "interventionist" category. With 1984 as the base year, the average agricultural terms of trade of the market-oriented group decline to 93 in 1995 (1984=100), whereas those of the interventionist group rise to 136.

11   Tables A.9 and A.18.

12   This conclusion was reached earlier by D. Ghai and L. Smith, "Food price policy and equity", in J. W. Mellor, C. L. Delgado and M. J. Blackie (eds.), *Accelerating Food Production in Sub-Saharan Africa* (Baltimore and London: Johns Hopkins University Press, 1987), pp. 284-285. Also, it has been shown in a study of East Africa that the heavy subsidization of food crops after 1973 meant that in most countries there was no net taxation of agriculture; see U. J. Lele and L. Meyers, "Growth and structural change in East Africa: Domestic policies, agricultural performance and World Bank assistance 1963-86", MADIA Discussion Paper No. 3 (Washington, D.C.: World Bank, 1989).

13   U. J. Lele, "Comparative advantage and structural transformation: A review of Africa's economic development experience", in G. Ranis and T. P. Schultz (eds.), *The State of Development Economics: Progress and Perspectives* (Oxford and New York: Basil Blackwell, 1988), p. 204.

14   Meerman, *op. cit.*

15   Results of studies of the supply response of individual export crops to changes in the real prices of those crops indicate that for annual crops (cotton and tobacco) short-run supply elasticities generally range from 0.2 to 0.7. For tree crops (coffee, cocoa and tea), the range is lower – from 0.1 to 0.3. Long-run elasticities are generally higher, but usually less than unity; see G. Helleiner, "Smallholder decision making: Tropical African evidence", in L. G. Reynolds

(ed.), *Agriculture in Development Theory* (New Haven and London: Yale University Press, 1975); and N. Mamingi, "How prices and macroeconomic policies affect agricultural supply and the environment", World Bank Policy Research Working Paper No. 1645 (Washington, D.C.: World Bank, 1998).

16 Surprisingly, in view of its importance to the adjustment process, there is little research into the aggregate supply response of agriculture to real output prices in Africa. The main multi-country empirical study (M. E. Bond, "Agricultural supply response to prices in sub-Saharan Africa", IMF Staff Papers, Vol. 30, 1983, pp. 703-726) is now 15 years old. For a set of nine SSA countries, Bond found that price elasticity was low and only significant in two countries – Kenya and Ghana. The estimates correspond to those for other low-income countries and suggest that a 10 per cent increase in real crop prices will elicit only a 1 or 2 per cent increase in aggregate agricultural output in the short run.

17 "Vent for surplus" is a generic term for models of trade and growth that involve the exploitation of resources which had previously been unused because they had no economic value.

18 J. C. Berthélemy and C. Morrisson, *Agricultural Development in Africa and the Supply of Manufactured Goods* (Paris: OECD Development Centre, 1989); and D. Bevan, P. Collier and J. W. Gunning, *Peasants and Governments: An Economic Analysis* (Oxford: Clarendon Press, 1989).

19 World Bank, *Tanzania Economic Report: Towards Sustainable Development in the 1990s*, Report No. 9352-TA (Washington, D.C.: World Bank, 1991); quoted in L. Putterman, "Economic reform and smallholder agriculture in Tanzania: A discussion of recent market liberalization, road rehabilitation, and technology dissemination efforts", *World Development*, Vol. 23, No. 2, 1995, p. 315.

20 O. M. Ogbu and M. Gbetibouo, "Agricultural supply response in sub-Saharan Africa: A critical review of the literature", *African Development Review*, Vol. 2, No. 2, 1990, p. 90.

21 On the time that women spend in transport activities in rural areas, see D. F. Bryceson and J. Howe, *African Rural Households and Transport: Reducing the Burden on Women?* (Delft, Netherlands: International Institute for Hydraulic and Environmental Engineering, 1992); and I. Barwell, "Transport and the village: Findings from African village-level travel and transport surveys and related studies", World Bank Discussion Paper No. 344, Africa Region Series (Washington, D.C.: World Bank, 1996).

22 See Bevan, Collier and Gunning, *op. cit.*, especially chapters 13-15.

23 World Bank, "Report and Recommendation of the President of the International Development Association to the Executive Directors on a proposed credit of SDR 52.6 million (US $70 million equivalent) to the Republic of Malawi for an agricultural sector adjustment programme", Report No. P-5189-MAI

(Washington, D.C.: World Bank, 1990), quoted (p. 869) in J. Harrigan, "Modelling the impact of World Bank policy-based lending: The case of Malawi's agricultural sector", *Journal of Development Studies*, Vol. 33, No. 6, 1997, pp. 848-873.

24 K. Savagodo, T. Reardon and K. Pietola, "Mechanization and agricultural supply response in the Sahel: A farm-level profit function analysis", *Journal of African Economies*, Vol. 6, No. 3, pp. 336-377.

25 T. S. Jayne, "Do high food marketing costs constrain cash crop production? Evidence from Zimbabwe", *Economic Development and Cultural Change*, Vol. 42, No. 2, 1994, p. 399. See also A. De Janvry, M. Fafchamps and E. Sadoulet, "Peasant household behaviour with missing markets: Some paradoxes explained", *Economic Journal*, Vol. 101, 1991, pp. 1400-1417.

26 C. Jones, "Intra-household bargaining in response to the introduction of new crops: A case study from North Cameroon", in J. L. Moock (ed.), *Understanding Africa's Rural Households and Farming Systems* (Boulder, Colorado: Westview Press, 1986).

27 Fertilizer costs in Africa are inherently high because of high transport cost, lack of competition in distribution systems and absence of economies of scale in procurement. International comparisons show the following median nitrogen fertilizer-maize price ratios: Asia (1980-1992): 2.7; Latin America (1980-1992): 3.8; Kenya (1980-1995): 7.3; Zimbabwe (1980-1994): 6.4; and Côte d'Ivoire (1980-1992): 5.4; see P. W. Heisey and W. Mwangi, "Fertiliser use and maize production", in D. Byerlee and C. K. Eicher (eds.), *Africa's Emerging Maize Revolution* (Boulder, Colorado, and London: Lynne Rienner, 1997), table 13.3. These ratios have been exacerbated by the failure to reduce import barriers; see D. Gisselquist, "Import barriers for agricultural inputs", UNDP-World Bank Expansion Program, Occasional Paper No. 10 (Washington, D.C.: World Bank, 1994).

28 See C. Poulton, A. Dorward and J. Kydd, "The revival of smallholder cash crops in Africa: Public and private roles in the provision of finance", *Journal of International Development*, Vol. 10, No. 1, 1998, pp. 85-104.

29 T. S. Jayne and S. Jones, "Food marketing and pricing policy in Eastern and Southern Africa: A survey", *World Development*, Vol. 25, No. 9, 1997, pp. 1505-1527; and C. B. Barrett, "Liberalization and food price distributions: ARCH-M evidence from Madagascar", *Food Policy*, Vol. 22, No. 2, 1997, pp. 155-173.

30 V. Kelly, B. Diagana, M. Gaye, T. Reardon and M. Sene, "Have structural adjustment programs compromised efforts to intensify sustainable African agricultural production: Empirical evidence from Senegal", paper presented to the Meeting of the International Association of Agricultural Economists, Sacramento, California, August 1997. See also T. Reardon et al., "Promoting sustainable intensification and productivity growth in Sahel agriculture

after macroeconomic reform", *Food Policy*, Vol. 22, No. 4, 1997, pp. 317-327.

31   Meerman, *op. cit.*, p. 156.

32   For a full discussion of rural financial markets in least developed countries, including policy implications, see UNCTAD, *The Least Developed Countries 1997 Report* (United Nations publication, Sales No. E.97.II.D.6), New York and Geneva, 1997.

33   See B. M. Desai and J. W. Mellor, "Institutional finance for agricultural development: An analytical survey of critical issues", *Food Policy Review*, No. 1, 1993; W. G. Donovan, "Agriculture and economic reform in sub-Saharan Africa", AFTES Working Paper No. 18, 1996, chapter 8; M. K. Nissanke, "Financing, enterprise development and export diversification in sub-Saharan Africa", UNCTAD/GDS/MDPB/Misc. 8 (Geneva, 1998); P. Mosley, "Micro-macro linkages in financial markets: The impact of financial liberalization on access to rural credit in four African countries", paper presented to the meeting of the UNU/WIDER Project on Impact of Liberalization on Key Markets in Sub-Saharan Africa, Addis Ababa, March 1998.

34   G. Kitching, *Class and Economic Change in Kenya* (New Haven: Yale University Press, 1980). See also T. Reardon, E. Crawford and V. Kelly, "Links between non-farm income and farm investment in African households: Adding the capital market perspective", *American Journal of Agricultural Economics*, Vol. 76, No. 5, 1994, pp. 1172-1176.

35   For a detailed discussion of trends in the ratio of value-added per worker in agriculture and non-agriculture during the reform period, see M. Karshenas, "Capital accumulation and agricultural surplus in Africa and Asia", UNCTAD/GDS/MDPB/Misc. 1 (Geneva, 1998).

36   See Barrett, *op. cit.*

37   R. Barrow and M. Roth, "Land tenure and investment in African agriculture", *Journal of Modern African Studies*, Vol. 28, No. 2, 1990, p. 296.

38   For overviews of the debate, see H.W.O. Okoth-Ogendo, "Agrarian reform in sub-Saharan Africa: An assessment of State responses to the African agrarian crisis and their implications for agricultural development", in T.J. Bassett and D.E. Crummey (eds.), *Land in African Agrarian Systems* (Madison, Wisconsin: Wisconsin University Press, 1993); J.-P. Platteau, "The evolutionary theory of land rights as applied to sub-Saharan Africa: A critical assessment", *Development and Change*, Vol. 27, 1996, pp. 29-86; E. Sjaanstad and D.W. Bromley, "Indigenous land rights in sub-Saharan Africa: Appropriation, security and investment demand", *World Development*, Vol. 25, No. 4, 1997, pp. 549-562. On the view that diversity of claims leads to inappropriate deployment of surplus, see S. Berry, *No Condition is Permanent: The Social Dynamics of Agrarian Change in Sub-Saharan Africa* (Madison: University of Wisconsin Press, 1993).

39   In the early 1990s, for example, a group of 18 countries in the humid and sub-humid tropics had only 63 kilometres of rural roads per 1,000 square kilometres. Taking account of population density difference, this was less than one sixth of the level in India in 1950; see D.S.C. Spencer, "Infrastructure and technology constraints to agricultural development in the humid and subhumid Tropics of Africa", Environment and Production Technology Division Discussion Paper No. 3 (Washington, D.C.: International Food Policy Research Institute, 1994).

40   J. Smith et al., "The role of technology in agricultural intensification: The evolution of maize production in the Northern Guinea Savanna of Nigeria", *Economic Development and Cultural Change*, Vol. 42, No. 3, 1994, pp. 537-554.

41   M. Gallagher, "Government spending in Africa: A retrospective of the 1980s", *Journal of African Economies*, Vol. 3, No. 1, 1994.

42   M. Lipton, "The place of agricultural research in the development of sub-Saharan Africa", *World Development*, Vol. 16, No. 10, 1988, p. 1231. Thirtle et al. found empirical evidence in favour of the need for critical mass, showing that large countries appear to fare better than small ones, possibly because of the existence of scale economies in R&D (C. Thirtle, D. Hadley and R. Townsend, "Policy-induced innovation in sub-Saharan African agriculture: A multilateral Malmqvist productivity approach", *Development Policy Review*, Vol. 13, 1995, pp. 323-348). If this finding were confirmed, it could contribute to explaining the good performance of Nigeria's domestic-market-oriented agriculture.

43   For an analysis of agricultural research expenditures, see P. Pardey, J. Roseboom and N. M. Beintema, "Investments in African agricultural research", *World Development*, Vol. 25, No. 3, 1997, pp. 409-423. Estimates of rates of return to maize research are from D. Byerlee and D. Jewell, "The technological foundation of the revolution", in Byerlee and Eicher (eds.), *op. cit.*

44   Y. Hayami and J.-P. Platteau, "Resource endowments and agricultural development: Africa vs. Asia", paper prepared for the IEA Round Table Conference on "The Institutional Foundation of Economic Development in East Asia", Tokyo, 16-19 December 1996, p. 34.

45   Cleaver, *op. cit.*, p. 23.

46   FAO, *Investment in Agriculture: Evolution and Prospects* (Rome: FAO, 1996), table 8.

47   A number of researchers have pointed to cases of positive supply response of peasant farmers to declining producer prices and the rising costs of inputs, which has taken the form of more intensive use of household labour and compression of household consumption. Empirical evidence is provided for Brazil (F. Contre and I. Goldin, "L'agriculture en période d'ajustement au Brésil", *Revue Tiers-Monde*, Vol. XXXII/12, April-June 1991), for Turkey (K. Boratav, "Inter-class and intra-class relations of distribution under structural adjustment: Turkey during the 1980s", in T. Aricanli and D. Rodrik (eds.), *The*

Political Economy of Turkey, (Basingstoke, UK: Macmillan, 1990)), and for the United States during the Depression years (H. Friedmann, "World market, State and family farm: Social bases of household production in the era of wage labor", *Comparative Studies in Society and History*, Vol. 20, No. 4, 1978). Such behaviour could help explain post-1985 productivity improvements in Africa in conditions of adverse price movements.

48   Recent research on 13 sub-Saharan African countries in the 1980s which compares export responses to currency depreciations in situations with different parallel currency premiums shows that "official depreciations which were preceded by relatively large exchange misalignment and were accompanied by a reduction in the latter, as proxied by the currency premium, exerted roughly twice as much positive effect on real exports as other official depreciations" (Z. Yiheyis, "Export adjustment to currency depreciation in the presence of parallel markets for foreign exchange: The experience of selected sub-Saharan African countries in the 1980s", *Journal of Development Studies*, Vol. 34, No. 1, 1997, pp. 111-130).

49   World Bank, *Adjustment Lending in Sub-Saharan Africa: An Update*, Operations Evaluation Department Report No. 16594 (Washington, D.C.: World Bank, 1997). In the present analysis, the following countries are excluded from the sample because of the effects of social unrest: Chad, Mozambique, Rwanda, Sierra Leone and Sudan, and also Sao Tome and Principe.

50   When countries are classified in terms of high, medium and low population densities, according to the classification of H. Binswanger and P. Pingali ("Technological priorities for farming in sub-Saharan Africa", *World Bank Economic Research Observer*, Vol. 3, No. 1, 1988), which takes account of agro-climatic potential, it is apparent that agricultural growth rates declined or were stagnant between the 1970s and the post-1985 period in 8 out of 10 low-density countries, 4 out of 11 medium-density countries and 3 out of 11 high-density countries.

51   J. Teranishi, "Sectoral resource transfer, conflict and macro-stability in economic development: A comparative analysis", in M. Aoki, H. K. Kim and M. Okuno-Fujiwara (eds.), *The Role of Government in East Asian Development: A Comparative Institutional Analysis* (Oxford: Clarendon Press, 1997).

Chapter IV

TRADE, ACCUMULATION AND INDUSTRY

A. Introduction

The major challenge facing a large number of low-income, predominantly agrarian economies in Africa is how to break out of the vicious circle of low productivity and heavy dependence on a small number of primary commodities. The challenge is a long-standing one. Efforts in most countries in the years following independence tended to concentrate heavily on developing import-substituting industries in order to increase productivity and diversify the production structure. Today the emphasis has shifted to improving export performance. It has been increasingly recognized that, given the limited size of domestic markets and the dependence on the import of intermediate and capital goods, expanding export capacity and increasing international competitiveness are vital for rapid growth and development.

Meeting this challenge requires a higher level of investment and establishing a virtuous link between trade and capital accumulation. The pattern of investment is a crucial determinant of such a link. It is evident that the competitive advantage of most economies in SSA lies in the exploitation of natural resources through diversification and increased processing of resource-based products. However, although it reduces risks, diversification as such does not ensure strong and sustained growth. The challenge is to identify, support and expand activities in areas where value-added is greater, productivity growth is faster and demand elasticities in world markets are higher.

For economies at higher levels of development, particularly with better endowments in physical and human capital, improving productivity and international competitiveness depends very much on the rehabilitation of industry, particularly as regards labour-intensive products. Many of the existing manufacturing industries in Africa were established in the context of the import-substitution strategies pursued in the post-colonial era. Much of their capacity is unviable because of rapid shifts over the past decade in the global and national policy environment and changes in some of the key parameters affecting their competitiveness. The lack of a positive response to such shifts reflects, to a great extent, the failure of these industries to advance beyond the infant industry stage and their continued dependence for survival on protection and on provision of foreign exchange earned by the primary sector or secured through foreign aid. Restructuring such industries into efficient and competitive units calls for substantial investment in both physical and human capital.

A strong and sustainable investment recovery is thus a necessary condition for more outward-oriented development strategies in Africa. Linking trade to the process of capital accumulation will mean that policies are based neither simply on a drive for greater openness, nor on "picking winners", but on widening as much as possible the choice of investment opportunities across the spectrum of more dynamic sectors.

The following section analyses the level and composition of Africa's trade. The analysis shows that Africa's marginalization in world trade is a reflection of its inability to sustain a rapid growth rate. This is followed by an examination of the region's endowments in human and physical capital and natural resources, which suggests that its export potential lies in the primary sector, even though there are unexploited opportunities in manufacturing in some countries. The subsequent section focuses on accumulation and export growth, emphasizing the opportunities for diversification and processing in the primary sector to promote non-traditional exports, and drawing on the experience of successful countries in East Asia and elsewhere. This is followed (in section D) by a brief analysis of the structure and performance of African industry and the potential for manufactured exports. The final section examines the market opportunities for exports from Africa both to the advanced industrial countries and through intraregional trade.

B. Main features of African trade

---

1. Level of trade

An indication of the marginal status of SSA in the world economy is the very low absolute level of its exports and its decreasing share in world trade during the past four decades, a trend which has worsened markedly since 1970. In 1995, the value of total merchandise exports from SSA, including South Africa, was $73 billion (of which South Africa alone accounted for $28 billion), which is close to the figure for Malaysia ($74 billion) but considerably less than that for the Republic of Korea ($125 billion). As table 14 shows, the trend in exports from SSA is in sharp contrast to that not only of the fast-growing East Asian NIEs, but also to that of most other developing regions. The consequence has been import compression, and, given the reliance of SSA countries on imported capital and intermediate goods, weak productivity and output growth, which adversely affect exports.

In some accounts the resistance of African policy makers to open trade regimes is advanced as an explanation of the poor overall economic performance of the continent,[1] and on this basis the conclusion is drawn that countries in SSA need to rapidly liberalize trade as the surest way of correcting the price distortions and misallocation of resources which have held back economic growth.

But do the economies of SSA indeed trade too little, given their levels of per capita income, population size and geographical characteristics?

Generally, the share of trade in GDP tends to be high in small countries because the limitations of the domestic market lead to production structures that are more specialized than in larger countries. Since higher income levels are often associated with larger imports of both primary products and manufactures, a commensurate increase in exports is needed if a country is to avoid balance-of-payments problems; hence, richer countries tend to trade more. Higher transport and transaction costs associated with a number of geographical features such as distance from the world's leading traders, the extent of common borders, weak infrastructure and land-locked status tend to reduce both the competitiveness of a country's products on export markets and the opportunity costs of producing a product at home rather than importing it. The regression results reported in table 15, taking into account these factors, suggest that the ratio of trade to GDP in countries of both sub-Saharan Africa and North Africa is very much in line with their population size and per capita income. Countries in Latin America and the Caribbean on average trade less than expected, while the East Asian NIEs trade more.[2]

It thus appears that the comparatively small share of SSA countries in world trade is primarily a reflection of their small share in global output. Slow growth in traded-goods sectors explains why SSA as a whole experienced a decline in the share of exports in GDP over the past two decades in a period of rapidly growing world trade, starting from a ratio which was similar to that of the East Asian NIEs in the 1970s. It follows that the SSA

Table 14

**SHARES OF DEVELOPING ECONOMIES IN WORLD EXPORTS AND IMPORTS,
BY REGION, 1950-1995**

(Percentages)

	1950	1960	1970	1980	1985	1990	1995
				Exports			
All developing economies	33.0	23.9	18.9	29.0	25.2	23.7	27.7
America	12.1	7.7	5.5	5.4	5.6	4.2	4.4
Africa	5.3	4.2	4.1	4.6	3.2	2.3	1.5
Sub-Saharan Africa	3.3	2.9	2.4	2.5	1.7	1.2	0.8
Asia	15.2	11.5	8.5	18.4	15.8	16.7	21.4
First-tier NIEs[a]	2.8	1.6	2.0	3.8	5.8	7.7	10.4
				Imports			
All developing economies	28.9	25.2	18.8	24.0	23.2	22.2	29.1
America	10.0	7.5	5.7	5.9	4.2	3.6	4.8
Africa	5.7	5.1	3.4	3.7	2.8	2.1	1.7
Sub-Saharan Africa	3.1	3.0	2.3	2.2	1.5	1.1	0.9
Asia	12.6	11.8	8.5	13.4	15.4	15.8	22.0
First-tier NIEs[a]	3.0	2.2	2.7	4.3	5.3	7.5	10.8

Source: UNCTAD, *Handbook of International Trade and Development Statistics, 1997.*
 a Hong Kong, China; Republic of Korea; Singapore; and Taiwan Province of China.

countries need to focus on growth-enhancing policies, rather than concentrate on trade liberalization. It is unlikely that a liberal trading regime will by itself generate a greater volume of trade unless it is accompanied by a faster rate of economic growth. An extensive econometric literature on the determinants of economic growth has been unable to confirm an independent role for openness.[3] Moreover, an examination of recent experience in East Asia as well as of specific liberalization episodes in the advanced industrial economies fails to show any direct causal link between openness and faster growth.[4]

2. Export composition and resource endowment

At least two statistical problems hamper the discussion of SSA's export structure: the un-reliability of trade statistics for many countries and the arbitrary classification in those statistics of products such as non-monetary gold, uncut precious stones and some natural-resource-based chemicals, which are very important export items for a number of SSA countries, as manufactured exports.[5] Table 16 compares a number of alternative estimates regarding the share of manufactures in SSA countries' exports. Whilst the estimates differ significantly, they all confirm the general impression that manufactures, on average, account for a small share of total exports, but that there is also much variation among countries. Even on the broadest definition, manufactures account for under 15 per cent of total exports in close to two thirds of countries in SSA; on a narrower definition, the proportion is less than 10 per cent in three quarters of the countries and under 5 per cent in half. By contrast, and on most accounts, the share in Mauritius is close to 70 per cent, in South Africa

Table 15

AFRICAN TRADE IN THE 1980s IN COMPARISON: SOME REGRESSION RESULTS

(Dependent variable: Sum of ratios of exports and imports to GDP, 1980-1989 average)

	Sub-Saharan Africa dummy	North Africa dummy	NIEs[a] dummy	Latin America dummy	OECD dummy	Log (Population)	Log (Per capita income)	Log (Distance)	Gravity component of openness	Constant	R-squared	Number of obser-vations
(1)	-3.5	0.4	27.9	-12.1	-5.5	-8.2	6.3			130.7	0.57	110
	(-0.6)	*(0.1)*	*(3.7)*	*(-2.7)*	*(-1.0)*	*(-8.3)*	*(2.6)*			*(4.2)*		
(2)	-2.6	-6.9	26.8	-17.2	-15.3	-8.6	8.0	-8.8		143.3	0.62	83
	(-0.4)	*(-0.8)*	*(3.7)*	*(-3.5)*	*(-2.2)*	*(-6.9)*	*(2.7)*	*(-1.8)*		*(4.1)*		
(3)	-12.1	-6.9	29.7	-16.6	-3.3	-9.8		-7.6		224.3	0.58	87
	(-2.6)	*(-0.8)*	*(4.0)*	*(-3.4)*	*(-0.6)*	*(-8.2)*		*(-1.5)*		*(11.6)*		
(4)	-4.9	-0.7	26.0	-4.6	1.5				0.8	30.4	0.45	116
	(-1.1)	*(-0.1)*	*(3.1)*	*(-0.9)*	*(0.3)*				*(8.8)*	*(7.1)*		

Source: Trade and population data from UNCTAD database; GDP data from Penn World Tables, version 5.6 (http://www.nber.org/ pwt56.html); "distance" from R. Barro and J.-W. Lee, "Data set for a panel of 138 countries", 1994 (http://www.nber.org/ pub/barro.lee); "gravity component of openness" from J. A. Frankel and D. Romer, "Trade and growth: An empirical investigation", NBER Working Paper No. 5476 (Cambridge, Mass.: National Bureau of Economic Research, 1996).

Note: t-statistics are shown in brackets. Dummy variables for the five country groupings are used to see whether Africa trades less than would be expected taking into account structural characteristics. The analysis was done for 1980-1989 because the availability of purchasing-power-parity-adjusted per capita GDP data is seriously constrained for earlier and more recent years. However, doing the analysis for the periods 1980-1992 and 1964-1992 on the basis of a reduced data set does not change the basic pattern of the results.

a Indonesia, Malaysia, Republic of Korea, Taiwan Province of China and Thailand; Singapore and Hong Kong, China, have not been taken into consideration because their very large share of trade in GDP makes them statistical outliers.

and Zimbabwe around 30 per cent, and in Kenya, Senegal and Sierra Leone around 20 per cent.[6]

The composition of African exports reflects in large part the underlying structural features of African economies, in particular their endowments in labour, human and physical capital, and natural resources. Indeed, it is generally agreed that differences in factor endowments are an important factor accounting for differences among countries in export structure. Moreover, it is recognized that there are strong complementarities between these factors, particularly between human and physical capital, which limit the possibilities of changing production and export structures. However, these factor endowments and their interrelationships are not permanently fixed. In particular, in a process of development the accumulation of capital and skills, and related changes in technological con-ditions, allow an economy not only to alter its growth path but also to deepen its integration into the world economy. Consequently, it is also necessary to consider the time horizon and the pace of accumulation and development when examining comparative export structures and performance.

Given that most manufacturing activities require a much higher input of capital and skill per worker than of land per worker, countries with a relatively high ratio of capital and skill per worker can be expected to export mainly manufactures, while those with a low ratio of skill per worker and a relatively high ratio of land per worker can be expected to export mainly primary products. SSA's export structure indeed corresponds to this pattern.[7] Among seven regional groupings SSA has been consistently the least skill-abundant, as measured by the number of average years of

Table 16

ALTERNATIVE ESTIMATES OF THE SHARE OF MANUFACTURES IN TOTAL MERCHANDISE EXPORTS OF AFRICAN COUNTRIES

(Percentages)

Country	UNCTAD	World Bank	Owens and Wood	Wood and Mayer	Amjadi, Reincke and Yeats	IDC[a]
	1990	1990 or 1989	1989	1989-1991	1990 or latest year available	1989-1991
Angola	6.3	0.1	..	0.3	1.0	4.8
Benin	12.4	..	26.9	4.5	3.4	..
Botswana	..	..	..	..	..	9.0
Burkina Faso	11.0	..	9.9	7.2	11.0	..
Burundi	2.0	2.0	8.7	4.0	2.0	..
Cameroon	8.4	8.5	24.7	8.2	15.2	..
Cape Verde	45.1	12.3	2.4	35.0	12.3	..
Central African Republic	48.2	48.2	29.9	2.2	48.2	..
Chad	12.7	9.0	3.8	4.7	9.0	..
Comoros	42.2	26.6	..	13.4	26.6	..
Congo	12.5	12.5	2.3	4.4	6.6	..
Côte d'Ivoire	16.8	16.8	12.3	5.7	16.8	..
Dem. Rep. of the Congo	16.6	16.6	8.7	5.1	16.6	..
Djibouti	..	7.8	11.1	57.2	7.8	..
Equatorial Guinea	..	..	..	8.9	4.0	..
Ethiopia	5.3	5.3	3.9	4.1	5.3	..
Gabon	3.4	3.4	4.8	4.0	3.4	..
Gambia	25.9	25.9	..	0.6	25.9	..
Ghana	13.4	13.4	..	3.2	13.4	..
Guinea	..	..	..	0.7	0.5	..
Guinea-Bissau	..	..	..	4.6	4.9	..
Kenya	17.3	17.3	24.2	21.1	17.3	..
Liberia	30.9	30.9	0.6	22.4	0.1	..
Madagascar	15.2	15.2	9.7	14.2	15.2	..
Malawi	4.8	4.8	8.9	4.9	4.8	9.2
Mali	1.6	1.6	2.7	0.6	6.8	..
Mauritania	0.5	0.5	6.7	0.8	0.5	..
Mauritius	68.1	68.1	26.9	61.2	68.1	64.9
Mozambique	..	17.5	..	46.4	17.5	28.4
Namibia	..	..	..	..	..	9.6
Niger	55.5	..	4.3	1.7	2.0	..
Nigeria	2.1	2.1	0.7	0.9	2.1	..
Rwanda	4.7	4.7	..	0.8	4.7	..
Senegal	22.5	22.5	21.9	13.5	22.5	..
Sierra Leone	26.1	26.1	24.3	2.6	26.1	..
Somalia	1.1	1.1	1.9	5.0	1.1	..
South Africa	34.4	34.4	28.7	28.6	34.4	28.6
Sudan	1.0	1.0	1.1	4.8	1.0	..
Swaziland	..	..	..	..	..	13.4
Togo	9.1	9.1	6.9	8.5	9.1	..
Uganda	1.1	1.1	..	0.8	1.1	..
United Rep. of Tanzania	17.5	11.8	3.6	9.9	11.8	17.8
Zambia	7.5	11.2	1.9	4.0	11.2	3.9
Zimbabwe	30.9	30.9	25.7	34.4	30.9	32.1

Source: UNCTAD, *Handbook of International Trade and Development Statistics, 1994;* World Bank, *World Development Indicators, 1997* (CD-Rom); T. Owens and A. Wood, "Export-oriented industrialisation through primary processing?", *World Development,* Vol. 25, No. 9, 1997, based on UNIDO data; A. Wood and J. Mayer, "Africa's export structure in comparative perspective", UNCTAD/GDS/MDPB/Misc. 4 (Geneva, 1998); A. Amjadi, U. Reincke and A. Yeats, "Did external barriers cause the marginalization of sub-Saharan Africa in world trade?", World Bank Policy Research Working Paper No. 1586 (Washington, D.C.: World Bank, 1996).
a Industrial Development Corporation of South Africa.

Chart 22

SCHOOLING AND LAND AVAILABILITY IN DIFFERENT GROUPS OF COUNTRIES, 1960-1990, AT FIVE-YEAR INTERVALS

(Years of schooling and land per worker)

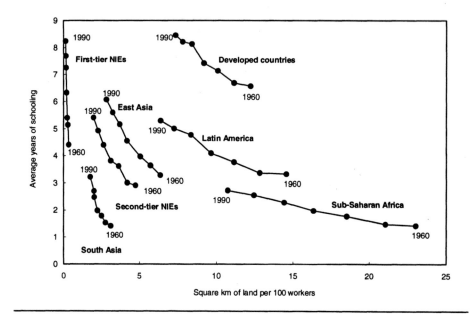

Source: R. Barro and J.-W. Lee, "International data on education" (Cambridge, Mass.: Harvard University), mimeo; and World Bank, *World Development Indicators, 1997* (CD-Rom).
Note: Data are for total land area ("land") and population over age 15 ("workers").

schooling (see chart 22). Its current resource structure is roughly the same as that of Latin America in the 1960s, and its skill-per-worker (but not its land-per-worker) endowment resembles that of the second-tier East Asian NIEs three decades ago. While the endowment structure of SSA is consistent with its low manufacturing to primary exports ratio, that ratio is actually lower than expected in comparison with other regions.

Arguments based on regional averages neglect the internal diversity of SSA. Human and, in particular, natural resources are widely dispersed among these countries. In chart 23 the actual manufactured export shares for SSA countries and South Africa are compared with the shares predicted on the basis of their relative re-

source endowments. Only one country in SSA – Mauritius – is predicted to be a manufacturing specialist, whilst a large majority of countries are predicted to have a manufactured export share below 20 per cent. The chart indicates, moreover, that the actual share of manufactures is lower than the predicted share for 29 of the 36 countries, equal to the predicted one in four countries, and higher in only three. The negative discrepancies exceed 10 percentage points in 17 countries and 20 percentage points in nine. It thus appears that most SSA countries export fewer manufactures relative to primary products than would be predicted from their resource endowments; this implies that they have some scope to increase the share of manufactures even without further accumulation of human and physical capital.

Chart 23

**ACTUAL AND PREDICTED SHARES OF MANUFACTURES IN TOTAL EXPORTS
OF AFRICAN COUNTRIES, 1990**

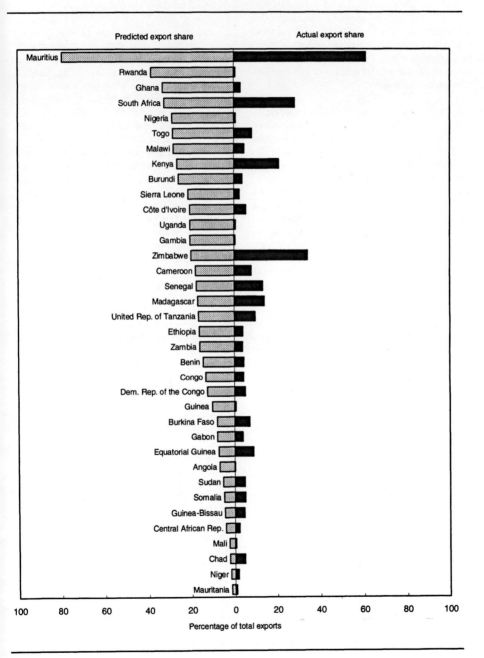

Source: A. Wood and J. Mayer, "Africa's export structure in comparative perspective", UNCTAD/GDS/MDPB/Misc. 4 (Geneva, 1998).

While the discrepancy between actual and predicted shares of manufactured exports may to some extent result from data errors, the evidence of untapped manufacturing export opportunities may also reflect a high degree of underutilization of human and physical capital. This means that manufactured exports may be increased without reducing primary production and exports, and thus be associated with a rise in total export earnings if conditions for greater efficiency and competitiveness can be secured.

The conventional analysis lays stress on inadequate infrastructure, inappropriate economic policies and unfavourable geography in explaining SSA's weak performance. However, the results of an analysis of the correlations for SSA countries of the discrepancies in actual and predicted manufactured export shares with variables which proxy these factors show that lack of openness, the most commonly cited measure of inappropriate policies in conventional analysis, does not provide a significant explanation. By contrast, levels of infrastructure development and the misalignment of exchange rates appear to be much more important.

Much of the unrealized potential in manufactured exports is concentrated in about a dozen countries, while in some two dozen others there is little or no immediate potential. Moreover, even where the potential exists, geographical conditions are likely to be a constraining factor, so that the possibilities of increasing the manufactured export share through improvements in policies and infrastructure may be overstated. Examples are some mineral-rich economies such as Ghana, Nigeria and Sierra Leone, as well as small land-locked countries such as Burundi, Malawi, Rwanda, Swaziland and Uganda, where high transport costs are less of an obstacle to increasing primary exports than manufactured exports, which latter depend heavily on imported inputs.

3. Diversification in the primary sector

Given SSA's resource endowments, the low share of manufactures and the high share of primary goods in its exports are not surprising. Another important aspect of SSA's export structure is that these primary exports are often concentrated on a limited number of traditional products. Consequently, SSA economies are more vulnerable to natural disasters and more exposed to adverse price movements and instability in export earnings than others. Also, they suffer more than other countries from the low price elasticity of demand for many agricultural products.[8]

Export dynamism and diversification away from primary commodities into new products with more favourable price and productivity prospects are often associated with an increasing share of manufactures in a country's export basket. However, this is too narrow an approach, particularly for countries in SSA. In the first place, emphasis solely on rapid diversification into manufactures can prejudice policy efforts aimed at maximizing the rents which arise from effective exploitation of natural resources in the initial stages of development. If properly used for investment in physical and human capital, these rents can provide a strong development stimulus. Moreover, with heightened global competition and the ability of transnational corporations to allocate different stages of production to different countries, some labour-intensive manufactures, such as apparel and computer chips, have begun to exhibit the kind of unfavourable price dynamics previously associated with primary commodities. Indeed, as discussed in *TDR 1996* (Part Two, chapter III), SSA may be particularly vulnerable to unfavourable price movements in these low-skill manufacturing activities. Finally, even though in general primary production has a smaller impact on development than manufacturing, it involves a range of activities of widely differing technological sophistication, and skill and capital intensity. Diversification into more sophisticated agricultural products can consequently provide more dynamic growth effects.

In assessing the scope for diversification within the primary sector, a distinction can be made between processed and unprocessed primary products. Although it is again difficult to avoid classification problems, processed primary products can be defined as those which are identified as manufactures in industrial and employment statistics but as primary products in trade statistics. Such goods are produced in factories but use large inputs of raw materials; they include canned food, cigarettes, paper and aluminium ingots. Processed and unprocessed primary products can be further broken down into agricultural products and minerals, metals and fuels, with a further subdivision of agricultural products into static and dynamic ones. The group of dynamic agricultural products includes items whose income elasticity of

Table 17

SHARES OF DIFFERENT CLASSES OF PRIMARY PRODUCTS IN TOTAL EXPORTS, BY REGION, 1990

(Percentages)

Region	Processed commodities			Unprocessed commodities		
	Minerals, metals and fuels	Dynamic agricultural products	Static agricultural products	Minerals, metals and fuels	Dynamic agricultural products	Static agricultural products
Sub-Saharan Africa	5.9	1.8	4.2	24.9	12.9	39.4
Middle East and North Africa	11.1	1.5	1.1	50.5	4.8	1.8
Latin America	12.3	3.5	4.9	18.5	13.6	19.0
South Asia	0.8	0.3	4.5	1.9	13.3	12.7
East and South-East Asia	3.2	3.6	5.0	13.0	6.0	9.2
First-tier NIEs	5.2	0.8	1.4	0.1	3.5	0.5
Second-tier NIEs	2.6	7.4	6.0	19.8	5.0	8.9
Developed countries	4.2	3.3	6.1	6.0	6.0	3.9

Source: See chart 23.
Note: For the distinction between static and dynamic agricultural products, see text.

demand is greater than unity and much higher than that of traditional agricultural products.[9]

Table 17 shows that agricultural products account for almost 60 per cent of SSA's exports, with nearly 40 per cent of all exports being unprocessed static products. It also shows that the share of processed exports of minerals, metals and fuels is comparable to that in other developing regions. However, processed copper from the Democratic Republic of the Congo and Zambia accounts for the bulk of these exports, and if those two countries are excluded the share is reduced considerably.

C. Accumulation and export growth

While manufactures could make a significant contribution to the growth of total exports in a small number of African countries, most countries will inevitably have to continue to rely on an expansion of natural-resource-based production. This expansion may be achieved in two ways: by increasing productivity and output in traditional products and regaining market shares; and by diversifying into more dynamic, processed primary products. Since attaining these objectives depends on technological change and creation of additional productive capacity, and hence on new investment, a sustainable growth process requires mutually reinforcing dynamic interactions between capital accumulation and exports, resulting in structural changes in the pattern of production and exports.

This dynamic is quite well known and is described in some detail in previous *TDRs* in relation to the evolution of the East Asian NIEs. In the earliest stage, when exports consist largely of primary commodities, the challenge is to maximize the rents and foreign exchange from the exploitation of natural resources, which calls for considerable investment in the primary sector, including public investment. Rising output in the primary sector then allows a surplus to be generated for investment to establish resource-based industries. As the scope for accelerating development through productivity improvement and diversification in the primary sector is exploited, sustaining growth will require a gradual shift to the production and export of manufactured goods, starting with technologically less demanding ones, and then gradually upgrading into more sophisticated products and industries.

Such a process is characterized by rising exports, savings and investment, both in absolute terms and as a share of GDP. Initial constraints on domestic resource mobilization mean that an important part of domestic investment will need to be financed by capital inflows. In this respect FDI can be one important means not only of reducing the resource gap, but also of creating employment and increasing output and exports of natural-resource-based industries. But the precise nature of its contribution will depend on how the increased current revenue and foreign exchange earnings are utilized. Over time, the resource gap should narrow as exports and domestic savings begin to grow faster than investment with the emergence of a strong national entrepreneurial class that is more inclined to reinvest profits.

Such a pattern has characterized the export-investment nexus in East Asian NIEs ever since their initial stages of development. Similar dynamic patterns have not been present in Africa, except in Mauritius and, to a lesser extent, Botswana, Egypt and Morocco (see table 18). Indeed, Mauritius provides an example of how a surplus generated in a traditional primary sector as a result of productivity gains can help to shift resources quickly into manufactured output and exports. At independence in 1968 Mauritius was still essentially a monoculture economy, dependent upon sugar exports for its foreign exchange. However, the accumulation of sugar profits saw the emergence of a local entrepreneurial class, and once the limits of import-substitution industrialization had been reached, government efforts to diversify into textile exports found a ready source of domestic savings which could be used to strengthen private and public investment in support of a more export-oriented industrial drive. In some cases sugar plantation owners themselves went directly into textile production and exports, while in others profits from sugar exports were channelled into investments in textiles through the domestic financial system.[10]

1. Expansion of traditional exports

As discussed in the previous chapters, agro-ecological conditions are difficult in many parts of SSA. However, undercapitalization is certainly a major factor in low productivity compared with other regions. Improvements in irrigation, fertilizer use and seed varieties could increase productivity and output considerably in much of SSA and at the same time make agricultural products more competitive in world markets. It is also important to note that tropical climatic conditions, seen by some as a major constraint on growth in SSA, have not prevented rapid growth in other developing regions, most notably South-East Asia.

More important, there is a large unexploited potential in minerals in some African countries. As a result of intensive exploration and prospecting, estimates of SSA's mineral reserves have been raised considerably over the past few years. Of the known world reserves, Southern Africa alone has nearly 90 per cent of platinum group metals, 85 per cent of chromium, 75 per cent of manganese and 50 per cent of gold.[11] Given the currently low level of exports in some countries, successful exploitation of mineral reserves could lead to a rapid and very substantial increase in export earnings. However, unless the physical infrastructure is improved significantly, the scope for expanding mineral exports will be limited mainly to high-value products and to countries with long coastlines.

While some minerals can be exploited by medium-sized companies with comparatively modest sunk costs, the exploitation of other minerals often requires substantial initial investments. Many existing state enterprises in the mining sector, which have traditionally involved high-cost and low-productivity operations, are unable to make these investments without major restructuring. It thus seems almost certain that FDI, whether through wholly owned operations or through joint

Table 18

GROSS NATIONAL SAVINGS, GROSS DOMESTIC INVESTMENT AND EXPORTS IN AFRICA

(Percentages of GDP)

Country	1968-1970			1975-1978			1986-1989			1990-1993		
	Savings	*Investment*	*Exports*	*Savings*	*Investment*	*Exports*	*Savings*	*Investment*	*Exports*	*Savings*	*Investment*	*Exports*
Benin	..	..	..	13.0	17.3	22.1	6.3	12.7	26.8	6.6	14.2	22.7
Botswana	..	..	..	8.0	35.7	42.5	34.3	24.8	71.8	31.9	36.7	66.7
Burkina Faso	..	..	..	18.1	23.2	8.7	19.8	21.0	10.4	20.9	21.4	11.6
Cameroon	..	..	..	16.1	25.4	23.6	17.5	22.3	19.3	13.4	16.1	19.4
Central African Republic	4.7	17.8	27.4	9.9	12.0	24.6	..	9.0	20.5	-2.3	8.8	17.1
Chad	13.0	18.0	21.1	15.7	20.1	22.2	6.0	9.0	33.9	-3.0	7.6	30.6
Côte d'Ivoire	21.2	20.1	37.6	20.7	26.5	39.5	6.1	13.9	8.7	7.1	9.8	6.9
Ethiopia	10.8	12.9	10.4	7.3	9.0	12.3	7.9	13.0	40.9	25.7	23.6	47.6
Gabon	..	..	..	54.4	58.5	51.7	20.8	35.5	52.6	24.9	20.4	60.8
Gambia	..	..	..	2.8	18.5	36.8	18.7	18.4	17.7	4.9	14.5	17.3
Ghana	8.7	12.5	20.5	7.5	8.2	11.3	6.2	11.6	22.9	15.6	19.4	30.6
Kenya	17.8	21.4	29.6	18.0	23.8	31.6	16.4	24.1	16.1	..	..	16.2
Liberia	..	..	..	29.9	31.9	55.4	..	..	..	..	..	..
Madagascar	..	..	..	5.4	8.5	16.2	11.2	11.9	22.8	4.9	11.9	21.0
Malawi	1.7	20.4	23.9	18.0	31.0	27.9	5.4	17.8	16.4	1.0	17.0	16.4
Mali	..	..	..	11.5	16.0	12.1	9.2	21.3	..	14.3	22.2	..
Mauritania	23.5	23.9	39.3	17.3	36.8	36.0	15.5	26.1	51.7	9.0	20.6	43.7
Mauritius	13.0	11.9	40.8	23.0	29.7	49.2	27.6	28.2	63.7	28.0	29.9	61.6
Niger	..	..	..	12.2	18.6	21.1	16.5	14.0	20.0	6.9	7.1	15.3
Nigeria	6.7	13.6	9.5	23.7	28.3	20.5	14.0	17.1	27.3	..	..	..
Rwanda	..	..	..	17.8	14.9	13.4	10.7	14.9	8.1	6.9	11.0	5.9
Senegal	5.5	13.6	24.3	11.7	17.3	37.1	0.5	12.0	25.0	2.9	13.2	23.9
Sierra Leone	11.2	14.4	30.3	3.6	12.5	24.7	1.1	9.7	15.9	-0.2	13.6	26.7
Togo	..	..	..	31.8	36.1	49.6	11.7	24.7	42.1	4.0	14.9	29.9
Uganda	13.5	13.5	22.5	5.1	6.7	10.3	2.9	10.8	8.0	2.8	15.1	7.6
Zambia	37.6	26.6	55.3	14.8	29.4	38.1	1.4	12.6	32.4	1.8	11.1	27.3
South Africa	24.6	28.5	23.9	24.4	26.2	30.4	22.7	19.9	29.0	16.5	15.7	24.0
Algeria	30.9	32.5	22.8	36.9	47.3	30.0	27.2	29.7	15.4	28.5	29.9	24.6
Egypt	8.8	13.2	13.9	18.4	30.5	21.8	10.0	22.4	20.9	19.3	19.0	29.5
Morocco	12.6	15.3	18.1	15.9	28.3	18.2	21.8	22.2	23.9	21.1	22.8	25.5
Tunisia	17.6	21.9	21.6	24.4	30.2	30.2	21.9	23.5	38.4	21.0	27.8	41.1

Source: UNCTAD secretariat calculations, based on World Bank, *World Tables* (tapes).

ventures, will play an increasingly important role in this sector in most African countries. Africa is home to some successful mining firms, including the world's largest mining company. But the export potential of this sector will continue to be determined by complementary public sector investments in infrastructure.

An expansion of mineral production will not by itself provide the missing economic linkages needed for a strong and sustained process of economic growth. Rather, it could offer an important source of foreign exchange earnings and government revenues which could be used to accelerate capital formation and structural change in other parts of the economy. This requires better management of the mineral sector than was often exercised in the past, when traditional concerns about ownership and control of extraction, processing and marketing activities dominated policy-making, as well as an effective macroeconomic response in order to avoid possible "Dutch disease" problems.

Botswana is a good example of a country with an effective mineral-led growth strategy and one of the highest growth rates in the world economy over the past three decades. The share of the mining sector in Botswana in GDP rose from zero in 1966 to close to 50 per cent in 1986 and currently stands at a little under 40 per cent. This development has been very closely tied to the exploitation of diamonds, which dominated foreign exchange earnings and are a major source of government revenues. Exploitation of diamonds has been carried out by a single large TNC, which, like the Government of Botswana, has a 50 per cent stake in the diamond mines. The key elements of Botswana's success have been the successful negotiation of contracts with transnational producers and the prudent management of mineral revenues, including their use for public investments in physical and human capital. Also, policy makers have avoided the urban bias common to many economies in Africa, and have channelled resources to improving agricultural growth and productivity. However, despite these achievements, serious doubts about its heavy dependence on a single commodity remain, and in recent years Botswana has tried to diversify the range of activities linked to the exploitation of diamonds as well as its range of primary exports.

A crucial question is to what extent attempts to expand traditional exports may encounter a fallacy-of-composition problem, leading to falls in prices and even in export earnings. Experience shows that such a possibility cannot be ruled out, particularly for the main export crops of the region.[12] However, rapid growth in the resource-poor Asian countries, including China and India, can alter the demand conditions for all sorts of primary products, including traditional agricultural commodities and minerals. Nevertheless, expansion in traditional products would require a careful assessment of potential costs and benefits, particularly if it needed substantial investment. Moreover, problems associated with shifts from food crops to export crops, discussed in chapter II, would also need to be kept in mind.

2.　Non-traditional exports

The case in favour of processing and diversification into non-traditional exports is well established. They should help improve the stability of export earnings and reduce the risks of investment.[13] Perhaps, and most significantly, they hold out the possibility of establishing activities which offer greater potential for deepening a country's technological base and skills profile, and of entering markets with a comparatively high income elasticity of demand.

However, the link between diversification into new primary products and overall export performance is not a simple one. While diversification may stabilize export earnings, it does not as such help establish a dynamic investment-export nexus. It has to encompass products with greater supply and demand potentials, and be accompanied by policies designed to translate increased incomes into faster capital accumulation. Moreover, new products may require considerably higher levels of capital and skill which may be more productively employed in the traditional sector in generating export earnings.

Again, processing does not always add value to primary products. When the technology is old and inefficient, it may be more rational to export the primary product without processing it; this appears to be the case, for example, regarding cashew nut exports in some Southern African countries. Sometimes inefficient processing can put domestic industries producing final consumer goods at a disadvantage in international markets if such industries are forced to purchase processed materials from high-cost domestic firms. That appears to be true of some consumer durable industries in Southern Africa, where metal sheets supplied by domestic producers cost much more than if obtained in world markets.[14]

Thus, not all economies with diversified production and export structures achieve a rapid rate of accumulation and income growth. Indeed, according to one study for the period 1970-1985, for nine of the 11 countries which diversified into new products, real export earnings actually declined or remained stagnant. Of the eight countries which experienced growth in real export earnings during this period, only two did so on the basis of a diversified export profile.[15]

As discussed earlier, there are some agricultural products which have a dynamic potential because of their high unit value and high income elasticity of demand. Successful diversification into such products generally requires introduction of new technologies, efficient management and marketing techniques. If these are put in place, positive linkages may be created with domestic industry in the food, beverages and tobacco sectors. Such linkages are likely to favour a greater export orientation, as well as the emergence of domestic firms processing agricultural commodities that are large enough to compete in international markets. The need to establish such firms is essential if a strong profit-investment-export nexus is to emerge in SSA.

East Asian experience holds some useful lessons in diversification and processing based on the primary sector. Unlike the first-tier East Asian NIEs, three economies of South-East Asia (Indonesia, Malaysia and Thailand) were able to exploit a rich natural-resource base which provided considerable scope for accelerated growth through diversification and increased processing of resource-based products. Between 1967 and 1975 the share of primary exports in total non-oil exports of these three countries fell, but the average in 1975 was still over 87 per cent. Moreover, the share of some key primary commodities rose during this period: in Indonesia the share of non-food primary products rose from 70 per cent to 73 per cent; in Thailand the share of food exports rose from 55 per cent to 64 per cent of total exports; and in Malaysia a more pronounced drop in the share of primary exports during this period coincided with a successful diversification into palm-oil and cocoa processing as well as into rubber, wood and paper products. In Thailand, too, there was diversification into food exports such as fish products, as well as into wood and paper products and non-metallic mineral products. In Indonesia, where diversification has been slower, there was a move into timber and from the mid-1970s into wood and paper products. Nevertheless, in 1985 more than two thirds of these countries' non-oil exports were accounted for by primary and resource-based industries with a low skill, capital and technology content, and for Indonesia alone the proportion was over 85 per cent.[16]

Even traditional products such as timber can offer considerable potential for diversifying into more processed products and into simple manufactures. In Indonesia, plywood exports grew significantly during the 1980s following the country's move into wood and paper products in the 1970s. Malaysia has also significantly increased its processed timber exports, particularly plywood and furniture.[17] Such processing is particularly relevant for countries such as Cameroon, Gabon and Ghana, which have already moved successfully into timber exports.

Attracting FDI offers possible advantages in these early stages of diversification, given the ready access of affiliates to capital, technology and marketing networks of the parent TNC. However, successful diversification experiences in these dynamic agricultural sectors suggest that public sector support and domestic investment are an equally crucial ingredient. For example, the great expansion of Chile's exports of non-traditional and dynamic agricultural goods such as fruit, forestry and wine products since the mid-1980s has been premised on a strong recovery in domestic private investment. However, it is difficult to imagine that this private investment would have materialized without earlier public investment in agricultural and forestry education, research and infrastructure development. Foreign direct investment has been an important source of new marketing channels and technology, which has been adapted by domestic producers.[18]

A similar experience characterizes the strong performance of South-East Asian agro-exporters.[19] Malaysia's highly successful development of dynamic agricultural exports such as palm oil, as well as of processed exports in the cocoa and rubber sectors, has been based on the emergence of comparatively large production units and strong policy support, particularly for product-specific research (see box 3).

Box 3

THE PALM OIL INDUSTRY IN MALAYSIA

The emergence and the rapid growth of export-oriented palm oil production and processing have been a remarkable factor in Malaysia's economic development.[1] In less than 20 years the palm oil refining industry, which had a capacity of less than 40,000 tons of crude oil feedstock in the early 1970s, grew into a large export-oriented industry. Today it processes 99 per cent of the domestic crude palm oil and crude palm kernel oil, i.e. 8 to 9 million tons per year. This is an estimated 60 per cent share of world refined palm oil products (or 70 per cent of their world trade) and about 10 per cent of world oils and fats (or 25 per cent of their world trade).

The Government encouraged diversification into palm oil in response to sharp fluctuations in rubber prices in the 1950s and declining rubber prices in the 1960s, as well as in anticipation of the inevitable exhaustion of tin deposits. Diversification into palm oil was favoured by a number of factors, including the growing international demand for palm oil, Malaysia's favourable factor endowment regarding both physical resources (climate, topography and plantation infrastructure) and human resources (plantation management and agro-economic expertise), and the lower labour intensity of palm oil production, compared with rubber production; this last factor became more important with the increasing shortage of labour on estate plantations.

Research efforts supported by both the Government and the private sector have been an important element in the success of the palm oil industry. In 1979, the Government established the Palm Oil Research Institute of Malaysia (PORIM) with a view to expanding the current consumption of palm oil products, finding new uses, improving production efficiency and product quality, and promoting the marketability of palm oil products. PORIM has two notable features: it has been funded mainly by the industry itself through a levy on production, and a joint committee of industry and government representatives has been in charge of deciding its research programme. These features have ensured both the continuous availability of research funding and the responsiveness of research to the needs of producers.

The Government has actively encouraged downstream processing and refining of palm oil, with a view to building a resource-based industrial sector. Crucial in this effort has been the policy to partially exempt processed palm oil products from export duties, depending on the degree of processing. The ensuing massive investment in processing capacity led to intense competition among refiners, which forced them to enhance their industrial and technological capabilities rapidly. As a result, within a decade Malaysia was able not only to reach the world technological frontier in palm oil refining, but even to push back this frontier.

---

[1] For a more detailed account of the role of government policies in the development of the Malaysian palm oil industry see M. Jelani and B.M. Malek, "Support policies for the Malaysian palm oil industry", paper presented at the FEDEPALMA International Conference, Barranquilla, Colombia, 2-9 June 1995; K.S. Jomo and M. Rock, "Economic diversification and primary commodity processing in the second-tier South-East Asian newly industrializing countries", UNCTAD Discussion Paper No. 136 (Geneva, 1998); and UNCTAD, "Analysis of national experiences in horizontal and vertical diversification, including the possibilities for crop substitution: Malaysia" (UNCTAD/COM/73, 1995).

A number of SSA countries have also diversified into dynamic agricultural exports during the 1980s and 1990s, although absolute export earnings are, in most cases, still small (table 19). Kenya, the United Republic of Tanzania and Zimbabwe have successfully developed horticultural exports, and other countries, such as the Gambia, are beginning to develop export capacity in these products. Apart from a number of small exporters that have been able to establish business connections overseas through family ties, foreign firms with easy access to production inputs and marketing networks have often been dominant in these cases.

The provision of high-yielding varieties and other commercially applicable results of agricultural research is likely to be an important element in SSA's strategy to increase productivity in agri-

Table 19

EXPORTS OF DYNAMIC AGRICULTURAL PRODUCTS[a] FROM SELECTED REGIONS AND COUNTRIES, 1980-1994

(Millions of dollars)

Region/country	1980	1985	1990	1992	1994
Africa	2 540	2 290	3 477	3 522	3 853
Sub-Saharan Africa	1 524	1 403	1 878	1 877	2 050
of which:					
Cameroon	25	12	58	74	97
Côte d'Ivoire	298	272	319	335	366
Kenya	79	79	125	142	153
Senegal	198	238	400	280	212
Zimbabwe	44	42	37	34	62
Egypt	131	168	159	206	158
Tunisia	138	146	311	310	352
Memo items:					
All developing countries	29 023	32 819	52 873	59 419	71 247
Brazil	3 965	4 997	5 636	5 793	7 244
Chile	585	887	1 840	2 322	2 406
Malaysia	1 724	2 237	2 551	3 178	4 488

Source: UNCTAD database.
  a Meat and meat products; dairy products; fish and fish products; fresh and processed fruit, vegetables and nuts; feedstuffs; oilseeds; vegetable and animal oils; and spices.

culture and to further shift exports towards dynamic agricultural products. However, as noted in the last chapter, research expenditure in SSA stopped growing in the late 1970s and has been considerably lower than elsewhere. Donor support for agricultural research has increased and somewhat compensated for declining government funding, but it is unlikely that such high levels of donor funding will continue indefinitely.[20] Strengthening African agricultural research needs to take into account the high degree of location specificity of agricultural technology which has made technology transfer from developed countries to SSA difficult. It is encouraging to note, however, that many SSA countries have recently strengthened their cooperation in agricultural research and that a number of regional projects have been implemented.[21]

D. Industry and competitiveness

While in many African economies there is considerable scope for increasing productivity in the primary sector, in the longer run a more determined shift towards promoting manufacturing production and exports will be required in order to maintain rapid productivity growth. So far, industrial performance has generally been poor, and in SSA only a few countries are currently able to move more strongly into labour-intensive manufacturing exports. On the other hand, some countries in Southern and North Africa are already close to the limits of the initial expansion of manufacturing that can be achieved on the basis of abundant labour alone and increasingly require upgrading of skills and technology for further manufacturing growth.

1.   The structure and performance of industry

Available data indicate that the manufacturing share in the GDP of Africa (excluding South Africa) is low even by the standards of other developing regions. In 1995, it was only 11.5 per cent compared with 21 per cent for Latin America and 24 per cent for South and East Asia. Africa's share in that year in the manufacturing value-added (MVA) of all developing countries was only 5.5 per cent, a decline from the already low level of around 6.9 per cent in the mid-1980s.[22] Moreover, in absolute terms MVA grew only slightly in SSA between 1980 and 1990 and has even fallen since then, in sharp contrast to developing countries elsewhere.

As a result, the absolute gap in manufacturing output between SSA and the rest of the world has increased significantly over the past 20 years. In the early 1990s, the MVA of all SSA countries was at about the level of Indonesia and Turkey, while it had been three times that of Indonesia in 1970. As regards the distribution in Africa, there is, as already noted, a wide dispersion among countries. South Africa accounts for about the same MVA as all SSA countries combined, among which Cameroon, Côte d'Ivoire, Kenya, Nigeria and Zimbabwe have the greatest manufacturing activity. In per capita terms, only Mauritius and South Africa have established a strong manufacturing base comparable to that of middle-income countries such as Turkey (chart 24). A number of North African economies, in particular Morocco and Tunisia, also compare favourably with successful second-tier East Asian NIEs, such as Indonesia. However, an examination of trends in per capita manufacturing output shows that while there were 14 countries in SSA with per capita manufacturing comparable to and in many cases considerably higher than that in Indonesia in 1980, all (for which data are available) had been overtaken by 1995.

Most countries in SSA have not reached the threshold level of manufacturing which could help them break out of the vicious circle restricting entry into foreign markets; output is mainly for their domestic markets. This situation contrasts with that of East Asia, where support and protection given to these industries were made conditional upon successful export performance from the very early stages of their establishment. Consequently, manufacturing industries in Africa have not been exposed to market discipline through exports, and in addition they have failed to benefit from the scale advantages needed to compete internationally. These factors have, in turn, further restricted the development of such industries to small and sluggish domestic markets, perpetuating high costs and giving rise to inefficiencies and low levels of productivity.

The food industry appears to dominate manufacturing in the non-mineral African economies, while the group of other manufactures, which includes petroleum and metals, accounts for a substantial share in the other countries (see table 20). The importance of the food, beverage and tobacco sectors in manufacturing and the small share of manufactures in total exports confirm the importance of the domestic market in the development of manufacturing in SSA. By contrast, the share of manufacturing activities which are most likely to provide strong developmental effects is very small.

This situation, in part, reflects mistaken policy choices in the first stages of industrialization. The principal role assigned to manufacturing in SSA countries even prior to independence was to produce non-durable consumer goods for the domestic market in an attempt to replace imports. This first attempt at changing the structure of domestic production did not in most cases require sophisticated government interventions to alleviate the market coordination failures which often characterize modern industrial activities. Moreover, since transportation costs were typically high in SSA, such goods could be cost-competitive with imports even when domestic production costs were high by international standards. However, in most cases, this strategy failed to strike the kind of balance between domestic and export-oriented activities which is needed in order to improve the balance-of-payments situation and promote industrialization. This lack of balance was reflected in the virtual absence of efforts to promote manufactured exports, and, together with high costs, it dampened any ambitions that manufacturers might have had to penetrate and secure a sure foothold in export markets.[23]

Chart 24

MANUFACTURING VALUE-ADDED PER CAPITA IN SUB-SAHARAN AFRICA, INDONESIA AND TURKEY, 1995

(In constant 1987 dollars)

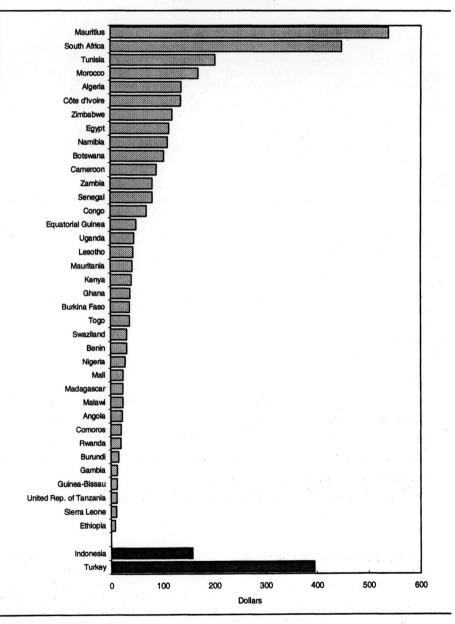

Source: World Bank, *World Development Indicators, 1997* (CD-Rom).
Note: Data for Benin, Burkina Faso, Equatorial Guinea and Namibia are for 1994, and those for Côte d'Ivoire and Zimbabwe are for 1993.

Table 20

SHARES OF SELECTED PRODUCT GROUPS IN TOTAL MANUFACTURING VALUE-ADDED IN AFRICA, BY COUNTRY, 1970 AND 1993

(Percentages)

Country	Food, beverages and tobacco		Textiles and clothing		Machinery and transport equipment		Chemicals		Other manufactures[a]	
	1970	1993	1970	1993	1970	1993	1970	1993	1970	1993
Algeria	32	13	20	14	9	15	4	5	35	54
Burkina Faso	69	..	9	..	2	..	1	..	19	..
Cameroon	50	26	15	12	4	1	3	8	27	54
Congo	65	..	4	..	1	..	..	..	29	..
Côte d'Ivoire	27	35	16	11	10	7	..	..	47	47
Egypt	17	21	35	13	9	13	12	13	27	40
Gabon	37	..	7	..	6	..	6	..	44	..
Ghana	34	36	16	5	4	2	4	10	41	47
Kenya	33	42	9	9	16	10	9	9	33	30
Libyan Arab Jam.	64	..	5	..	0	..	12	..	20	..
Madagascar	36	..	28	..	6	..	7	..	23	..
Malawi	51	..	17	..	3	..	10	..	20	..
Mali	36	..	40	..	4	..	..	..	20	..
Mauritius	75	..	6	..	5	..	3	..	12	..
Mozambique	51	..	13	..	5	..	3	..	28	..
Rwanda	86	..	..	..	3	..	2	..	8	..
Senegal	51	58	19	2	2	3	6	14	..	23
Sierra Leone	..	69	..	1	..	..	..	..	..	30
Somalia	88	..	6	..	..	..	1	..	6	..
South Africa	15	16	13	8	17	18	10	10	45	48
Sudan	39	..	34	..	3	..	5	..	19	..
Swaziland	37	..	2	..	..	..	..	..	60	..
Tunisia	29	..	18	..	4	..	13	..	36	..
U. R. of Tanzania	36	..	28	..	5	..	4	..	26	..
Zambia	49	..	9	..	5	..	10	..	27	..
Zimbabwe	24	33	16	16	9	6	11	4	40	41

Source: World Bank, *World Development Indicators, 1997* (CD-Rom).
   a Wood and related products, paper and related products, petroleum and related products, basic metals and mineral products, fabricated metal products, and professional goods and miscellaneous manufactured articles.

2. The competitiveness of manufacturing exports

As noted earlier, there is potential for expanding manufactured exports in a small number of countries in SSA. However, the question arises whether current manufacturing structures lend themselves to a more export-oriented development path. In the absence of selective export promotion policies, competitiveness depends on the behaviour of real wages, on productivity growth and on the real exchange rate. A comparison of unit labour costs in African countries and some potential competitors in a number of manufacturing sectors in 1995 shows that in most cases costs

Table 21

UNIT LABOUR COSTS IN SELECTED COUNTRIES AND INDUSTRIES, 1980 AND 1995

(Ratios to the United States level)

Country	Textiles		Clothing		Transport equipment		Footwear	
	1980	1995	1980	1995	1980	1995	1980	1995
Ghana	0.79	1.05	0.53	..	0.84	..	5.26	..
Kenya	0.97	1.61	1.07	0.65	1.57	2.25	0.43	1.13
Madagascar	0.75	0.49	0.59	1.24	0.73	1.28	0.77	0.59
Mauritius	0.67	0.96	1.08	1.53	1.02	1.28	0.81	0.57
United Rep. of Tanzania	0.90	..	0.87	..	0.64	..	1.23	..
Zimbabwe	0.71	0.69	1.07	1.30	1.01	0.98	1.02	0.97
South Africa	1.01	1.45	1.45	1.88	1.23	1.35	1.22	1.48
Egypt	1.28	1.45	1.15	1.02	1.55	1.48	1.50	0.30
Morocco	1.16	1.33	1.45	1.64	1.33	1.24	1.46	..
Tunisia	1.37	..	1.24	..	0.95	..	1.15	..
Bangladesh	1.04	1.81	0.77[a]	0.87	0.73	0.35	0.49	0.71
Indonesia	0.58	0.32	1.14	0.95	0.40	1.46	0.45	0.85
India	1.16	1.09	1.19	0.46	1.25	1.46	1.65	0.60
Republic of Korea	0.74	0.81	0.79	0.91	0.76	0.80	1.01	1.03
Turkey	0.69	0.42	0.71	0.39	0.98	0.63	1.06	0.60

Source: UNCTAD secretariat calculations, based on UNIDO, *Handbook of Industrial Statistics, 1988*, and *International Yearbook of Industrial Statistics*, various issues.

a 1983.

in Africa were much higher than in competing countries such as Bangladesh, India and Indonesia (table 21). Moreover, in general, unit labour costs in Africa actually increased after 1980 relative to those in competing countries, even though in many cases real wages stagnated or even declined.[24] On the other hand, some African economies with relatively high wages, such as Mauritius, Morocco and South Africa, have been among the region's most successful exporters of goods such as textiles, clothing and footwear. Strong productivity growth in these economies has been a key ingredient of their export success.

A more comprehensive competitiveness indicator, taking into account exchange rate, wage and productivity movements, is presented for selected African countries in table 22. From the early 1980s to the mid-1990s, the aggregate competi-

tiveness indicator improved for some of these countries, and for Egypt quite spectacularly. However, it appears that this was largely due to a combination of currency depreciation and significant cuts in real wages; investment has actually fallen significantly. In a number of countries strong productivity and investment growth has been offset by currency appreciation or rapidly rising wage costs. The pattern of strong investment and productivity growth, combined with moderate growth in real wages and relatively stable currencies – a pattern found in India, Indonesia and Turkey – still appears to be absent from Africa.

Many African firms which have moved successfully into exports in areas such as textiles and clothing have done so because substantial investment in new equipment and quality control facilities has made it possible to build links with foreign dis-

Table 22

COMPETITIVENESS INDICATORS FOR MANUFACTURES IN SELECTED COUNTRIES, 1995

(Index numbers, 1985 = 100)

	(1)	(2)	(3)	(4)	(5)	(6)
					Memo items	
Country/region	Real exchange rate[a]	Real wage costs in manufacturing[b]	Labour productivity[c] in manufacturing	Aggregate competitiveness indicator[d]	Employment in manufacturing	Investment[e]
Ghana[f]	250.8	259.1	187.5	181.4	128.2	105.2
Kenya[g]	85.2	76.3	69.6	77.7	108.4	93.2
Mauritius[h]	84.5	165.5	165.6	84.5	150.4	108.3
Zimbabwe[i]	143.7	81.1	82.7	146.5	90.2	103.5
South Africa[f]	66.9	105.7	118.0	74.7	94.3	95.2
Egypt[f]	180.2	63.5	121.3	344.2	116.0	90.3
Morocco	78.3	101.6	144.3	111.1	167.2	92.9
Indonesia	140.5	155.8	182.0	164.1	248.6	111.6
India[f]	169.8	116.1	167.2	244.6	119.0	100.6
Republic of Korea	71.3	248.3	283.4	81.4	119.6	107.5
Turkey[h]	121.5	181.2	237.8	159.4	110.6	105.1

Source: Exchange rate and price data from IMF, *International Financial Statistics Yearbook 1997;* investment and GDP data from World Bank, *World Development Indicators, 1997* (CD-Rom); all other data from UNIDO, *International Yearbook of Industrial Statistics,* various issues.
   a Price-deflated bilateral exchange rate with the dollar; an index number higher than 100 indicates a real depreciation of the local currency since 1985.
   b Nominal wage costs deflated by the index of wholesale prices, where available, otherwise by that of consumer prices.
   c Real value-added per worker.
   d Calculated by multiplying the ratio of value-added per worker in manufacturing (column 3) to real wage costs in manufacturing (column 2) by the real exchange rate (column 1).
   e Index of the ratio of gross domestic investment to GDP.
   f 1985-1993.
   g 1991-1995.
   h 1985-1994.
   i 1994 (1989 = 100) except for investment/GDP, which is for 1993 (1989 = 100).

tributors.[25] Effective marketing is closely tied to product quality and reliability even for labour-intensive products, and investment in human and physical capital is often a prerequisite for establishing a reputation as a reliable trading partner. Successful African manufacturing firms have invested in marketing either in-house or through links with marketing services, and in some countries public institutions have been particularly important through organizing trade fairs and handling trade formalities. Where foreign marketing firms have been used extensively there does not appear to

have been, except in Mauritius, the transfer of capabilities that was typical of the East Asian experience.

The experience of the second-tier NIEs in South-East Asia is again instructive for SSA. As in the case of their north-eastern neighbours a decade or more earlier, a decisive element in the shift of these economies to labour-intensive manufactured exports was the combination of private and public investment with supportive trade and industry policies.[26] Manufacturing became the leading economic sector, in terms of share of GDP, in the late 1970s in Thailand and in the early 1980s in Malaysia, but in Indonesia not until the early 1990s. In all these countries manufacturing was built up through a fairly prolonged period of import-substitution industrialization (ISI), which helped to build local capabilities in light and resource-based manufacturing. As in SSA, food, beverages and tobacco were the dominant sectors in MVA in these countries. However, a more diversified manufacturing structure emerged under

ISI than has been the case in most SSA countries, and these sectors subsequently formed an important part of the exporting capacity of countries in South-East Asia, often through the close involvement of foreign firms, particularly in labour-intensive clothing and electronics sectors.[27] In all three countries a number of resource-intensive sectors emerged under ISI, which subsequently acquired export capacities, including jewellery, food processing and wood-based products.

E. The markets for African exports

For developing countries, success in entering the expanding areas of international trade holds the key to sustaining growth based on successful export performance. Such trade is not always confined to products with high income elasticities. International trade can expand for different reasons and with vastly different implications for the longer-term growth of national economies. Liberalization in fairly sluggish but large markets and in products with moderate or even low income elasticities can offer ample export opportunities for small developing countries, particularly in OECD markets, where expansion of trade is associated not so much with rapid growth as with shifting competitive positions. However, only a handful of developing countries have so far been able to penetrate and increase their shares in expanding areas of trade in these highly competitive markets.

The potential for increasing manufactured exports, particularly at the lower end of the skill spectrum, is also considerable not only to advanced economies but also to the NIEs, where rapid economic growth and industrial upgrading have opened up new market opportunities for less developed countries. Moreover, the possibilities for greater trade with other developing countries, and particularly intraregional trade, also need careful consideration in the creation of more export-oriented manufacturing sectors in SSA. Intraregional trade can provide an initial step in the acquisition of the necessary skill and know-how before the challenges are met in the more demanding markets of advanced economies.

1. OECD markets

African countries have been much less successful in the markets of advanced industrial economies than most other developing countries over the last decade. The shares of both SSA and North Africa in total OECD imports have dropped significantly since the beginning of the last decade (chart 25). From 1980 to 1995 the share in both cases declined from more than 3 per cent to around 1 per cent, whereas the share of the first-tier East Asian NIEs rose from 3.5 per cent to 5.8 per cent, and that of Latin America was relatively stable at around 5.0 per cent. Moreover, SSA had a share similar to that of the second-tier East Asian NIEs in 1980, whereas the share of the latter group of countries had risen to three times that of SSA by 1995.

A more detailed analysis, based on data from ECLAC's Comparative Analysis of Nations (CAN) system, permits a classification of exports by their dynamic market position in OECD markets.[28] As explained in detail in *TDR 1996*, a dynamic/competitive position materializes when a country increases its share in the market for a dynamic product, defined as one for which trade is growing faster than the average for all products; such a product is called a "rising star". Similarly, an undynamic/competitive position is one where a country's share is rising in the market for a product for which trade is growing more slowly than the average for all products; such a product is called

Chart 25

SHARES OF SELECTED REGIONS IN TOTAL IMPORTS OF OECD COUNTRIES, 1980, 1990 AND 1995

(Percentages)

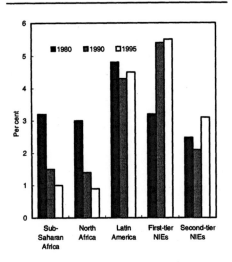

Source: OECD, *Monthly Statistics of Foreign Trade*, various issues.
Note: First-tier NIEs are Hong Kong, China; Republic of Korea; Singapore; and Taiwan Province of China. Second-tier NIEs are Indonesia, Malaysia and Thailand.

a "declining star". The corresponding positions where a country is becoming uncompetitive are called "lost opportunities" (trade for the product is growing above average) and "setbacks" (trade for the product is growing below average).

A country should strive to have a large number of rising stars, i.e. aim at increasing the share of dynamic products in its total exports. This has been the basis of the success of many East Asian economies. Having an increasing share of its exports in the lost-opportunities category means that while these dynamic products have secured a higher share in the country's export basket, the country itself has lost market shares for these products. An increasing share of declining stars in a country's export basket means that these products have become more important in the country's exports, indicating that the country itself has become

more competitive in these sectors, but that the sectors' evolution in world trade is below average. Even though such a position has positive aspects from the point of view of competitiveness and may increase exports, a growing share of these stagnant products in a country's export basket will not improve the economy's dynamic potential over the medium term. A number of Latin American countries are in this position.[29]

A comparison of the evolution between 1985 and 1995 of the shares for the four product categories in total exports of four developing regions shows that both Africa as a whole and SSA have increased the share of rising stars in their export baskets (chart 26). Moreover, they have by and large kept constant the share of the other group of dynamic products (lost opportunities). However, the share of these products in Africa's exports is far smaller than in the other regions; they account for about one fourth of the total for the whole of Africa and about one fifth for SSA, compared with more than half for Latin America and about 90 per cent for the East Asian tigers. In general, Africa, and in particular SSA, export a relatively high proportion of products for which growth is not above average.

2. Opportunities for intraregional trade

At various times during the past three decades, SSA countries have, with varying degrees of determination, made efforts towards regional integration. Increased regional trade and investment indeed offer a means of overcoming the constraints on individual countries related to their small size and of breaking away from their traditional export structure. Moreover, the regional context is useful for learning to adapt to the pressures of international integration, particularly the challenges of increased global competition. For manufacturing sectors which are traditionally oriented towards the domestic market and internationally uncompetitive, increased regional trade and investment can be a first step towards closer integration with the world economy. It would allow enterprises to gain experience in competing in foreign markets and dealing with customs and other trade-related regulations; hence, they would gradually enhance their capacity to export to more demanding global markets. Moreover, certain types of exports in such areas as agricultural machinery and other farm implements can often capture a

DYNAMISM AND COMPETITIVENESS OF EXPORTS FROM SELECTED DEVELOPING REGIONS, 1985 AND 1995

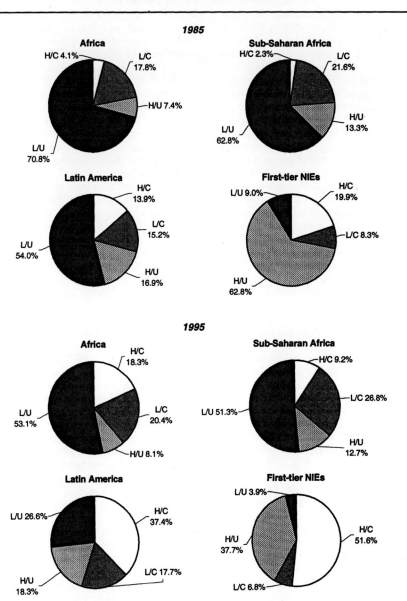

1985

Africa
H/C 4.1%
L/C 17.8%
H/U 7.4%
L/U 70.8%

Sub-Saharan Africa
H/C 2.3%
L/C 21.6%
H/U 13.3%
L/U 62.8%

Latin America
H/C 13.9%
L/C 15.2%
H/U 16.9%
L/U 54.0%

First-tier NIEs
L/U 9.0%
H/C 19.9%
L/C 8.3%
H/U 62.8%

1995

Africa
H/C 18.3%
L/C 20.4%
H/U 8.1%
L/U 53.1%

Sub-Saharan Africa
H/C 9.2%
L/C 26.8%
H/U 12.7%
L/U 51.3%

Latin America
L/U 26.6%
H/C 37.4%
L/C 17.7%
H/U 18.3%

First-tier NIEs
L/U 3.9%
H/C 51.6%
L/C 6.8%
H/U 37.7%

Source: ECLAC, Comparative Analysis of Nations database.
Note: H/C: highly dynamic/competitive position (rising market share for highly dynamic products);
L/C: less dynamic/competitive position (rising market share for less dynamic products);
H/U: highly dynamic/uncompetitive position (falling market share for highly dynamic products);
L/U: less dynamic/uncompetitive position (falling market share for less dynamic products).

wider regional market because they have to suit local climatic and physical conditions. In learning to adapt to these conditions firms can also build up innovative capacities which can subsequently be used to enhance their competitiveness in other markets.[30] Similar considerations can apply to labour-intensive products such as textiles and clothing, jewellery products and wood products, where design can provide regional niche markets.

A regional pattern of industrialization involving a progressively deeper regional division of labour where trade and investment flows link developing countries at different levels of development has been an important part of successful growth stories in East Asia. Replicating this kind of experience is an attractive prospect for SSA. But greater intraregional trade can also have benefits globally. The immediate impact of additional exports from one SSA country to another may be a reduction in the share and level of imports from developed countries, i.e. trade diversion. However, given that the increased exports are likely to lead to faster economic growth, imports from developed countries can over time also grow faster, thereby making up for the initial loss. Hence, ultimately, increased intraregional trade among developing countries can have a global trade-generating effect.

Table 23 suggests that between 1988 and 1996 most SSA countries shifted their exports away from industrialized countries, and that intra-African trade expanded considerably, while the opposite occurred in North African countries.[31] For example, in 1996 five countries – Côte d'Ivoire, Kenya, Malawi, Senegal and Zimbabwe – exported more than 20 per cent of their products to Africa, while in 1988 only three of them did so. However, this increased intra-African trade is dominated by only a few countries: Côte d'Ivoire, Ghana, Kenya, Nigeria and Zimbabwe account for about two thirds of all SSA exports to other countries in the region, including South Africa. Moreover, the increase has been due to a small number of primary commodities. Petroleum alone accounts for one third of the increase, with cotton, live animals, maize and cocoa accounting for another 18 per cent. The small share of regionally traded manufactures is confined to products with a large natural-resource content, such as cement, aluminium, iron plate and sheet, and woven cotton fabrics.[32]

Intraregional trade in SSA in 1996 amounted to about $9.5 billion (equivalent to about 8.6 per cent of the region's total exports), a level which is often considered too low for enhancing welfare and growth. It reflects the comparatively low level of SSA trade overall, but also the relatively high cost of regional trade, which is determined by, in addition to excessive transport costs, political barriers to trade and factors influencing the general business environment such as ethno-linguistic fragmentation and political instability.

What, then, is the potential for greater intra-SSA trade? It may be quantitatively assessed by the value of goods which are currently imported from the rest of the world but for which at least one SSA country is successfully exporting to the rest of the world to a significant extent. Trade between the Southern African Customs Union (SACU), which comprises Botswana, Lesotho, Namibia, South Africa and Swaziland, and the non-SACU members of the Southern African Development Community (SADC) Angola, Malawi, Mauritius, Mozambique, the United Republic of Tanzania, Zambia and Zimbabwe (hereinafter SADC-7), has greater potential for expansion than trade among other SSA countries.[33] This is because of the substantially greater differences in per capita GDP[34] and in current production and export structures between the two groups of countries.

Given the overlap in the product composition of exports by non-SACU members of SADC to the rest of the world with SACU's imports from the rest of the world, there is an untapped potential for trade between the two groups. Apart from petroleum, where the overlap is greatest, this potential mainly concerns primary products (including meat, tropical beverages, cotton, diamonds and non-ferrous metals) and a few resource-intensive basic manufactures (such as cotton yarn, cement and some types of woven fabrics); for other manufactures the potential is limited (table 24).

A trade potential identified in this way can, however, only be a rough estimate because it is based on actual trade flows rather than on their determinants. Therefore, supply capabilities in the potential exporting countries and market access conditions in the potential importing countries have also to be taken into account. For example, the current subregional trade pattern in Southern Africa has been strongly influenced by the asymmetrical pace of trade liberalization. Most SADC-7 countries, specifically Angola, Malawi, Mozambique, Zambia and Zimbabwe, have implemented substantial trade liberalization

Table 23

THE DESTINATION OF AFRICAN EXPORTS, 1988 AND 1996

(Millions of dollars and percentages)

Exports from	Year	Total exports ($ million)	Per cent share in African exports					
			Industrial countries	Developing countries	Africa	Developing Asia	Middle East	Latin America
Africa	**1988**	**64 300**	**67.6**	**16.2**	**6.2**	**4.5**	**1.4**	**1.6**
	1996	**110 900**	**64.7**	**26.0**	**10.1**	**9.1**	**1.9**	**2.8**
Cameroon	1988	1 582	85.0	13.9	11.4	0.6	0.1	0.4
	1996	2 222	83.9	16.1	9.2	5.7	0.2	0.1
Côte d'Ivoire	1988	2 780	65.3	31.0	21.7	3.2	..	0.4
	1996	4 996	65.4	33.8	23.3	3.5	0.5	2.2
Gabon	1988	1 207	78.9	20.6	5.0	3.4	1.5	9.2
	1996	2 850	85.4	14.2	2.9	6.5	0.3	3.3
Ghana	1988	874	79.5	15.9	2.0	3.2	1.0	3.3
	1996	1 704	68.2	26.6	15.8	7.3	0.7	0.1
Kenya	1988	1 073	60.0	34.8	24.6	6.1	3.5	0.1
	1996	2 203	46.3	48.3	32.1	9.0	6.5	0.1
Malawi	1988	280	77.9	19.2	18.0	..	..	..
	1996	494	55.0	38.0	23.6	4.3	2.2	1.0
Mauritius	1988	1 001	93.9	6.0	3.5	2.0	0.5	..
	1996	1 573	87.7	9.8	6.7	2.5	..	0.1
Nigeria	1988	6 884	88.1	11.5	6.5	0.5	0.1	4.2
	1996	14 836	79.9	20.1	8.5	7.5	..	3.7
Senegal	1988	591	59.1	34.1	18.7	14.4	0.1	0.1
	1996	806	43.3	46.8	22.1	20.2	2.3	2.0
Uganda	1988	323	89.5	9.6	0.5	6.7	11.5	..
	1996	559	82.1	17.9	2.4	2.8	1.9	0.1
Zambia	1988	871	72.0	28.0	6.2	15.2	5.5	..
	1996	1 000	41.3	58.7	13.9	33.8	9.8	..
Zimbabwe	1988	1 396	58.8	40.6	29.9	5.8	1.7	0.6
	1996	2 343	46.9	53.0	38.4	8.1	2.4	0.4
South Africa	1988	21 830	42.8	12.0	4.4	5.2	0.7	0.7
	1996	35 682	43.3	30.5	12.5	12.9	1.7	2.2
Egypt	1988	2 120	50.4	44.9	3.5	8.2	15.6	0.3
	1996	5 239	51.9	46.3	2.0	6.6	15.9	..
Morocco	1988	3 464	70.2	29.4	2.5	11.9	7.0	2.2
	1996	6 973	81.2	18.8	3.0	7.3	..	2.2
Tunisia	1988	2 393	76.8	20.3	4.0	6.7	4.9	0.3
	1996	5 519	82.4	14.4	3.1	3.3	5.7	0.6

Source: IMF, *Direction of Trade Statistics Yearbook*, various issues.

Table 24

ACTUAL AND POTENTIAL SADC-7 EXPORTS TO SACU, 1995

(Millions of dollars)

Product	Actual SACU imports from SADC-7	Potential SACU imports from SADC-7	Current main SADC-7 exporters
Petroleum (SITC 33)	0.2	2 775	Angola
Non-ferrous metals (SITC 68)	9.3	325	Zambia, Zimbabwe
Cement and diamonds (SITC 66)	15.0	264	Angola, Mauritius, Zimbabwe, United Republic of Tanzania
Iron and steel (SITC 67)	5.0	225	Zimbabwe
Cotton (SITC 26)	35.7	191	United Republic of Tanzania, Zimbabwe, Mozambique
Cotton yarn and textile fabrics (SITC 65)	20.7	158	Mauritius, Zambia, Zimbabwe
Clothing and accessories (SITC 84)	27.9	139	Mauritius, Zimbabwe, Malawi, United Republic of Tanzania
Cocoa, coffee, spices, tea (SITC 07)	11.3	117	United Republic of Tanzania, Malawi, Zimbabwe
Meat (SITC 01)	4.1	97	Zimbabwe
Memo item:			
All products	402.2	8 822	

Source: F. von Kirchbach and H. Roelofsen, "Trade in the Southern African Development Community: What is the potential for increasing exports to the Republic of South Africa?", UNCTAD/GDS/MDPB/Misc. 11 (Geneva, 1998).
Note: Trade potential is calculated as the overlap between SADC-7 exports to the world and SACU imports from the world.

programmes during the past 10 years, thus effectively opening their markets to South Africa and the rest of the world, while South Africa appears to have adopted a more gradual approach. Although more recently there has been some improvement in the access of, for example, Zimbabwean textiles, clothing and agricultural products to the SACU market, a further levelling of the current regional asymmetries regarding market access would probably be needed in order to increase the scope for SADC-7 exports to SACU.

International competitiveness and supply capacities also affect intraregional trade potential. For example, to the extent that SADC-7 exporters

to the EU are supported by preferential market access conditions under the Lomé Convention, it is not clear whether these exporters could compete on an equal footing with SACU's imports from elsewhere, or whether they would be competitive only if SACU granted them preferential conditions similar to those granted by the EU. Moreover, SADC-7 would need to create sufficient supply capacities so that increased exports to SACU would lead to trade creation rather than simply replace its exports to the EU.

If conditions regarding the competitiveness and supply capability of SADC-7 exporters are fulfilled, increased intraregional trade in Southern Africa could help reduce regional trade imbalances in the context of growing exports and imports for all the countries concerned. Given that South Africa runs large trade surpluses with SADC-7 countries, the increased exports by the latter to SACU will reduce bilateral imbalances. However, since a growing share of imports by SADC-7 countries now comes from South Africa, greater export earnings by those countries will also translate into increased sales by South Africa to neighbouring countries. In this sense, intraregional trade involving initially a diversion of SACU imports from advanced countries to SADC-7 can be trade-generating for all the parties concerned.

These prospects for increased intra-SSA trade are not independent of the wider efforts to accelerate accumulation and restore sustained growth. However, even small increases in intraregional trade help develop new export capacity which can generate a virtuous circle of regional growth dynamics by easing the balance-of-payments constraints on imports and providing learning effects which will eventually make African exporters more competitive globally. However, it is likely that trade within SSA will initially be confined to subregions centred on comparatively more advanced countries such as South Africa, Kenya and perhaps Côte d'Ivoire, while the prospects for enhanced trade among these subregions will evolve more slowly alongside improvements in transportation and communication facilities.

Notes

1   See, for example, D. Dollar, "Outward-oriented developing economies really do grow more rapidly: Evidence from 95 LDCs, 1976-1985", *Economic Development and Cultural Change*, Vol. 40, 1992, pp. 523-544; and J.D. Sachs and A.M. Warner, "Sources of slow growth in African economies", *Journal of African Economies*, Vol. 6, 1997, pp. 335-376.

2   For similar results see D. Rodrik, "Trade policy and economic performance in sub-Saharan Africa", NBER Working Paper No. 6562 (Cambridge, Mass.: National Bureau of Economic Research, 1998).

3   In their "Economic reform and the process of global integration" (*Brookings Papers on Economic Activity*, No. 1, 1995) Sachs and Warner have offered the most cogent version of the "open economies converge" thesis. In commenting on this work, Stanley Fischer noted that: "The strength of the Sachs-Warner results is surprising, given that the question that is being looked at, that of the influence of openness on growth, has been extensively studied before ... It is particularly surprising that this paper reaches stronger conclusions than the World Bank's famous 1987 *World Development Report*, which was so roundly criticized for overreaching" (*Ibid.*, pp. 103-104). More sophisticated versions of the "open economies converge" thesis now stress a package of market-liberalizing and macroeconomic disciplining policies. The empirical evidence in support of this approach is stronger – though still far from conclu-

sive – than for the simpler versions, but is very much contingent upon the level of income and development achieved by countries. See P. Mosley, "Globalization, economic policy and convergence", in UNCTAD, *International Monetary and Financial Issues for the 1990s*, Vol. X (United Nations publication, Sales No. E.97.II.D.5), New York and Geneva.

4   For further discussion of these and related points regarding the links between trade policies and economic growth, see *TDR 1997*, Part Two, chapter II. section E, and R. Rowthorn and R. Kozul-Wright, "Globalization and economic convergence: An assessment", UNCTAD Discussion Paper No. 131 (Geneva, February 1998).

5   An additional problem is that disaggregated export data become available only after much delay, which is why tables 16 and 17 refer to 1990 data (three-year averages for 1989-1991). More recent data available for a few SSA countries suggest that the share of different product categories in total merchandise exports has not changed significantly since then.

6   Some trade statistics reveal a relatively high share of manufactures for the Central African Republic, Sierra Leone and Zambia, but this is because gold and uncut diamonds are counted as manufactures. Similarly, Niger's large share, on the basis of data in the UNCTAD *Handbook of International Trade and Development Statistics*, is due to the classification of uranium exports as manufactures.

7   The empirical analysis in this section draws on A. Wood and J. Mayer, "Africa's export structure in comparative perspective", UNCTAD/GDS/MDPB/Misc. 4 (Geneva, 1998). The interpretation of the results here may, however, be somewhat different from that of the authors.

8   See T. Akiyama and D.F. Larson, "The adding-up problem: Strategies for primary commodity exporters in sub-Saharan Africa", World Bank Policy Research Working Paper No. 1245 (Washington, D.C.: World Bank, 1994).

9   This group includes meat and meat products, dairy products, fish and fish products, fruit, vegetables, nuts, spices and vegetable oils. For further discussion of this product classification, see Wood and Mayer, *op. cit.*

10   For a discussion of the Mauritian experience see L. Darga, "A comparative analysis of the accumulation process and capital mobilisation in Mauritius, Tanzania and Zimbabwe", UNCTAD/GDS/MDPB/Misc. 3 (Geneva, 1998); and T. Meisenhelder, "The developmental state in Mauritius", *Journal of Modern African Studies*, Vol. 35, No. 2, June 1997. As discussed in these papers, some special conditions - in particular, favourable access to the EU market - helped accelerate growth in Mauritius. However, only through effective policies was Mauritius able to make full use of these opportunities.

11   Data contained in a recent report by the United States Bureau of Mines, as cited in "Survey of African Mining", *Financial Times*, 15 September 1997. Known reserves are not, of course, the same as profitable production opportunities; whether it is worthwhile to invest in exploiting such reserves will depend on the actual costs of exploitation and the future world market prices of the respective commodities.

12   For a discussion of this experience see *TDR 1993*, Part Two, chapter II, section C.

13   For a discussion of the definition of non-traditional exports and its relation to diversification see G. Frazer and G. Helleiner, "Non-traditional exports and export diversification: Alternative definitions and methodologies", paper prepared for the WIDER Project on Growth, External Sector and the Role of Non-Traditional Exports in Sub-Saharan Africa, Helsinki, May 1997.

14   High costs may also be a feature of the early stages of infant industries which are promoted in the context of a longer-term development strategy. In this case it is necessary to avoid a situation in which domestic firms receiving inputs from these industries have to bear the difference between world market prices and the higher cost of domestic supplies. This can be achieved through the provision of temporary price or cost subsidies.

15   See P. Svedberg, "The export performance of sub-Saharan Africa", in J. Frimpong-Ansah, S.M. Ravi Kanbur and P. Svedberg (eds.), *Trade and Development in Sub-Saharan Africa* (Manchester: Manchester University Press, 1990).

16   This category includes food products, other primary commodities, wood and paper products, and non-metallic mineral products. See *TDR 1996*, Part Two, chapter II, section C.

17   See UNCTAD, "Analysis of national experiences in horizontal and vertical diversification, including the possibilities for crop substitution: Malaysia" (UNCTAD/COM/73), 1995, and *TDR 1996*, Part Two, annex to chapter II.

18   M. Agosin, "Export performance in Chile", paper prepared for the WIDER Project on Growth, External Sector and the Role of Non-Traditional Exports in Sub-Saharan Africa, Helsinki, May 1997.

19   K.S. Jomo and M. Rock, "Economic diversification and primary commodity processing in the second-tier South-East Asian newly industrialized countries", UNCTAD Discussion Paper No. 136 (Geneva, 1998).

20   See P. Pardey, J. Roseboom and N. Beintema, "Investments in African agricultural research", *World Development*, Vol. 25, No. 3, 1997, pp. 409-423.

21   See, for example, A. Taylor et al., "Strengthening national agricultural research systems in the humid and sub-humid zones of West and Central Africa", World Bank Technical Paper No. 318 (Washington, D.C.: World Bank, 1996).

22   UNIDO, *International Yearbook of Industrial Statistics 1998*, table 1.3.

23   R.C. Riddell, "Manufacturing Africa. Reflections from the case-studies", in R.C. Riddell with P. Coughlin, C. Harvey, I. Karmiloff, S. Lewis Jr., J. Sharpley and C. Stevens, *Manufacturing Africa* (London: Overseas Development Institute and James Currey; and Portsmouth, New Hampshire: Heinemann, 1990), p. 36; and L. Mytelka and T. Tesfachew, "The role of policy in promoting learning during the early industrialization: Lessons for African countries", UNCTAD/GDS/MDPB/Misc. 7 (Geneva, 1998).

24   From 1975-1979 to 1987-1991 manufacturing real wages in Zimbabwe, Mauritius, Kenya and the United Republic of Tanzania declined by 32 per cent, 37 per cent, 40 per cent and 83 per cent, respectively; see ILO, *World Employment Report 1996/97* (Geneva: ILO, 1997).

25   See S. Wangwe, "Conditions under which African manufacturing industries in sub-Saharan Africa have been able to break into export markets", UNCTAD/GDS/MDPB/Misc. 5 (Geneva, 1998).

26   See *TDR 1996*, Part Two, chapter II, section C.

27   See R. Rasiah, "The export manufacturing experience of Indonesia, Malaysia and Thailand: Lessons for Africa", UNCTAD Discussion Paper No. 137 (Geneva, 1998).

28   See also E. Rodriguez, "Export diversification by region", paper prepared for the WIDER Project on Growth, External Sector and the Role of Non-Traditional Exports in Sub-Saharan Africa, Helsinki, 1998.

29   For further discussion see *TDR 1996*, Part Two, chapter II, section D.

30 See Wangwe, *op. cit.*

31 It could be argued that this increase in recorded intra-SSA trade is misleading because the incentives to circumvent official trade channels have greatly diminished with trade and exchange-rate reform. However, even where unrecorded trade flows are large, they have usually concerned goods imported from outside SSA or goods of domestic origin but destined for export outside SSA. Hence, such goods would in any case not qualify as true intraregional trade.

32 A. Yeats, "Problems and prospects for African regional trade arrangements: Some empirical evidence" (Washington, D.C.: World Bank, 1997), mimeo, p. 40.

33 This analysis draws on F. von Kirchbach and H. Roelofsen, "Trade in the Southern African Development Community: What is the potential for increasing exports to the Republic of South Africa?", UNCTAD/GDS/MDPB/Misc. 11 (Geneva, 1998). The Democratic Republic of the Congo and Seychelles are also non-SACU members of SADC, but they joined SADC only in 1997, so that their trade data could not be taken into account.

34 Countries with similar living standards are likely to engage in enhanced bilateral trade only if they have a significant level of industrial production and hence trade in specific intermediate goods and production inputs, as well as in brand-name finished goods.

Chapter V

POLICY CHALLENGES AND INSTITUTIONAL REFORM

A. Introduction

Any long-run improvement in living standards in Africa can be achieved only through a sustained rise in productivity. Increasing investment is a prerequisite, if not a guarantee, of rapid productivity growth, because the latter requires the use of more productive technologies and higher skill levels, which are usually embodied in, or closely related to, new plant and equipment. Furthermore, strong complementarities between public investment and private investment mean that these should rise together if the fast and continuous pace of economic growth which has so far eluded the majority of countries in SSA is to be achieved.

In most countries, higher investment will be closely linked to an export-oriented development strategy and a shift in the structure of output and employment from agriculture to industry. As noted in chapter IV, resource endowments limit this investment-export nexus in the early stages of development. However, these endowments are themselves transformed with a successful take-off into sustained economic growth. Also, faster economic growth makes possible closer integration into the world economy, ensuring that international factors reinforce the domestic determinants of the growth process. The possibility of growth impulses being transmitted to neighbouring countries through trade and investment links can often give a strong regional dimension to that process.

Clearly, Africa needs structural reform and adjustment in order to overcome many of the impediments to capital accumulation and economic growth. In the view of some observers, such impediments result primarily from government interventions in economic activity; new investment opportunities should ensue quickly if such practices are abandoned and the logic of price reform dictated by global markets is accepted. The analysis in the last four chapters has raised serious doubts about such expectations. Liberalization and privatization, even to the extent that they are desirable, can hardly exhaust policy options in Africa. Policies need to be based on greater realism, in recognition of the fact that economic activity is undertaken by fallible economic agents in both the private and the public spheres, that markets and other institutions needed for the efficient functioning of a market economy are missing or highly imperfect, and that initial weaknesses and asymmetries in supply capabilities are as likely to be reinforced as removed by closer integration into world markets.

B. Policy options

1. Elements of a pro-investment climate

Present conditions in SSA do not preclude a take-off into rapid and sustained economic growth (see box 4). At the same time, it is far from certain that the recent recovery constitutes a turning point, given the generally weak investment performance and the failure to increase the level and diversify the structure of exports. Raising investment from its currently depressed levels thus assumes particular importance.

Policy intervention of various kinds can play a key role by setting the general conditions for a fast pace of capital accumulation and correcting specific market failures impeding it. Such intervention should, however, be founded upon the recognition that in market-based systems capital accumulation is closely linked to the consolidation of private property rights and the emergence of a strong domestic entrepreneurial class willing to commit its resources to investment rather than personal consumption.[1] The combination of public and private initiatives needed to stimulate rapid economic growth is perhaps best illustrated by the East Asian NIEs. However, a similar picture can be found in Latin American countries such as Chile, as well as in better-performing African economies such as Mauritius, Morocco and Tunisia.

The tissue of a modern entrepreneurial class is very thin in most African countries. To some extent, this may reflect the suspicion with which governments viewed modern and large-scale enterprises in their countries because they were owned or managed either by persons belonging to ethnic minorities or by nationals of the former colonial power. This reaction, however, was common to many other post-colonial experiences. Rather, stalled growth across much of SSA is linked to the failure of the State to gradually cede its initial economic power to a nascent independent entrepreneurial class which could assume the lead role in a dynamic accumulation process.

A more rapid pace of capital accumulation depends, *inter alia*, on the availability of resources

for both the public and the private sector, as well as on incentives for private investment. As discussed in chapter I, rapid and substantial debt relief for a number of countries in SSA could provide a significant boost to public investment while at the same time increasing the availability of foreign exchange needed for imports of capital goods. As for the mobilization of domestic resources, experience suggests that it is much easier to increase savings from a growing level of income than from a stagnant one. Consequently, to the extent that output and income could be increased by greater and better utilization of existing resources, they could provide a basis for higher rates of domestic savings and investment. Such an opportunity appears to exist particularly in countries which have recently achieved significant increases in output and income.

Improvements in economic conditions need to be accompanied by policies designed to encourage savings and investment. While interest rate policies have an uncertain, and even perverse, influence on savings, fiscal, trade and credit policies can play crucial roles in creating conditions that favour saving over consumption. In countries with a developed corporate sector, a range of fiscal instruments can be used to encourage retention and reinvestment of profits, including tax exemptions and special depreciation allowances applied on a general level or targeted at specific industries. Again, measures such as controls on luxury imports, restricted access to consumer credit and public appeals to wealth holders to show self-restraint can provide incentives to increase the savings ratio.[2]

However, the principal policy challenge in many countries is to create a pro-investment climate so as to raise productivity levels and initiate the necessary structural changes. There is a consensus that political stability, a good legal structure and effective contract enforcement are needed in order to ensure rising levels of private investment. A stable macroeconomic climate is also desirable, although actual rates of inflation, and the size of the budget and current account deficits consistent

Box 4

INITIAL CONDITIONS AND ECONOMIC TAKE-OFF

Modern growth theory emphasizes the path dependence of economic development. It has been argued that because of the weakness of its initial economic and social conditions, a sustained acceleration of growth in SSA is precluded. Moreover, the relative success of countries in other developing regions over the past three decades may pose greater obstacles to rapid growth in SSA than were faced by previous generations of latecomers to development.

In point of fact, present economic conditions in SSA are not uniformly less favourable than were conditions in the East Asian countries on the eve of their take-off into sustained growth. As the table shows, the conditions are similar in many respects to those in East Asia in the mid-1960s, and in some respects they are better than those in South-East Asia in the mid-1970s, when the countries in that region launched into two decades of very fast economic growth and structural change.

MAJOR ECONOMIC AND SOCIAL INDICATORS FOR THE REPUBLIC OF KOREA, THE SECOND-TIER NIEs AND SUB-SAHARAN AFRICA

	Republic of Korea	Second-tier NIEs[a]	Sub-Saharan Africa
	1960	1975	1995
GDP per capita *(at constant 1987 dollars)*	768	692	598
Agricultural value-added *(per cent of GDP)*	36.7	28.3	29.2
Manufacturing value-added *(per cent of GDP)*	13.8	15.1	11.4
Gross domestic savings *(per cent of GDP)*	11.6 [b]	24.6	7.6
Gross domestic investment *(per cent of GDP)*	13.0 [b]	25.2	19.9
Exports of goods and services *(per cent of GDP)*	3.3	28.4	33.4
Urban population *(per cent of total population)*	27.7	24.1	34.3
Primary school enrolment *(per cent gross)*	103.0 [c]	86.7	75.0
Secondary school enrolment *(per cent gross)*	42.0 [c]	29.3	27.0
Telephones in use per 1,000 inhabitants	4.4	7.8 [c]	9.5 [d]
Life expectancy at birth *(years)*	53	55	52

Source: UNCTAD secretariat calculations, based on *World Development Indicators 1998*, The World Bank, Washington, D.C., 1998.
Note: Figures for regions are mean values.
   a   Indonesia, Malaysia, Thailand.
   b   1962.
   c   1970.
   d   1988.

In two important respects, however, present conditions in SSA do not match those in East Asia prior to the latter's growth take-off. First, the physical and social infrastructure, particularly the education base, is generally poorer. Secondly, to judge from the levels of savings and investment the accumulation process is much weaker. However, changes in these conditions can be quite rapid. Both the Republic of Korea and Taiwan Province of China, for example, made great strides in the 1950s in raising the level of basic education, often from a lower starting point than some countries in SSA. In the 1960s, and again from quite modest levels, a shift of resources to higher levels of education and training further enhanced the human capital stock in those countries.[1] In communication and transport infrastructure, too, the push in these countries came after 1970. Similarly, during the 1950s gross national savings were less than 4 per cent of GDP in the Republic of Korea and less than 10 per cent in Taiwan Province of China. In both countries they rose rapidly in the 1960s, more than doubling by the end of the decade, and exceeding 30 per cent by the early 1980s.

---

[1]   Although the second-tier East Asian NIEs began with comparable, and in some cases considerably better educational and infrastructural starting points than the first-tier NIEs, their subsequent growth was slower. Indeed, one of the slower growing East Asian economies over the past three decades – the Philippines – began with one of the best educational endowments.

with high rates of investment, fall within a fairly wide band.[3] Furthermore, it is generally agreed that abrupt policy shifts should be avoided so as to allow investors to take a long view.

But it is also important to ensure that markets do not generate impulses that undermine incentives and opportunities for investment. In this respect, it is a matter for concern that some recent policy reforms which are aimed at correcting price distortions and improving allocative efficiency in SSA may have damaging consequences for both private and public investment. This is true particularly of financial liberalization, but also of some trade liberalization measures (see subsection 3 below).

(a) Avoiding financial instability

The conditions that gave rise to rapid financial liberalization in many countries in Africa, as in developing countries elsewhere, are quite familiar.[4] Generally, it was introduced as a reaction to excessive and often misguided government intervention in the financial sector, including public ownership of banks and controls over interest rates and credit allocation, which often resulted in negative real deposit and lending rates and preferential treatment for public entities. Initially, reform efforts were directed towards improving government intervention, such as lifting interest rate ceilings above inflation, phasing out directed credit allocation and reducing public sector deficit financing from the banking system, but they were soon abandoned in favour of market-determined interest rates and privatization and deregulation of the banking system. Simultaneously, there has been a shift in public sector deficit financing to private markets through the issue of bills and bonds. This was thought to bring about not only greater price stability but also better fiscal discipline, as well as a shift to indirect control in the conduct of monetary policy, and hence give a greater role to market forces.

It is generally agreed that a number of conditions have to be satisfied for orderly and successful financial liberalization. First, a relatively high degree of price stability is needed in order to avoid sharp increases in interest rates. Second, the government budget should be brought under control in order to prevent a public sector debt spiral of high interest rates, deficits and debt, which could necessitate large cuts in primary spending to avoid debt explosion. Third, there should be relatively well developed, sound financial institutions that would give depth to markets and ensure healthy competition. Fourth, it is important to ensure that the corporate sector is not highly vulnerable to increases in interest rates. Finally, effective prudential regulations and strict bank supervision should be put in place in order to reduce the likelihood of financial instability.

Many of these conditions were not satisfied before the implementation of financial liberalization in SSA. Consequently, the experience with such reforms has been rather disappointing.[5] First of all, because fiscal adjustment was slower than expected, the switch to bond financing has led to very high and variable real interest rates since the market for government debt turned out to be very thin, consisting of only a few banks. This has resulted in a rapid accumulation of domestic debt and fiscal instability. High intermediation costs and large amounts of non-performing loans carried by the recently privatized and/or deregulated banks are another reason for high interest rates. Finally, although a large number of locally incorporated commercial banks have been established, their low level of capitalization, combined with weak prudential regulations and poor lending practices has caused banking crises in several countries. In Kenya, for example, 14 commercial banks and non-bank financial institutions failed in 1993 alone, compared with three in 1984-1988.[6]

The combination of high interest rates and increased financial instability has placed a considerable burden on the private sector even where the rates were technically efficient and competitive. Increased debt charges on profits, together with the higher cost of finance, have discouraged private investment. Public investment has been equally hit by rising interest payments on domestic debt, since it is often easier to shift the burden onto capital than current spending.

While there should be no illusions about the difficulty of reforming the financial sector in SSA, there is little reason in principle to assume that the institutions developed in East Asia to mobilize domestic savings, or the measures of financial restraint employed there, are incompatible with existing conditions in many countries.[7] Given the difficulties associated with ensuring the depth and soundness of financial markets and institutions, it might prove wiser to move towards administered interest rates while making every effort to avoid the kind of problems encountered in the past. This could also help to check the accumulation of domestic debt and fiscal instability. Under a regime of measured financial restraint, policymakers not only have greater leverage on capital accumulation, but also assume the important role of a risk-sharing partner at a critical stage of economic development.[8] Although strict government control of credit allocation is neither a necessary nor a desirable feature of financial restraint, institutional arrangements, including development banks, are still needed to channel credits to agricultural smallholders and small and medium-sized industrial enterprises.[9]

The liberalization of foreign trade and foreign-exchange markets has taken a course similar to that of domestic liberalization. Initially, exchange rates remained regulated and currency devaluation was the most frequently and intensively used tool in adjustment programmes in SSA. But subsequently many countries moved towards market-determined exchange rates and current account convertibility. As a result, the extensive restrictions on access to foreign exchange for current account transactions, which were the norm during the early 1980s in the vast majority of SSA countries, no longer exist: as of September 1997 more than 30 countries had formally subscribed to the Article VIII obligations of the IMF and by 1996 foreign exchange markets had been unified and the previously often substantial black market premium on foreign exchange had been eliminated in all SSA countries except Burundi, Ethiopia, Liberia and Nigeria.[10]

Again, the markets for foreign exchange have proved to be very thin, resulting in excessive volatility. Exchange rate instability has been further exacerbated by arrangements that have resulted in de facto liberalization of the capital account. As part of their foreign exchange reform, many countries have introduced "own-funds" import schemes, under which no questions are asked about the source of finance for imports, as well as foreign exchange bureaux. The bureaux system was in principle designed for all current account transactions, while some control over capital movements would be retained; it was assumed that the source of funds for the bureaux system would be unrecorded exports and workers' remittances. However, owing to inadequate monitoring and supervision of bureaux transactions, this system has also been used for a wide range of capital transactions, resulting in a de facto liberalization of the capital account. Currently enforced recording procedures do not allow a clear separation to be made between current and capital transactions which go through the bureaux system, but it has been estimated that the scale of capital flows to SSA countries in relation to the size of the latter's economies is comparable to that in other regions if the unrecorded flows from the bureaux system are taken into account.[11]

Available evidence for a number of countries in SSA suggests that private capital flows have been an important cause of increased exchange rate instability. For instance, during the first half of the 1990s Kenya and Uganda experienced sharp appreciations when private transfers and access to short-term credits increased markedly. Zambia experienced a depreciation of the real effective exchange rate in 1991, followed by an appreciation in 1992 and 1993 and another depreciation in 1994. South Africa has experienced similar fluctuations.[12]

Establishing an investment-export nexus in SSA depends to an important extent on the maintenance of stable and competitive real exchange rates. There was certainly a need to move towards more realistic and flexible exchange rates from the earlier regimes of rigid and overvalued rates. Indeed, evidence cited in chapter III suggests that devaluations assisted some African agricultural exporters in achieving competitiveness. However, again, the pendulum appears to have swung too far, giving rise to instability. An appropriate management of exchange rates requires, *inter alia*, the kind of regulation and control of capital flows discussed in *TDR 1998*, Part One, chapter IV.

(b) Curbing capital flight

The available, albeit limited, evidence on capital flight suggests that SSA is one of the regions most affected. For example, it has been estimated that 70 per cent of privately owned wealth (excluding land) was held abroad in 1992, and that Africa's private capital stock would be about three times higher than it currently is if that wealth had simply been retained at home.[13] Assets of such a magnitude could make a crucial contribution to Africa's economic take-off if they could be mobilized for productive investment.

It is often held that overvalued exchange rates, the absence of profitable investment opportunities and economic and political instability were the main reasons for capital flight in SSA. It is not clear, however, whether the expatriation of these assets was motivated by a simple economic calculus of risk and return. More likely, much of it appears to have originated from the illicit diversion of public funds rather than to have been constituted by business incomes seeking economic stability or high yields abroad. To that extent, market confidence and policy credibility considerations probably play a minor role in decisions about where the money is invested. A change in the banking regulations of those developed countries where these funds tend to be invested would probably be a more effective measure towards their repatriation.

Nevertheless, consideration of risk and return are not irrelevant. The appropriate policy response is not to ease restrictions on capital account transactions, which would be inappropriate for most countries in SSA, but to pursue measures which can lock domestic investors into a growth take-off in a relatively secure environment. Greater political stability, effective property rights, investment incentives and stable exchange rates are needed to prevent further capital flight from aborting faster growth in SSA.[14]

However, capital flight is not exclusively a financial problem. The emigration of highly skilled individuals ("brain drain") has contributed to a shortage of skilled personnel and qualified workers in SSA, depriving its economies of a crucial and desperately needed factor for growth and development. It is estimated, for example, that 60,000 doctors, engineers and university staff left Africa during 1985-1990 and that as many as 20,000 a year have left since 1990.[15]

It is difficult to determine cause and effect between the supply of a skilled labour force and private investment. The fact that the level of investment flows from developed to developing countries is less than would be expected from economic theory has been explained by some authors in terms of the absence of an appropriately skilled labour force in developing countries.[16] However, new investment increases the demand for skilled workers and hence provides incentives for individuals to invest more in their education and to stay in their own country. Hence, policies conducive to private investment are also a crucial element of a strategy for skill accumulation, including the return of skilled workers from abroad.

An equally effective measure that could reduce the pull factor and facilitate the return of skilled workers to Africa is their greater use in operations in the region by international financial institutions (IFIs) and aid agencies. This could have other benefits as well. For instance, it has been argued, in relation to development research, that:

> IFI professionals cost much more than professionals living in their native developing countries and having similar qualifications; moreover, these professionals in developing countries also have the comparative advantage of knowledge with respect to domestic institutions and idiosyncracies ... For example if the equivalent of 50 per cent of the resources used in Washington to finance 1,000 World Bank economists were used in 100 developing countries to finance 1,000 graduate domestic economists (on average 10 per country), the policy reform advice and development research would be greatly improved; there would also be spillovers and domestic externalities increasing local research and development. At the same time, there would be an important saving of resources in Washington D.C. World Bank expenditures.[17]

(c) Using foreign direct investment

Africa needs to attract private capital with a long-term commitment to the region. Foreign direct investment can make a growing and positive contribution to the extent that it brings productive assets to complement domestic resources and improves linkages with overseas markets. Many SSA governments have, over the past decade, made concerted efforts to attract FDI by liberalizing their investment laws, including easing restrictions on entry and on profit remittances and strengthening protection of intellectual property, as well as by offering generous fiscal incentives.[18] However, the flow of FDI to Africa continues to be minimal, a situation which reflects the weak growth performance of the region. Whether in search of markets or cost advantages, FDI is attracted by success.

Nevertheless, FDI can be attracted in some sectors, the most important of which is probably mining although in many cases it will require improving public infrastructure. More stable legislative and contractual arrangements have helped to reduce the risk in mining projects with long gestation periods and could encourage TNCs to establish more processing facilities in such areas as petroleum.[19]

The availability of unskilled labour and a strong raw material base should also prove attractive to international agribusiness, particularly where technological requirements are not too demanding. Moreover, the strong backward and forward linkages associated with these activities make such investments particularly attractive. As noted in chapter IV, a number of countries in Latin America and South-East Asia have struck a balance between private and public sector investment, and between domestic and foreign producers, that has allowed a rapid expansion of non-traditional agricultural exports. Some countries in SSA have also been successful in this regard. Tourism is another sector which could be quickly and effectively developed in cooperation with TNCs, particularly through the use of management contracts and licensing arrangements.

To the extent that countries are ready to begin exporting manufactures, closer links with international firms will be desirable. However, securing the right kind of FDI and making a judicious choice of instruments for technology transfer and marketing become even more important at this stage in terms of indigenous capacity-building and long-term productivity growth. While there are obvious advantages which a foreign affiliate can bring to a production location, TNCs are generally attracted by a strong growth performance rather than leading the process of growth, and too much should not be expected from export-oriented manufacturing FDI in most countries in SSA.[20] Moreover, the strategy pursued by some African countries – immediately following independence – of reliance on FDI, external advisers, expatriate technical personnel and turnkey operations, with the aim of leapfrogging the initial stages of industrialization, prevented the development of important domestic production linkages.[21] In any case, FDI in manufacturing, where international competition is more intense, is perhaps even more cautious than in other sectors. In this respect, closer regional links could be particularly useful in bringing FDI to some countries neighbouring South Africa.

The policy challenge for countries with considerable foreign investment in mining and agriculture is how to capture an important part of the rents from the exploitation of natural resources, and also to avoid the "Dutch disease" problem that may be associated with an expansion of exports of the latter, as well as to invest efficiently in non-traditional export sectors the financial resources thus generated (see chapter

IV). Establishing linkages with local suppliers and securing technology spillovers become more important objectives for activities in the secondary sector. It is essential to remember that TNCs are driven by their own narrow objectives which are different from, and potentially at odds with, the host countries' objectives of building up local capacities and a strong domestic supply base. Moreover, even a successful policy of attracting FDI must be vigilant as regards TNCs' rapidly exiting from cost-sensitive sectors when domestic wages start rising or lower-cost locations begin to emerge.[22]

2. Agricultural policies

A central objective of agricultural development policy is to promote private farm investment and sustainable productivity growth amongst smallholders. This objective is founded on two premises. First, strategies which focus exclusively on promoting capitalist agribusinesses have often not had the desired economic or social results. Second, the key problem facing smallholders is undercapitalization. Without assets they cannot generate a surplus for investment, and are forced to adopt risk-minimizing behaviour which tends to reduce output and productivity; furthermore, agricultural intensification is likely to promote land degradation.

However, throwing more money at the problem is not likely to do much good if priorities are not carefully selected. Past agricultural development projects channelled resources into areas with limited productivity potentials, and often with multiple objectives. Agricultural growth may be better promoted by focusing policies and targeting resources on areas with the highest productive potential and high population density. Also, their effectiveness should not be undermined, as it was in the past, by gender biases in the provision of agricultural services.

The analysis in the previous chapters strongly suggests that an exclusive emphasis on either export crops or food crops needs to be avoided. The desirable mix has been elusive, in part because policies have been overburdened with the goals of poverty reduction and self-reliance. Certainly, in most countries in SSA agricultural exports need to expand, particularly in those without mineral resources and immediate opportunities for manufactured exports. However, it should be borne in mind that higher productivity in food production and lower prices can make a significant contribution to export expansion by reducing wage costs. This can be particularly important where much of domestic food consumption is in commodities which are non-tradable outside the region.

The profitability of agricultural production and investment depends on a host of factors, including input and output prices, productivity and transaction costs. Concentrating on producer prices alone does not always bring about higher production and investment when other factors influencing costs are unfavourable. Leaving these to markets does not always generate the right incentives for farmers. Moreover, even where incentives are generated, supply response does not always follow if there are legal, financial and technical constraints on the capacity to invest and produce.

Experience elsewhere, particularly among the most successful NIEs in East and South-East Asia, suggests that it is possible to achieve high rates of agricultural growth even when farmers are taxed, but only if the overall configuration of factors that determine profitability stimulates investment and production. One important factor is the large amount of public investment needed to raise productivity and reduce transaction costs. Again, the way in which agriculture is taxed impinges directly on incentives. Elsewhere, for example, land taxes had the effect of promoting, rather than discouraging, productivity growth, and the relevance of such schemes to Africa can be explored. But what may be more important immediately is the reform of local government to ensure that local taxes are collected fairly and efficiently and used for local development purposes. Progress in this area can be rapid.[23]

The low productivity of African agriculture, when combined with declining and volatile world prices, creates a vicious circle. When world prices decline, private investment in agriculture is increasingly unattractive; but without investment, productivity will remain low. This situation arises partly because governments in the past may not have made the best use of gaining from commodity booms, devoting revenues to other purposes rather than supporting agricultural productivity growth through investment. But today's problems cannot be solved by simply passing the world prices to producers. It is essential to increase public investment in agriculture and there may also

be a case for treating certain crops at certain times as "infant industries" by implementing sector-specific supply-side policies. Such policies would seek to reduce costs through measures designed to improve the technological capacities of farmers, achieve economies of scale and specialization, and encourage market development. In this regard, much experience has been acquired in Africa for certain export crops, such as tea in Kenya and cotton in francophone West Africa, and also for food crops, such as maize in Zimbabwe.

The disappointing past performance of many marketing boards and *caisses de stabilisation* (which often date from colonial times) does not imply that the original reasons for their establishment no longer hold; these reasons included the desire to improve marketing channels, guarantee minimum prices, and (in the case of the latter) stabilize prices and provide other services connected to agricultural development. They have failed for other reasons, notably on account of inefficiencies in their operation and of political interference. The recent wave of privatization and liberalization in Africa has reduced the role of these boards and *caisses*, but has failed to solve the major problems confronting farmers. These entities were established to counter real weaknesses due to the lack of marketing arrangements for both inputs and products, the unavailability of credit and storage, and the absence of competition; and, despite their deficiencies, they did provide a measure of price stability for farmers, ensure quality control, serve as a focal point for forward sales, and negotiate international financing at attractive rates. In consequence the reduced role of these institutions in some African countries has left commodity trade in disarray and farmers much more exposed to volatility in world commodity markets.

These problems can be avoided by actions which include adaptation of official rules and regulations to ensure that modern techniques for commodity trade, financing and risk management are available to the private sector,[24] stimulating local banks to play a more active role in these areas, strengthening farmers' associations, better dissemination of information, promoting organized markets in certain cases, and the provision to both farmers and traders of risk-management services. The private sector and competitive markets can help in meeting many of these needs but the possible scope of their role is limited. Modern techniques to hedge against price instability are beyond the individual means of most African farmers and traders and, owing to their imperfections, domestic capital markets provide little opportunity for consumption smoothing over time. Moreover, competitive markets are lacking in many areas of African commodity trade, and the private sector is likely to be unwilling or unable to provide much of the other infrastructure required for such trade. Thus government action remains indispensable in areas such as market development (which is not an automatic process but requires public-sector support), financing and risk management, and the provision of other services and infrastructure; and under many of these headings an important role can be played by reformed and depoliticized marketing boards and *caisses*. Indeed, in present circumstances there is a strong case for institutional pluralism in which marketing boards and *caisses* are part of a landscape that also includes private organizations, parastatals and cooperatives.

Land reform is also a key policy issue in SSA. Customary land tenure arrangements can hamper the development of rural labour and capital markets and divert entrepreneurial energies towards gaining access to local resources rather than improving productivity. They are characterized by significant gender and generational biases which undermine incentives for key social groups. On the other hand, individual titling will not lead to increased private farm investment unless other constraints are also removed. Critical in this regard are the dissemination of locally adapted technologies for increasing productivity, and the provision of special credit facilities and institutions. Greater availability of, and higher remuneration from rural non-farm employment opportunities also play an important role because income from these activities increases the surplus available for investment in agriculture and can provide a buffer against risk.

3. Trade policies

Unquestionably, in the past many countries in SSA raised their levels of protection to excessive levels. The absence of competitive pressures eventually precluded higher productivity and improvements in managerial and technological capabilities, and prevented the graduation of infant industries to a higher level of maturity because it protected inefficiency and created windfall profits for those with privileged access to import licences.

In most countries quantitative restrictions on imports have been eliminated and replaced by tariffs, and tariff structures have already been drastically compressed and their scale reduced over the past decade or so. However, there have also been cases of policy reversal in this area, partly as a result of the impact of tariff reductions on budget revenues, and partly because economic costs exceeded gains.

However, although import-substitution policies have proved unsuccessful in much of SSA, rapid and comprehensive import liberalization is not the only, or the most desirable, alternative. A gradual approach is warranted, in part because little is known about the link between trade policies and productivity growth.[25] But perhaps more significantly, an extensive examination of trade liberalization experiences suggests that strong prior export expansion is critical for sustaining any moves towards greater openness to imports, and that it is wrong to see export expansion and import substitution as mutually exclusive strategies. The case for infant industry protection and industrial policies to promote learning and develop managerial and other capabilities in domestic firms is no less relevant in SSA today than it has been for all successful late developers over the past century.[26]

A trade regime designed to promote investment and exports should have a number of basic features. First, it should allow exporters to have easy and reliable access to inputs at world prices. Second, it should facilitate investment. Third, it should discourage luxury consumption. Finally, it should protect domestic producers against damaging competition. From this point of view, the trade policy reforms adopted in SSA are not always satisfactory.

While attainment of the above objectives requires selective liberalization and differentiated tariff structures, reform in Africa, as elsewhere in the developing world, has been governed by a desire to attain a relatively uniform tariff structure with low tariff rates in the belief that this minimizes distortions while generating budget revenues. However, this approach has often resulted in the taxation of exporters. Efforts to establish duty drawback schemes have not generally succeeded in according duty-free status to exporters for their imported inputs. An alternative would be to exempt all key inputs from import duties while raising the tariffs on others. This would be a rational option particularly in countries lacking domestic industries that provide inputs to other sectors. Furthermore, value-added taxes could be used, where necessary, to discriminate against uses of such inputs for domestic consumption as well as to make up for revenue losses. Such a scheme could also be effectively applied to capital goods imports, since most countries lack domestic capital goods industries. However, import charges on capital goods continue to be comparatively high in many countries in Africa, and this appears to be a reason for the lower than expected investment response to import liberalization.

Regarding the evidence on tariff structures across countries and product categories in the most recent year available, several features are noteworthy.[27] Imports of machinery and equipment are in general subject to lower charges than other manufactures. However, consumption goods are to be found in both groups. With regard to the structure of charges within the group of machinery and equipment imports, the evidence suggests that the North African countries (with the exception of Tunisia) and South Africa, i.e. the relatively more industrialized African countries, have significantly lower charges on machinery than on transportation equipment. This feature is most striking when compared with the structure of charges in Côte d'Ivoire and, to a lesser extent, Kenya, Madagascar and Malawi (a country where this feature was much more pronounced at the end of the 1980s), which is relatively favourable to imports of transportation equipment compared with imports of machinery. To the extent that this tariff structure is a reflection of a comparatively favourable treatment of imports of luxury consumer goods (such as expensive passenger cars) relative to those of production facilities which are required in industry, it would appear to be particularly inappropriate.[28]

An accurate description of the trade regimes in Africa is complicated by various exemptions such as those for public purchases and in the use of donor aid. In some countries, export retention schemes have allowed exporters to use their proceeds to import not only duty-free intermediate goods but also consumer goods. These, together with large-scale smuggling and reduction in tariffs on consumer goods, have created serious difficulties for local firms in competing with imports. One recent study of Zambia has noted that basic consumer goods industries such as textiles and leather and wood and furniture products have been hit hardest by trade liberalization; under normal circumstances, those industries are likely to form the basis of a more export-oriented industrial base.[29]

Phased and differentiated import liberalization needs to be complemented by an efficient system of export promotion through fiscal, credit and other incentives. State assistance with market information and export penetration strategies, trade banks, insurance mechanisms for exporters, and the rationale for export taxes and direct subsidies all need to be examined carefully in this context. Export-processing zones, widely used in East Asia, might provide a context in which to experiment with many of these policy initiatives.[30] However, in all cases, support must be timebound and linked to technological and skill development, productivity growth, the emergence of complementary supply industries and scale considerations, as well as to explicit export targets. More sophisticated technology and training policies will be needed, particularly once initial resource advantages have been fully exploited, in order to address the small base of managerial and technological capabilities in SSA, and to facilitate the switch to new and more dynamic areas of competitiveness.

C. Constraints of the new trading regime

It is increasingly argued that the adoption by developing countries of selective strategies may no longer be possible because the intensification of multilateral trade disciplines and the extension of their scope as a result of the Uruguay Round

prohibit the use of some key policy tools to promote exports and protect infant industries. It is pointed out in particular that the WTO regime has reduced the scope for using measures such as trade-related subsidies and imposing conditions on FDI, and for practices such as lax enforcement of intellectual property rights; all these were integral parts of the East Asian development strategy.

Certainly, the more generalized protection which provided a backdrop for targeted policies in East Asia is no longer possible. It may also be true that the new trading regime will reduce the scope for policy manoeuvre for those developing countries that wish to pursue a strategy involving vigorous infant industry protection and export subsidies. Tighter constraints may in particular arise from the Agreement on Trade-Related Investment Measures (TRIMs) and the Agreement on Trade-Related Aspects of Intellectual Property Rights (TRIPs). However, although the Uruguay Round has clearly imposed greater discipline, it has also improved security of market access for exports from developing countries. This represents an improvement on the conditions faced by many East Asian NIEs.[31]

With respect to infant industry protection, to the extent that tariff rates remain unbound or bound at ceilings above currently applied rates, they can be increased to protect infant industries. The Agreement on Subsidies and Countervailing Measures perhaps contains the most meaningful provisions on differential and more favourable treatment for poorer countries, some of which are not subject to any precise time limits. For example, the least developed countries and 20 other countries with GDP per capita of less than $1,000 are exempt from the prohibition on export subsidies so long as they remain in these categories and certain thresholds, based on shares of world markets for products benefiting from export subsidies, are not reached. These exemptions cover most countries in SSA.

Thus, while the WTO multilateral agreements have reduced the scope of some policy options, selective strategies can still be applied. The main

constraint would seem to be the necessity for such strategies (particularly those which involve negotiations with developed countries or TNCs) to respect the specific time frame laid down in the different agreements. In this context, both formal and informal government-business links, which played such an important role in East Asia's success, are likely to be of growing importance. As discussed in the next section, measures to strengthen government-industry partnerships deserve closer attention. Also, technical assistance should place more emphasis on informing countries in SSA of the full extent of these possibilities, and incorporating them into larger development strategies.

Furthermore, it should be noted that there are many policy measures that remain outside the scope of WTO obligations. Many of the policies identified earlier with a dynamic investment climate can still be so designed as to be permissible under the new trading rules. These include general fiscal concessions to corporations, the provision of subsidized R&D, measures to promote corporate savings and investment, and differential taxes (VAT and excise tax) on domestic consumption and production. Since these policies can have considerable influence on promoting technological upgrading and international competitiveness, their importance cannot be emphasized too strongly.

Arguably, slow growth in the North and the persistence there of high tariffs and subsidies in some agricultural and food-based products, together with the erosion of preference margins for African countries, are greater obstacles to raising export levels and entering some non-traditional lines of export.[32] Action is needed by OECD countries to improve access for African exporters of both traditional agricultural products and processed raw materials; this would also help to improve market knowledge and marketing skills that will be needed for such products as textiles.

. D. The institutional hiatus and reform

Social divisions, particularly those linked to ethnic differences, have often been cited as an important reason for low investment and slow growth in SSA because they have given rise to excessive

rent-seeking behaviour, political instability and poor public services. Certainly, a number of countries in SSA suffer from civil strife or external conflicts, and some still lack some of the basic social and political conditions for initiating sustained growth. However, social conflict and division are not an intrinsically African problem, but rather are linked to the debilitating effects of poverty, growing inequality and heightened factional competition in situations of severe economic decline.[33] As discussed at length in *TDR 1997*, political and social instability tend to be greater where social stratification and inequalities are associated with widespread poverty. This can threaten to generate a vicious circle whereby political instability and social unrest give rise to greater uncertainty, lower investment and slower growth, which in turn lead to greater poverty and further instability.[34]

Global comparisons show that, contrary to a widespread perception, even though SSA has the largest number of politicized communal groups, it experiences less economic and political discrimination than most other regions, thanks in large part to efforts by many post-independence States to build multi-ethnic political coalitions.[35] These efforts, however, have not been without large economic costs. Redistributive measures based on the politics of inclusion have in many cases reduced microeconomic efficiency and dissipated investment funds, and at worst have generated a system of spoils for the wealthy and well-connected. But it does not follow that ethnic multiplicity is necessarily an impediment to growth. A number of successful East Asian NIEs, for example, have faced serious ethnic tensions in the course of their development, which were once seen as obstacles to growth. The experience of Malaysia illustrates how it is possible to manage ethnic divisions whilst nevertheless accelerating growth.

There is a widespread belief that countries in SSA still lack much of the basic institutional infrastructure to manage complex economic policies. However, healthy scepticism about excessive claims regarding what policymakers can achieve needs to be distinguished from simple prejudice against public action in general, and myths about African managerial capacities in particular.[36] There is little doubt that the economic stagnation of the 1980s, the accompanying fiscal crisis of the State and the ideological shift away from public activities have all seriously weakened governments in SSA, and in particular have eroded state managerial capacities, thus making it difficult to pursue certain types of policy. But the warning of an ill-fated marriage between complex policies

and unsophisticated States in SSA is a false one. On the one hand, it ignores those successful experiences which evolved out of a period of deep economic and political crisis, and often on a weak bureaucratic base.[37] On the other hand, whilst the policy rhetoric of the past decade has denied the existence of the requisite state capacity in SSA to pursue demanding national development strategies, the alternative has called for a daunting combination of closer links with the world economy through trade and financial liberalization, stabilizing the economy, downsizing state agencies and privatizing public assets, financial deepening, fiscal discipline, good governance, democratization and the creation of an "enabling environment" for the private sector. Often, the recommendation has been to pursue all reforms simultaneously and at a fast pace.

A take-off to growth requires that governments pursue general policies aimed at raising the level of investment, together with a more limited number of selective interventions in certain key import-substitution and export-oriented industries which contribute to the accumulation of capabilities and know-how. In SSA, as earlier in the second-tier NIEs, these policies will need to target resource-based activities and some simpler labour-intensive manufactures. There is little reason, *a priori*, to deny that engagement in a limited number of policies during the initial stages of export promotion in SSA will allow governments to learn how to design sectoral policies, to find out what incentives are effective and for what purpose, and to learn about the loopholes that a policy that looks good on paper may have in practice. More sophisticated policies needed for promoting the next generation of industries can build on these experiences.

After a decade or more of reform in SSA premised on the assumption that government failures are far worse than market failures, the need for a different emphasis is now increasingly recognized, stressing the complementarity between the State and the market and promotion of the developmental State. The latter term was coined to describe the set of government institutions which aim to promote entrepreneurship, profits and capital accumulation without compromising a wider set of development objectives beyond those narrowly prescribed by business interests. Certainly, in SSA, this requires capacity building in the public and private sectors; also, it is necessary to avoid the capture of state agencies by special interest groups. However, a developmental State will also seek to fill gaps and repair failures across a range of institutions in SSA.

This is a daunting task, and any comprehensive agenda of institutional reform can emerge only at the country level, where ownership of the reforms can be ensured and the chances of success thereby enhanced.[38] However, in the light of the policy suggestions discussed above, two closely related sets of reforms can now be considered by many countries in SSA: the creation of a competent and independent state bureaucracy, and the building of closer ties between such a bureaucracy and the emerging private sector.

The need to restore an effective policymaking machinery depends in part on recovering the bureaucratic momentum which was present in many countries in SSA in the early post-independence years but was subsequently lost. According to one recent study:

> In many countries in sub-Saharan Africa, the civil service has sharply deteriorated in almost every way since the 1970s ... Beginning in the 1980s, a succession of fiscal stabilization programs has reduced government employment in Africa to the lowest level of any developing region. Thus although additional downsizing may be necessary, most do not need to shrink the workforce but to overhaul the entire civil service system.[39]

This overhaul will have various dimensions. First of all, the core of the bureaucracy needs to be strongly insulated from political pressures. Total insulation is neither possible nor desirable (as it could make the bureaucracy unresponsive to an important source of change), but if the bureaucracy is unduly subject to the pressures of day-to-day politics, it will be less able to devise and modify policies in the light of its own experience, and is more likely to become overburdened with multiple objectives, many of which will be short-term in nature.

A second feature involves the degree of personnel continuity in the civil service. Policymaking cannot be embodied only in organizational structure and rules. Much will depend on the accumulated knowledge of civil servants, and it is necessary to find ways to maximize the application of such knowledge. A career structure is needed that rewards ability in a manner competi-

tive with the private sector. Remuneration may not need to be equivalent to the private sector, but there must be a combination of salaries, job satisfaction, perquisites, security and prestige that ensures that public sector managers match those in the private sector.[40]

Thirdly, it is absolutely indispensable that the core bureaucrats have substantial learning capabilities if policies are to be improved over time.[41]

Reforms of the civil service need not advance on all fronts simultaneously. Indeed, in the light of their recent history an excessively ambitious reform package is unlikely to succeed in SSA. In East Asia elements of the bureaucratic structure retained old-fashioned practices even as key ministries were undergoing significant reform. Thus, whilst confronting vested interests, disrupting established repertoires and changing prevailing norms are always difficult, the emergence of a few centres of excellence can make a considerable difference.

Given a capable, internally coherent state bureaucracy, the next challenge is to connect bureaucrats and entrepreneurs, a challenge that should be pursued on at least two different levels. On the most general level, governments need to diffuse a sense of shared commitment to a collective project of national development. The essential complement to this broad ideological commitment is a more concrete set of ties that enable specific agencies and enterprises to construct joint projects at the sectoral level.[42]

Cooperating with the private sector does not mean taking it for granted that local business groups will behave like Schumpeterian entrepreneurs. Instead, an approach combining engagement and support with scepticism and pressure is needed, in order to transform the character of private corporate elites. Specifically, policies of rent creation and discipline are called for so as to better manage profits and investment. However, the danger must be avoided of rents becoming more permanent, which in the long run would weaken entrepreneurship and hamper productivity growth, a feature which has been all too common in SSA. There are two possible solutions. The first is to establish policy mechanisms and institutions to ensure that creating the initial rents is essentially a "priming" exercise and that the support and protection are eventually withdrawn as the industry matures. The second is to impose performance criteria, in particular by using the discipline of the international market through, for example, export targets – a process sometimes described as establishing "contests".[43] In this way, infant industries promoted through state-created rents are expected to eventually prove themselves by the standards of the international market, to have their import protection gradually removed and/or to be pushed by the government to start exporting at a relatively earlier stage of development.

Behind any successful management of rents lies a much deeper process of building a robust network of government and business institutions consistent with strategic development goals. This will involve creating a series of formal and informal links with the entrepreneurial classes to assist in the design, implementation and coordination of policy measures. Such links can be established through sector-specific agencies within existing bureaucracies or the creation of specialized institutions. Deliberation councils are perhaps the archetypal forum for private entrepreneurs to filter policy proposals. But other organizational tools can serve a similar purpose, including task forces led and managed by the private sector, and major conferences bringing together business leaders, academics and government technocrats.[44] Such arrangements cannot be artificially imposed on countries in SSA and should, in any case, begin modestly. However, there are already some successful examples, such as in Ghana and Mauritius, which suggest that efforts in this direction can provide a fruitful avenue for building trust between the State and private actors.[45]

Notes

1   For further discussion see *TDR 1997*, Part Two, chapter V.

2   For further discussion of such measures see *TDR 1997*, Part Two, chapter VI.

3   For a useful discussion of what is known about those limits, see J. Stiglitz, "More instruments and broader goals: Moving toward the post-Washington Consensus", The 1998 WIDER Annual Lecture, Helsinki, January 1998.

4   These issues are discussed at greater length in *TDR 1991*, Part Two, chapter III.

5   For a discussion of these issues, see M. Nissanke, "Financing enterprise development and export diversification in sub-Saharan Africa", UNCTAD/GDS/MDPB/Misc. 8 (Geneva, 1998); and N. Lipumba, "Liberalisation of foreign exchange and financial markets: What have we learned?" (Helsinki: WIDER, 1998), mimeo. For evidence on financial market liberalization in Uganda see L. A. Kasekende and M. Atingi-Ego, "Impact of liberalisation on key markets in sub-Saharan Africa: The case of Uganda" (Kampala: Bank of Uganda, 1998), mimeo.

6   See N. S. Ndung'u and R. W. Ngugi, "Impact of liberalisation on key markets in sub-Saharan Africa: The Kenyan case" (University of Nairobi, 1998), mimeo.

7   See J. Stiglitz and M. Uy, "Financial markets, public policy, and the East Asian miracle", *World Bank Research Observer*, Vol. 11, August 1996.

8   See T. Hellman et al., "Financial restraint: Toward a new paradigm", in M. Aoki et al. (eds.), *The Role of Government in East Asian Economic Development* (Oxford: Clarendon Press, 1997); and M. Nissanke and E. Aryeetey, "Comparative institutional analysis: Sub-Saharan Africa and East Asia", paper prepared for the African Economic Research Consortium (AERC) Conference on Comparative African and East Asian Development Experience, Johannesburg, November 1997 (mimeo).

9   See N. Lipumba, "Structural adjustment policies and economic performance of African countries", in UNCTAD, *International Monetary and Financial Issues for the 1990s,* Vol. V (United Nations publication, Sales No. E.95.II.D.3), New York and Geneva, 1995.

10 For the evolution of exchange rate arrangements in SSA see IMF, *Exchange Rate Arrangements and Exchange Restrictions* (Washington, D.C.: IMF), various issues. See also Lipumba, *op. cit.*

11 See L. A. Kasekende, D. Kitabire and M. Martin, "Capital inflows and macroeconomic policy in sub-Saharan Africa", in UNCTAD, *International Monetary and Financial Issues for the 1990s,* Vol. VIII (United Nations publication, Sales No. E.97.II.D.5), New York and Geneva, 1997.

12 *Ibid.*, p. 71. For a discussion of these issues see, for example, P. K. Asea and C. M. Reinhart, "Le prix de l'argent: How (not) to deal with capital inflows",

Journal of African Economies, AERC Supplement, Vol. 5, 1996, pp. 231-271.

13 P. Collier and J. Gunning, "Explaining African economic performance", *Journal of Economic Literature*, Vol. 37, No. 1, pp. 64-111.

14 See Lipumba, *op. cit.*

15 H. Körner, "The 'brain drain' from developing countries: An enduring problem", *Intereconomics*, Vol. 33, No. 1, 1998, p. 27.

16 R. Lucas, "Why doesn't capital flow from rich to poor countries", *American Economic Review*, Vol. 80, 1990, pp. 92-96.

17 P. Meller, "The role of international financial institutions: A Latin American perspective", in G. Helleiner (ed.), *The International Monetary and Financial System* (London: Macmillan, 1996), p. 268.

18 See UNCTAD, *Foreign Direct Investment in Africa* (United Nations publication, Sales No. E.95.II.A.6), New York and Geneva, 1995.

19 See M. Odle, "Foreign investment opportunities in Africa", paper prepared for the International Conference on Reviving Private Investment in Africa: Partnerships for Growth and Development, Accra, Ghana, June 1996.

20 See R. Rasiah, "The export manufacturing experience of Indonesia, Malaysia and Thailand: Lessons for Africa", Discussion Paper No. 137 (Geneva, 1998).

21 L.K. Mytelka and T. Tesfachew, "The role of policy in promoting enterprise learning during early industrialization: Lessons for African countries", UNCTAD/GDS/MDPB/Misc. 7 (Geneva, 1998).

22 On the role of FDI in East Asia and the policy lessons see *TDR 1996*.

23 For a clear argument in support of local government reform, see M. Mamdani, *Citizen and Subject: Contemporary Africa and the Legacy of Late Colonialism* (Princeton, N.J.: Princeton University Press, 1996).

24 See UNCTAD, "National institution building to facilitate access to risk management markets for small producers and traders" (TD/B/CN.1/GE.1/2), Geneva, 1 August 1994.

25 Stiglitz, *op. cit.*, p. 16.

26 See *TDR 1994*, Part Three, chapter I; G. Helleiner, *Trade Policy and Industrialization in Turbulent Times* (London: Routledge, 1994); T. Biggs and P. Srivastava, "Structural aspects of manufacturing in sub-Saharan Africa: Findings from a seven country enterprise survey", World Bank Discussion Paper No. 348 (Washington, D.C.: World Bank, 1996); and S. Lall, "Trade policies for development: A policy prescription for Africa", *Development Policy Review*, Vol. 11, 1993.

27 See UNCTAD, *Directory of Import Regimes* (United Nations publication, Sales No. E.94.II.D.6), New York, 1994; and UNCTAD, TRAINS [Trade Analysis and Information System], CD-Rom (Geneva: UNCTAD, 1998).

28 It is interesting to note in this context that, according to the Uganda Investment Authority, cars currently account for 16 per cent of Uganda's imports compared with only 8 per cent for machinery (*Le Monde*, 3 March 1998).

29 See H. Tokeshi, "Trade reform in Zambia", Informal Discussion Paper 1, World Bank Macroeconomic Unit for Southern Africa (Washington, D.C.: World Bank, 1997).

30 For a useful discussion see P. Harrold et al., "Practical lessons for Africa from East Asia in industrial and trade policies", World Bank Discussion Paper No. 310 (Washington, D.C.: World Bank, 1996).

31 Japan faced discriminatory quantitative restrictions for many years after joining GATT, as many countries invoked the non-application clause against it. Other East Asian countries faced a series of non-tariff barriers, including voluntary export restraints in textiles and clothing and other sectors, as well as the threat of countervailing duties applied without the "injury test" by the United States (until the acceptance of the Tokyo Round Code).

32 According to the UNDP *Human Development Report 1997*, industrial countries spent $182 billion on agricultural subsidies, equivalent to 65 per cent of African GDP. See also UNCTAD, *International Trade Liberalization Measures and Implications for Export Diversification in Africa*, ITCD/COM/1, July 1998.

33 See UNCTAD, *The Least Developed Countries, 1997 Report* (United Nations publication, Sales No. E.97.II.D.6), New York and Geneva, 1997, Part III.

34 See *TDR 1997*, Part Two, chapter V.

35 See T. R. Gurr, *Minorities at Risk: A Global View of Ethnopolitical Conflicts* (Washington, D.C.: United States Institute of Peace Press, 1993).

36 On myths about African States, see T. Mkandawire, "Thinking the impossible? Developmental States in Africa", UNCTAD/GDS/MDPB/Misc. 9 (Geneva, 1998); and for a general review of the social science literature on the African State, see C. Gore, "Social exclusion and Africa south of the Sahara: A review of the literature", International Institute for Labour Studies Discussion Paper 62, Geneva, 1994, chapter 5. A useful antidote to excessive pessimism about African development management is D. K. Leonard, *African Successes: Four Public Managers of Kenyan Rural Development* (Berkeley and London: University of California Press, 1991).

37 East Asian bureaucracies were often accused, by outside observers, of harbouring conservative practices and of being unable to organize their economic development. It is instructive to recall that until the 1960s, for example, the Republic of Korea sent its bureaucrats to Pakistan for training in economic policymaking.

38 See I. Elbadawi and G. Helleiner, "African development in the context of the new world trade and financial regimes: The role of the WTO and its relationship to the World Bank and the IMF", paper for the AERC project on Africa and the New World Trading System, Nairobi, April 1998.

39 S. Schiaro-Campo, "Reforming the civil service", *Finance and Development*, Vol. 33, No. 3, 1996, p.10.

40 East Asian experience points to a diversity of options aimed at producing parity. See J. Campos and H. Root, *The Key to the Asian Miracle: Making Shared Growth Credible* (Washington, D.C.: Brookings Institution, 1996).

41 The Republic of Korea attempted a much wider reform of the civil service and relied more on dedicated career bureaucrats, whereas Taiwan Province of China was more willing to identify special career tracks and recruit external people in mid-career using the Taiwan National University and successful completion of graduate training abroad as selection tools. Singapore is different again: potential recruits are identified in secondary schools and given government scholarships for higher education in return for a commitment to enter the civil service; see P. Evans, "Transferable lessons? Re-examining the institutional prerequisites of East Asian economic policies", *Journal of Development Studies*, Vol. 34, No. 6, August 1998.

42 It is worth noting that in East Asia these connections did not spring into place fully developed. Indeed, according to one recent assessment, "the evolution of government-business ties in East Asia has been even more convoluted and counter-intuitive than the evolution of the bureaucracy itself"; see Evans, *op. cit.*, p. 74.

43 See World Bank, *The East Asian Miracle: Economic Growth and Public Policy* (New York: Oxford University Press, 1993).

44 See Campos and Root, *op. cit.*

45 Harrold et al., *op. cit.*

Lightning Source UK Ltd.
Milton Keynes UK
UKOW03f2005070417

298609UK00001B/137/P